Practical Theology

Practical Theology

"On Earth as It Is in Heaven"

TERRY A. VELING

ORBIS BOOKS

Maryknoll, New York 10545

Copyright © 2005 by Terry A. Veling

Published by Orbis Books, Maryknoll, N.Y. 10545-0308

Library of Congress Cataloging-in-Publication Data

Veling, Terry A.
    Practical theology : on earth as it is in heaven / Terry A. Veling.
       p.   cm.
    Includes bibliographical references (p.   ).
    ISBN-13: 978-1-57075-614-6 (pbk.)
    1. Theology, Practical.   I. Title.
BV3.V45 2005
261 – dc22
                                                        2005016712

Both doors of the world
stand open:
opened by you
in the twinight.
We hear them banging and banging
and bear it uncertainly,
and bear this Green into your Ever.

—Paul Celan

CONTENTS

Part One
ON EARTH AS IT IS IN HEAVEN

FOREWORD

At the beginning of his poem "The Love Song of J. Alfred Prufrock," T. S. Eliot invites readers to learn a place by walking past sawdust restaurants with oyster shells, on half-deserted streets that weave through a town like a tedious argument. Then he says, "Oh, do not ask, 'What is it?' Let us go and make our visit." This book by Terry Veling makes a visit to practical theology. When you get to the close of it, you've learned much by the visit. You know the town well. Veling's kind of walk is thorough, and in the mood of Gabriel Marcel, systematically unsystematic! It is Terry Veling's insistent refusal to let practical theology become the next *scholastique* that I admire about this book.

One of the human delights is to behold something very interesting and important in the process of becoming. Reading the chapters of this book, one by one as they were written, was that kind of experience. Practical theology, in the senses unfolding here, is a somewhat recent development in Catholic culture in the United States, especially in Catholic colleges and universities with graduate programs in ministry. It is still in the making. It is not a branch of theology, but a form of theology that operates strategically in all the traditional branches of theology, e.g., Christology, ecclesiology, etc.

"Practical theology" has multiple meanings. A common one in Protestant circles, reflected in the dictionary definition, is "the study of institutional activities of religion (as preaching, church administration, pastoral care, and liturgics)." Another meaning, common in Catholic culture, makes practical theology and pastoral theology interchangeable. Still another meaning of practical theology is that it is applied systematic theology.

But it is also emerging as a new genre of theology in Catholic culture in this country. In the European context it is sometimes known as political theology. In Latin America, liberation theology. In the United States, practical theology — but with ambiguity in our context because of alternative renderings of "practical" already noted, and also because practical connects with "pragmatic," a stream of meaning that is both philosophical and popular, but not right on target. "Practical theology" in this book needs two important glosses for clarification, one from Aristotle, the other from a long Hebrew tradition.

In his *Nicomachean Ethics* Aristotle names several kinds of knowledge and the practice of the knowledge. One kind of knowledge is about what kind of world we should be making together: *phronesis*. The actual use of that knowledge is *praxis* — and that is where our meaning of practical resides. One cannot truly know what kind of a world we should be making, be able to help it come into existence, and then, failing to do it, still be called virtuous. *Knowing* what we need to do implicates us. When the dialogue between faith and experience elucidates the world that cries out to come into existence, we are called! Practical theology always has this strategic character. Paul Hanson, in his book *The People Called: The Growth of Community in the Bible*, says that such a community is driven by a double exegesis: interpreting the world accurately and interpreting the Word accurately, and being implicated by the dialectic between them.

Practical theology, in the sense of this book, also shares deep affinities with the Hebrew world. The Hebrew word for "word" is *dabhar*. Unlike English, where a word represents some object or some idea, by speaking, *dabhar* is an extension of a person into the outer world, one that has effects. *Dabhar* words *do things, make things, bring things into existence, have effects*. The effects belong to the meaning of the words. It is in that sense that practical theology is strategic. Reflection on the world in the light of faith by its nature perhaps compels the doing of what the words say.

Now Terry Veling gets this so very well because of his personal acquaintance with such extensive Hebrew sensibilities. He knows the materials. He has lived in Israel. He feels it in his theological bones. Thus this book does theology in a nonlogocentric way. In many ways, the power of this work reflects the incorporation of Hebraic instincts into its inner workings.

I'd be hard-pressed to name the genre of this book. It doesn't read the way most theological books read, but it is that. It doesn't read the way books on spirituality read, but it is that. It doesn't read the way autobiographies read, but there is a lot of that. I think I would say, finally, that this is an extraordinary conversation because it is so personal from the author's side, and evokes response from our side. It's a conversation book.

But the judgment I'd like to make is this. This book is a way of actually engaging in practical theology. In fact, it engages in the development of this genre. That is why some of the delight in reading this book is watching the becoming of practical theology take place in our company.

Bernard J. Lee, S.M.

PREFACE

"In the Vineyard of the Text"

TO YOU, THE READER

Even though I do not know you, I've often thought of you through the long writing of this book. Who are you? I imagine you as a teacher or a student of theology — surrounded by books and deeply buried questions, by half-written papers and faintly gleaned responses. I imagine you as a pastoral worker or a minister — shepherding the lives of those in your care, anointing the young and the old, tending to the "least" and the "last." I imagine you as a parent who belongs to a small faith community, who has carved out a small slice of time for conversation and for drawing breath — for prayer and for reflection amidst "all the things denied us by modern society, a society of noise, of covetousness, and of possession."[1] I imagine you as a social worker who is out on the streets, along the highways and the byways, seeking justice and mercy for those whose voices are drowned and ignored. I imagine the "crowds" that Jesus gazed upon when he "went up the hill" and, seeing their faces, began to speak: "Blessed are you..." (Matt. 5:1–10).

In writing this work, I have tried to keep in mind the words of St. Paul, who, as we know, spent much of his time *writing letters* to the "people of God." Over and over again, we find him saying:

I write these things ... for building you up and not for tearing you down. (2 Cor. 13:10; 10:8)

Let no evil come out of your mouths, but only what is useful for building up ... so that your words may give grace to those who hear you. (Eph. 4:29)

What should be done then, my friends? When you come together, each one has a hymn, a lesson, a revelation, a word, or an
interpretation. Let all things be done for building up. (1 Cor. 14:26)

Finally, beloved, whatever is true, whatever is honorable, whatever is
just, whatever is pure, whatever is pleasing, whatever is commend-
able, if there is any excellence and if there is anything worthy of
praise, think about these things. (Phil. 4:8)

This book is not the result of an uninterrupted, continuous, or systematic reflection. All writing is punctuated, and this has certainly been
the case for me, progressing through periods of exclamation, long pauses,
complete stops, dashes, interruptions, and fragments. Writing proceeds
by episodes, by phases, and by interludes. Sometimes it is smooth and
flowing, other times it is caught in the nettles of human existence. It
seems to me that nothing approximates the word of God that hasn't itself
descended into the word of humanity. This is one of Christianity's great
mysteries: "He descended because of us; we ascend because of him."[2]

This book is written for you — with you in mind — like a "message in a
bottle," as Paul Celan says, always with the faint and yet earnest hope that
it may "wash up somewhere," perhaps on "heartland" — on a shoreline of
the heart.[3] The great preacher and writer St. Augustine said, "As far as I
can, I'm turning myself inside out for you."[4]

LECTIO DIVINA — "SACRED READING"

Many of the early Christian theologians were not simply great system-
atizers of thought. Rather, they spent much of their time composing and
preaching sermons and homilies in an effort to persuade, to exhort, or to
console their audiences.[5] I find this style of homiletic writing very attractive, for it invites the reader to listen and to hear, to reflect and to engage
with the text, rather than to merely "take in information."

I always *read aloud* the words that I write. I've also had the opportunity to practice this "oral reading" of my chapters with students in my
class. In many ways, we moderns have lost the sense of the power of
the spoken word.[6] For the ancients, however, the practice of *lectio div-
ina* or "sacred reading" was very much an *active* reading.[7] They usually

read, not as today, principally with the eyes, but with the lips, pronouncing what they saw, and with the ears, listening to the words, hearing what is called the *voces paginarum* — "the voices of the pages."[8] This type of reading is a real acoustical reading — an *activity* which, like chant and writing, requires the participation of the whole body and whole mind. The reader's ears pay attention, and strive to catch what the reader's mouth pronounces — embodying and incorporating the "sounding pages." For the ancients, in Christian as well as rabbinic tradition, "to meditate is to read a text and to learn it 'by heart' in the fullest sense of this expression, that is, with one's whole being: with the body, since the mouth pronounced it, with the memory which fixes it, with the intelligence which understands its meaning, and with the will which desires to put it into practice."[9]

This commitment to sacred reading is of Jewish, rabbinical origin. Gregorian chant, for example, takes its inspiration from that of the synagogue. Like the plainchant that anchors the lines of the text in the heart, pupils in Talmudic schools mouth and chant the text they are reading. The "house of study" is at the same time the "house of prayer." Sacred reading "implies thinking of a thing with the intent to do it; in other words, to prepare oneself for it, to desire it, to practice it."[10] The rabbis often refer to the passage in Ezekiel 3, where God's messenger holds out a scroll to his servant. Ezekiel is bidden to "eat the scroll," to "ingest it." And, "as he swallows the scroll...it tastes as sweet as honey."[11]

The text is like a vineyard. The lines on the page are the thread of a trellis which supports the vines. The reader harvests these lines as one who picks berries, and like ripe fruit the *voces paginarum* drop from his mouth.[12] Along the "trellis of the vineyard," each word catches hold of one or several other words that become linked together in rich associations. These verbal echoes excite the imagination and spontaneously evoke other scriptural allusions, phrases, and quotations. The reader savors the text as one who savors the fruit of the vine. The ancient writers (when composing sermons, for example) made the utmost use of this literary freedom. One digression may lead to another or to several others, without distraction. They felt free to wander and play in the "vineyard of the text," to harvest its fruits, to let the text intoxicate their imaginations.

Today, our imaginations are lazier. For the ancients, however, imagination was vigorous and active. It permitted them to picture and to "make present."[13] They were keenly aware of the evocative power of biblical language — concrete, full of imagery, and poetic in essence. They were keenly aware, as Paul Ricoeur suggests, that "the symbol gives rise to thought."[14]

"THE SYMBOL GIVES RISE TO THOUGHT"

We do not first have ideas or thoughts, and then (in a secondary way) seek to clothe these thoughts in symbol or metaphor, in an attempt to aid their expression. It is not a matter of first thinking abstractly, and then trying to find ways to express our abstract thought into something more symbolic, poetic, or metaphorical. Rather, Ricoeur suggests that the symbolic world is always prior as the genesis of all our thinking and acting in the world. Our thoughts, our theories, our articulations of meaning — these arise from the symbolic or metaphorical apprehensions of the way we experience the world around us. It is "the symbol" that gives rise to thought, and not our thinking that gives rise to symbols.

I have tried to follow this approach in writing this work. Many chapters, for example, take shape around a guiding metaphor, such as "the open book," "the field," "the gate," or a biblical verse, "we will do and we will hear," or a rabbinic and Gospel parable, "go and study — go and do likewise." I have tried to avoid complex, academic, or technical language and to move instead within the realm of symbol and metaphor. Having the scriptures close at hand is always a great help, because the words of scriptures are laden with richly symbolic and evocative language — "the word become flesh," for example — which gives rise to much thought and to the contours and practices of Christian existence: through God and through each other, with God and with each other, in God and in each other.

The guiding metaphor for this work comes from the prayer that Jesus taught. When you pray, pray that God's name may be hallowed, that God's kingdom may come, that God's will may be done — "on earth, as it is in heaven" (Matt. 6:10).

As it is with God, so too with us — that certainly gives rise to much thought, to new ways of living and acting — "Whoever says, 'I abide in him,' ought to walk just as he walked" (1 John 2:6).

This book is divided into three parts. *Part One: On Earth as It Is in Heaven* begins with an introductory chapter titled, "What Is Practical Theology?" It sets the scene for the work that follows. The following three chapters explore the crucial role that *hermeneutics* or *interpretive practices* play in any theology that deems itself "practical." "Searching the scriptures" and "studying tradition" means paying attention to the biblical testimony and the way this testimony has been lived and received across generations of people of faith. It is an interpretive and communal exercise that links us with a rich tradition of faith, filled with commentary and teaching, liturgy and art, prophetic witness and saintly lives. "Reading the signs of the times" is concerned with the way this tradition of faith opens onto our present reality. God's word is always a word addressed to us and for us — a word that calls forth our response. Reading the signs of the times means paying attention to God's concern for the world. It means listening and responding to the questions and issues that are circulating within our culture and society, within our own lives, within our parishes and congregations, our workplaces, our local neighborhoods.

Part Two: May Your Name Be Held Holy turns its attention to the sanctification or hallowing of God's name that takes place through the sanctification or hallowing of our own humanity and the relations between us. To hallow God's name is to hallow each other. This mode of thought is profoundly Jewish. One might suspect that it is also profoundly Christian (and rightly so), but I have found that it was my exposure to Jewish thinkers — Buber, Heschel, Levinas, for example — that deeply provoked my own latent apprehension that everything *of God* is ultimately concerned with everything *of humanity*. If symbol gives rise to thought, then the Jewish tradition gives rise to thinking that is preeminently practical in its deepest instinct and orientation. "I consider the human person," Buber says, "to be the irremovable central place of the struggle between the world's movement away from God and its movement towards God."[15] *Divinitas* can never be separated from *humanitas*.

Part Three: Your Kingdom Come seeks to let the overflowing and yet concrete symbol of "God's kingdom" stir and provoke our own thinking and acting "on earth" — here and now — "as it is in heaven." It takes up some of the more usual or expected themes of practical theology — culture and context, for example — along with less anticipated themes, such as the chapter titled, "To Dwell Poetically in the World." Nothing, perhaps, seems less practical than poetry — yet perhaps nothing is less theological than a crudely pragmatic and utilitarian life. "What does it profit them," Jesus wonders, "if they gain the whole world, but lose or forfeit themselves?" (Luke 9:25).

While there are those who say that the ideal is illusory and unreal, there are also those who say that "only the paradigmatic is real."[16] I do not know how to pray "thy kingdom come" unless I am, at the same time, gripped by the amazing and yet abrasive reality of God.

THANK YOU

To my students who graciously read my text, quite "orally," sounding every word and offering their own voices in response. To Mary Veling, Bernard Lee, and Matthew Del Nevo, who read each chapter as it came along and who responded with only one motivation — to improve and "to build up." To Robert Ellsberg at Orbis Books, who patiently stood by this work, sensing something of value even in its most rudimentary form. To my colleagues at St. Thomas University in Miami who kept me going with words of encouragement and support. To my parents and family and friends. And also to you, whom I do not know, yet I pray for your well-being — the *shalom* and wellness of God — for our sake and for the sake of our salvation. In the end, the kingdom of God is about friendship and human warmth — "I have called you friends" (John 15:15). We cannot be saved alone. Finally, to Con Power, who forever reminds me that "a light shines in the dark, a light that darkness could not overpower" (John 1:5). I dedicate this book to all those who struggle with faith — in God, and in humanity.

"You must believe in the book in order to write it," Edmond Jabès says. "The time of writing is the time of this faith."[17]

PART ONE

ON EARTH
AS IT IS IN HEAVEN

ONE

What Is Practical Theology?

There is an inherent difficulty in describing practical theology. For a start, it is often dogged by what Edward Farley calls the "fragmentation of theology," the division of theology into defined and specialized fields (as when we speak, for example, of systematic theology, or pastoral theology, or historical theology, etc.).[1] Into this scenario comes yet another branch called "practical theology," which leads many to ask, "So what does practical theology specialize in?" However, there is an important sense in which practical theology is an attempt to heal this fragmentation of theology, such that it resists being slotted into yet another theological specialty.

In his book *The Love of Learning and the Desire for God*, Jean Leclercq paints a wonderful picture of monastic culture in which we get a feel for what theology was like before it became fragmented and specialized.[2] Leclercq evokes a time when study and the love of learning was part and parcel of the desire for God, and was never divorced from liturgy and prayer, human work and labor, contemplation of the scriptures, the search for wisdom (in philosophy and the arts), or pastoral concern and the "love of neighbor."

While this may sound like a serene and untroubled scenario, it nevertheless presents an image of what practical theology is perhaps seeking to reclaim — a certain reintegration of theology into the weave and fabric of human living, in which theology becomes a "practice" or a way of life. This is what makes practical theology difficult to define, as though it were one "type" of theology as opposed to another "type." It resists a certain branding or labeling, and makes its appeal to a more integrated theological sensibility that attempts to honor the great learnings of theological

3

wisdom with the desire for God and the coming of God's kingdom "on earth, as it is in heaven."

There is another particular difficulty with defining practical theology. In asking, "What is practical theology about?" we are asking about its "theory." In our highly specialized world, we have grown accustomed to first clarifying the "theory" of something and then, as a second step, seeking its practical application. However, as might be expected from its very name, the "theory" of practical theology, as Karl Rahner suggests, "indwells the practice itself."[3] Theory "indwells" practice, not in the sense that we *put* theory *into* practice; rather, in the sense that it is only in the practice or doing of theology that we begin to realize and understand its meanings and its workings more deeply. As the Christian community, for example, engages in the practices of prayer, study, hospitality, forgiveness — as we do these things — we begin to deepen our understanding of what the kingdom of God is all about, and what it means to be a people of God.

Anyone who writes "about" practical theology faces the peculiar quandary of falling into either one of the "traps" named above, that is, turning it into a theological discipline that exists alongside other theological disciplines, or bringing it to theoretical clarity so that people can then know what to do with it. There is no assured way of avoiding this struggle, but we need to begin somewhere, and so in this introductory chapter I would like to present some "snapshots" of practical theology that attempt to open the scene for the chapters ahead. Practical theology is a large subject matter. Indeed, Rahner goes so far as to say that "*everything* is its subject-matter."[4] So there is little hope of really capturing it; rather, there is the hope of "whetting our appetites" for the love of learning and the desire for God.

PRACTICAL THEOLOGY IS NOT A "THING"

"To think and act practically in fresh and innovative ways," writes Don Browning, "may be the most complex thing that humans ever attempt."[5] Practical theology, as its name suggests, is less a thing to be defined than it is an activity to be done. In this sense, it resists our attempts to pin it down and define it. Practical theology is more "verb-like" than "noun-like." In many ways, we would be better to speak of "practicing theology" rather than "practical theology." So a better question to ask would be, "What does it mean to practice theology?"

Theology is often seen as a speculative enterprise in which people think about important questions concerning God, faith, belief, and the religious meaning of life. And most people, if you were to ask them about "practical theology," would probably say, "Oh, that's about applying our faith and our beliefs to life in the real world." There is the "world of theology" — somewhat abstract and aloof — and then there is the "real world" where theological knowledge is applied and put into practice.

This is a fairly common understanding of theology. Indeed, it is reflected in the long-standing division of theology into two primary areas, namely, "systematic theology" and "pastoral theology." Systematic theology is where we do all our theoretical work, and pastoral theology is where we apply this learning to the life of the church and the needs of the world. According to Thomas Groome, this is the standard paradigm of theology. We begin with heavy doses of theology's theoretical disciplines (systematics, church history, scripture studies, etc.) and then tag on, almost as an afterthought, some training in pastoral skills in order to apply this theory to practice. Such a paradigm "presumes a one-way relationship between theory and practice with theory always the point of departure; theory is something from 'outside' to be applied and practice something to receive it."[6] Practical theology is an attempt to heal this division, so that pastoral theology is never simply an afterthought or a derivative of systematic theology. So that theological reflection can regain its intrinsic connection to life. So that we can overcome the artificial distinction between thinking and acting and become more serious about both.

LIFE IN THE WORLD

One of the greatest philosophers of the twentieth century, Martin Heidegger, delivered somewhat of a jolt to his contemporaries when he suggested that philosophy is concerned with our life in the world. Hardly a mind-blowing thought, you might say! However, Heidegger was suggesting that the Western philosophical tradition had spent so much time inquiring into life and its meaning that it had forgotten to attend to life itself. He spoke of this forgetfulness as a "forgetfulness of Being."[7] How is it possible, one may wonder, to inquire into life's "being" and yet be forgetful of life at the same time?

Heidegger's response is that we have forgotten that "Being" carries the resonance of a verb rather than the "thingness" of a noun. We have tended to treat Being as though it were some*thing* that we can approach and gain knowledge of, as though it were some*thing* that we can know and apprehend, as though it were some*thing* "out there" that we can probe and analyze. Rather than seeing Being as a thing "out there" — aside and apart from us — Heidegger preferred to speak of our "being-in-the-world." He suggested that we do not stand over the world in order to know the world. We are not bare, thinking subjects who reach out to know a world of objects. Rather, we are absorbed and immersed in the world, never over against it as a subject to an object.

Life means living, and living is preeminently what we *do*. We do not simply exist; rather, we are alive and we *live* — and our living is vital and dynamic, whereas much of philosophy's talk about Being always seems so detached and lifeless. Heidegger sought to renew our appreciation of the verblike quality of Being — "to be" — not what is, but the verb, the very "act" of being. Knowledge of the world can never be detached from being-in-the-world, and if we want to know (if we want to understand), we need to engage our whole way of being — our memories, our feelings, our imagination, our thinking, our actions.[8]

In a similar fashion, practical theology suggests that we cannot separate knowing from being, thinking from acting, theological reflection from pastoral and practical involvement. Theology is always shaped by and embodied in the practices of historical, cultural, and linguistic communities. Our understandings always emerge from our practices, or from the "forms of life" in which we participate.

Practical theology does not really have a head for great systems of thought, even though it may admire these systems as one admires a great cathedral. There is something wonderful about towering thoughts, but even so they still cast a shadow. Our serene theories with their grand visions of life too often deny to knowledge any origin in the practical difficulties of life, but rather seek to transcend these difficulties into a vision of Being that is pristine and unaffected by human affairs.

What is typically called "systematic theology" is often tempted to gather everything into a "grand narrative" as though it already knew the story's whole plot — the beginning, the middle, and the end. Systematic theology seems to soar on eagle's wings, flying high above life and offering us a spectacular, God-like view. What it then leaves for us is to take this grand vision and to apply it to our lives, a task typically associated with the role of "pastoral theology" — taking what we have learned in the great system and applying it to the more lowly and everyday practices of Christian living.

Life, however, is not very "systematic." As Rowan Williams suggests:

> A religious discourse with some chance of being honest will not move too far from the particular, with all its irresolution and resistance to systematizing: it will be trying to give shape to that response to the particular that is least evasive of its solid historical otherness *and* that is also rooted in the conviction that God is to be sought and listened for in all occasions.[9]

According to the Brazilian educator and thinker Paulo Freire, the danger with intellectual systems is their tendency to confuse thought with existence. The speculative thinker forgets that knowledge involves passion, struggle, decision, and personal appropriation, that we must live and act out of our knowing. "Knowledge emerges only through invention and re-invention," writes Freire, "through the restless, impatient, continuing, hopeful inquiry people pursue in the world, with the world, and with each other."[10]

Practical theology wants to keep our relationship with the world open, so that we are never quite "done" with things; rather, always undoing and redoing them, so that we can keep the "doing" happening, passionate, keen, expectant — never satisfied, never quite finished. "Be perfect as your Father in heaven is perfect" (Matthew). Perhaps practical theology — as a constant "doing" — is a passion for perfection in an imperfect world. Impossible! Yet that is probably why all the "perfect" systems are left feeling so uneasy and insecure when poets and prophets show up. Practical theology is suspicious of any theology that is too solid, too well-built, too built-up. Rather, it is a theology that is given over to a passion for what could yet be, what is still in-the-making, in process, not yet, still coming ("Thy kingdom come!").

THE PEOPLE OF OUR TIME

When theology pays renewed attention to life in the world, a wonderful theological creativity emerges. Rather than operating in a detached, abstract realm of theological speculation, practical theology seeks to pay attention to people's various life situations and contexts. It seeks to align itself, as the Second Vatican Council so eloquently reminded us, "with the joy and hope, the grief and anguish of the people of our time, especially of those who are poor and afflicted in any way."[11]

We can think, for example, of Gustavo Gutiérrez, the "father" of liberation theology. Born in Lima, Peru, he was a mestizo, sometimes condescendingly referred to as a "half-caste" (part Hispanic and part Quechuan Indian). He grew up in a poor village and suffered physically as a child, often bed-ridden, with a severe case of osteomyelitis which left him with a permanent limp. However, he managed to go to college, where he first studied medicine, but changed direction and took various studies in theology and philosophy leading to his ordination as a priest. Although trained in classical European theology, he found it increasingly difficult to reconcile this highly systematic theology with the situation of the poor and the oppressed in Latin America. His own social class and suffering helped him to see the world from the "underside of history," with the eyes of the poor — and he began to sketch a rough draft of what became a major theological work, *A Theology of Liberation*, of which Henri Nouwen wrote:

> There is a little man in Peru, a man without any power, who lives in a barrio with poor people and who wrote a book. In this book he simply reclaimed the basic Christian truth that God became human to bring good news to the poor, new light to the blind, and liberty to the captives. Ten years later this book and the movement it started is considered a danger by the greatest power on earth.[12]

The story of Gutiérrez, "that little man from Peru," is a poignant reminder that theology — which means the "word of God" — is always addressed to particular situations of human life. It is also a poignant reminder that nothing that is genuinely human is alien to the gospel. On the contrary, the human story is the very "site" of God's revelation. This is why practical theology is always attentive to the *context* of human culture and human experience in its unique singularity and concrete particularity. Not only is Gutiérrez's story important, but so is every human story — my story, your story, the stories of women, the stories of indigenous peoples, the stories of humanity embodied in diverse cultural expressions, the stories of the saints — because it is in the human story that we hear the word of God who, as the Christian tradition affirms, "was made flesh and pitched his tent among us" (John 1:14).

VOCATION

The great philosopher of dialogue Martin Buber tells a story about an event that became a fundamental turning point in his life.[13] He was sitting in his office, seemingly enjoying the delights of studying and reading — a morning of "religious enthusiasm," he calls it. Then an unknown young man came to see him. Buber responded to the young man with friendly conversation, but wasn't really present to him "in spirit." He listened and was not disrespectful, but this was just another one of those usual visits from students, and he paid it no more or no less attention.

Later, not long after this visit, Buber learned that the young man had taken his own life. "I learned that he had come to me not casually," writes Buber, "but borne by destiny, not for a chat but for a decision. He had come to me, he had come in this hour." Reflecting further on this event, Buber says that he finally came to realize that religious experience is not meant to "lift you out of the world," but to lead you into the world. He writes:

> Since then I have given up the "religious" which is nothing but exception, extraction, exaltation, ecstasy; or it has given me up. I possess nothing but the everyday out of which I am never taken. The mystery is no longer disclosed, it has escaped or it has made its dwelling here where everything happens as it happens. I know no fullness but each mortal hour's fullness of claim and responsibility. . . . I do not know much more. If that is religion then it is just *everything*, simply all that is lived in its possibility of dialogue.[14]

Buber goes on to give the example of prayer, suggesting that when we pray, we do not remove ourselves or our lives from our prayer; rather, we bring our very lives to our prayer. Prayer does not remove us from life; rather, when we pray, we "yield" or refer our life to God. We listen. We seek to align ourselves with God's will, with God's heart, with God's good intentions for the world. And then, in the experience of prayer, a surprising transformation occurs, and we find that God is referring to us. "You are called from above," writes Buber, "you with this mortal bit of life are referred to . . . required, chosen, empowered, sent. . . ."[15]

According to the Jewish philosopher and Talmudic commentator Emmanuel Levinas, life is *vocational.* It addresses me. It calls out to me. It asks after me. It asks me to respond, to answer, to say, "Here I am . . . for you . . . in the Name of God." Practical theology shows a preference for the stranger in our midst, for the neighbor who is close to us, for the one who pleads for mercy or who cries out for justice, the one who says, "Love should be put into action!" This is when God comes between us and gets in my way, refuses to let me pass by — looks at me and commands me, pleads with me — respond! Act! "Going towards God is meaningless," writes Levinas, "unless seen in terms of my primary going towards the other person."[16] How can we say we love God, whom we have not seen, unless we love a brother or a sister whom we have seen? (1 John 4:20–21). Or as Levinas puts it, "The invisible but personal God is not approached outside of all human presence. . . . It is our relations with men that give theological concepts the sole signification they admit of . . . without which they would remain empty and formal frameworks."[17]

TO BE THOUGHTFUL AND ATTENTIVE

Practical theology displays a general wariness toward great systems of thought, yet it by no means advocates a simplistic return to theology as a "practical doing" over against theology as a "theoretical thinking."

Thoughtfulness is important to theology, just as it is important to human living. We all know what it means to speak of a "thoughtful" person or, by contrast, a "thoughtless" person. A thoughtful person is someone who is concerned and who cares. When someone acts in an especially generous or caring way, we often say how thoughtful that person is. Yet when someone acts in a careless or reckless manner, we wonder how such a person could be so thoughtless in their actions.

Practical theology is more about "understanding" than it is about "knowing." To understand is very different than to know. Indeed, an "all-knowing" person often strikes us as arrogant. Who does not feel a resistance toward the "know-it-all"? On the other hand, the person who understands is usually someone who feels great sympathy, who listens and seems to understand what we are going through. The understanding person is compassionate — "suffering with" — rather than bellowing with supposed wisdom.

In a brief and yet beautiful essay, Simone Weil reflects on "the right use of school studies with a view to the love of God" (the title of her essay). "Although people seem to be unaware of it today," writes Weil, "the development of the faculty of attention forms the real object and almost sole interest of studies."[18]

Weil suggests that *thoughtful attention* is crucial to the pursuit of learning, and that this pursuit will, in turn, aid us in living attentive and responsive lives. She writes:

> Not only does the love of God have attention for its substance; the love of neighbor, which we know to be the same love, is made of this same substance.... The capacity to give one's attention to a sufferer is a very rare and difficult thing; it is almost a miracle; it *is* a miracle. Nearly all those who think they have this capacity do not possess it.[19]

Woody Allen once quipped that 90 percent of humanity simply "shows up." We go about our lives almost in stunned resignation, hardly giving it a thought. In a similar way, the ancient philosopher Socrates said that a life lived *unreflectively* is a life lived in only half-measure. In other words, to truly live a full and worthwhile life is to *attend* to life, to be fully involved and immersed in life's great project. Otherwise, our lives are only half-lived, just touching the surface, rather than attentively present and fully engaged. Only the one "who is capable of attention," says Weil, "can do this."[20]

In his work on the Hebrew prophets, the Jewish theologian Abraham Heschel tells us that "the ultimate element of theological reflection is transcendent divine attention to man, the fact that man is apprehended by God."[21] The prophets *felt* this divine attention to humanity; they saw and felt the world as God sees and feels the world — with God's eyes, God's heart, God's mercy and justice. "The primary content of the prophet's consciousness," writes Heschel, "is this *divine attentiveness and concern*." He goes on to say that it is this "divine attentiveness to humanity, an involvement in history, a divine vision of the world, which the prophet shares and which he tries to convey." It is God's concern for humanity that lay at the root of the prophet's work. "Sympathy opens man to the living God. Unless we share His concern, we know nothing about the living God." Prophetic theology "may be defined, not as what man does with his ultimate concern, but rather *what man does with God's* concern."[22]

A WORK — NOT JUST "DOING"

In many ways, we live in a society that is always *doing*. Our lives are filled with busyness, and perhaps it is not surprising that this busyness is often linked with the constantly churning wheels of "business." Our calendars always seem full — how many times have I heard the reply, "Let me check my schedule." Moreover, we do all we can to ensure we don't miss a beat of all this rushed activity, armed with our indispensable cell phones, e-mails, faxes, and beepers.

But are we about the "work of God," of which Jesus says, "My Father is working still, and I am working" (John 5:17)? Jesus does the work his Father gave him to do (John 17:4), to "bring good news to the poor, to proclaim liberty to the captives, and to the blind new sight, to set the downtrodden free, to proclaim the Lord's year of favor" (Luke 4:18). During his time, there were some who wondered if Jesus was the anointed one of God. Jesus simply pointed to his activity among the people — teaching, healing, loving, forgiving...(Luke 7:18–23). His work is "pleasing to God" (John 8:28) and reveals the very nature and activity of God: "the work my Father has given me to do...the very work I have in hand, testifies that the Father has sent me" (John 5:36).

The work of practical theology is *vocational* work, in which our purpose for being in the world is related to the purposes of God. We would miss the mark of practical theology if we associate the word "practical" with the gross pragmatism and busyness of our age, where every "truth" boils down to its "usefulness" or its "application" or its "relevance" — or is otherwise dismissed as irrelevant and useless. Practical theology can never be reduced to the appeal of the pragmatist, "Let's get practical!" Rather, practical theology is a *response* to the call of God in which we come to realize that our purpose for "being in the world" is to respond to the "purposes of God." And sometimes, the purposes of God are very different to the purposes of the world. Indeed, as John Caputo notes, in the eyes of the world they can often seem rather foolish and impracticable:

> From time to time, here and there, it happens that men and women respond, answer a call, spend themselves, using themselves up entirely for the Other. They spend years, maybe a lifetime, serving others, giving themselves up for the good of others. . . . Fools spend their lives working to feed and house the poor, or teaching in crime-ridden schools, or protecting defenseless wildlife; they lead a celibate life serving the peasants in Central America, only to be dragged out of bed one night and shot to death by right-wing gangsters; they spend the better part of their adult life in prison, refusing to cut a deal with a racist government, trying to make a point.[23]

We may consider them fools, but in the end the lives of these obsessive and mad saints *do* make a point; we know that "what matters is the amazing grace, the amazing gift they make." As St. John reminds us, "Those who do what is true come to the light, so that it may be seen that their deeds have been done in God" (John 3:21). The work of practical theology is the work of the kingdom of God, and of the Spirit given to us: "Whoever has faith in me will do what I am doing, they will do even greater things . . ." (John 14:12).

TRUTH AND GOODNESS

Living attentive, thoughtful lives is important to practical theology. To try to live reflectively is to try to live in truthful ways — with integrity and honesty. It is to try to live responsibly, rather than with numbed silence or cold indifference. However, the test of truth is not so much measured against our great theories of life. Rather, truth is measured by the fruit it bears. When I am in the presence of a good and holy person, I am amazed at the truth I see — more than I have gleaned from books alone.

Emmanuel Levinas says that Goodness should always preside over the work of truth. The question of meaning and existence carries no sense on its own, unless it is first underwritten by the question of the ethical and the Good. This is the crux of Levinas's insistence: Whether or not existence is ethical and carries the value of the "Good" is a more urgent question and claims priority over whether or not existence is meaningful and carries the clarity of the "True." "Morality," writes Levinas, "presides over the work of truth."[24] The Good must preside over the True, in the sense that the value of my life for you presides over the meaning of my life for me. The question of existence cannot be answered within the realms of my own self or from the resources of my own self-reflection. Rather, it is given to me by the other who *provokes* the question of my existence, even as I try to justify its meaning. It is given to me by the one who is suffering, even while I live. It is given to me by the stranger and the immigrant, even while I recline at home. What is always first, what is always prior, is not the meaning of my existence as "being-there," but the responsibility of my existence as "being-for." All of Levinas's thinking hinges on this one crucial affirmation, that we are responsible for each other, that my existence is not an existence unto myself, but an existence "to you" and "for you."[25]

In the Jewish tradition, when the rabbis come across a difficult biblical text, they always look for the *ethical* message of the text, even when it is not especially evident. If the ethical message is not immediately apparent to them, it must be that they are not reading or interpreting the text correctly. They will stay with the text, bending and twisting it until its ethical import rings free. God's word, the Torah, is always about the *way one should live*, and the meaning of a text is always determined according to its ethical truth.[26]

In a similar way, in the Christian tradition, Augustine proposed that a basic principle of a *good* interpretation of scripture is whether or not the interpretation leads to a greater love of God and neighbor. The *good* interpretation will never lead one astray even if it may fall short of being the "true" or "correct" interpretation. Augustine writes that if someone "is deceived in an interpretation which builds up charity, which is the end of the commandments, he is deceived in the same way as a man who leaves a road by mistake but passes through a field to the same place toward which the road itself leads."[27]

Knowing the truth means little, according to St. Paul, unless it is infused with love. "If I have all the eloquence of men or angels, but speak without love, I am simply a gong booming or a cymbal clashing" (1 Cor. 13:1). Love and goodness must always lead the way, presiding over the work of theology, and not merely relegated into an "afterthought" — as happens, for example, when we create a subset of theology and call it "moral" or "pastoral" theology. Questions of morality, ethics, justice, and mercy must accompany all our theological work, such that the "theoretical" and the "practical" are not originally distinguishable.

A CRAFT MORE THAN A METHOD

It is not uncommon to read books on practical theology that devote considerable time to the question of methodology, that is, how we can best proceed with the task of practical theology. Learning the various methods of practical theology is important, but we should be wary of turning these methods into a simple "how to." Our world is inundated with "how to" books.

In his best-known work, the philosopher Hans-Georg Gadamer draws a distinction between "truth and method" (his book's title). Gadamer felt that our approaches toward reading and interpreting life were too captivated by methodological concerns.[28] He felt that we had become too preoccupied with finding the best methods to analyze human life, be it ancient texts, historical periods, other cultures, religious symbols. Getting the method right seemed as important, if not more important, than the truth we were seeking to discover. Moreover, our attachment to method gave us a smug sense that we were in control of our search and that all discoveries were finally in our hands.

In contrast to method, Gadamer preferred to speak of "truth" or "understanding." Whereas method tends to distance us from what we seek to know — as though we were mere observers of life — understanding seeks to invite our very selves into the interpretive process. Rather than standing apart, analyzing and probing with our refined methods, understanding seeks to draw us in. Inevitably we will lose something of the "control" that our methods afforded us, but we will become more receptive and open to that which is seeking to speak to us, to show itself to us, to reveal its truth to us.

In an interesting passage, Martin Heidegger offers the analogy of a woodworker learning the craft of cabinetmaking. He writes:

A cabinetmaker's apprentice, someone who is learning to build cabinets and the like, will serve as an example. His learning is not mere practice, to gain facility in the use of tools. Nor does he merely gather knowledge about the customary forms of the things he is to build. If he is to become a true cabinetmaker, he makes himself answer and respond above all to the different kinds of wood and to the shapes slumbering within the wood — to wood as it enters into man's dwelling with all the hidden riches of its nature. In fact, this relatedness to wood is what maintains the whole craft. Without that relatedness, the craft will never be anything but empty busywork.... Every handicraft, *all human dealings*, are constantly in that danger.[29]

Along with learning the "tools" and methods of practical theology, we must also develop an essential "relatedness" to theology, whereby theological practice becomes a way of life, where it enters our dwelling in the world and reveals "all the hidden riches of its nature." Practical theology is a craft in which we continually "answer and respond" to the call and vocation of apprenticeship and discipleship in God's ways.

In philosophy this process is known as *phronesis* — a "practical wisdom" that is shaped over years of practicing the wisdom of a craft, a teaching, or a discipline that becomes a "way of life." For practical theology, this process is known as a *habitus*, a disposition of the mind and heart from which our actions flow naturally, or, if you like, "according to the Spirit" dwelling within us.[30]

ON EARTH

Practical theology necessarily attends to the *conditions* of human life. It is concerned with the unique, the particular, the concrete — this people, this community, this place, this moment, this neighbor, this question, this need, this concern. Vatican II's Pastoral Constitution (*Gaudium et spes*) reminds us that without attention to "the joy and hope, the grief and anguish of the people of our time," practical theology would have little or no connection to the coming of God's kingdom "on earth." That same document tells us that "*at all times*, the Church carries the responsibility of reading the signs of the times and of interpreting them in the light of the Gospel" (nos. 1, 4).

"At all times" is another way of saying that the theological task must be performed *each* and *every* time — not *once* and *for all time*. In many ways, all good theology is practical theology — attentive, searching, responsive. Indeed, even the great classic works of theology (Augustine or Aquinas, for example) represent theological responses worked out in response to contemporary pastoral situations — bold and innovative attempts to listen to and understand present realities rather than simply regurgitating answers from the past.

There is nothing easy about practical theology. Trying to interpret present realities is an incredibly difficult and complex task. Often, it will require of theology a partnering with other disciplines, especially the social sciences, to help us get a better "read" of what is actually going on in our situation. Another valuable resource for "reading the signs of the times" can be found in our poets and songwriters, novelists and artists — those who are best able to unmask our cultural blinders to current realities.

It is easy to be lulled into our present, and to fail to notice how askew things really are. In Luke's Gospel, Jesus says to the crowds, "When you see a cloud looming up in the west you say at once that rain is coming, and so it does. And when the wind is from the south you say it will be hot, and it is. Hypocrites! You know how to interpret the face of the earth and the sky. How is it you do not know how to interpret the present time?" (12:54–56). How indeed? There is a reproof in this question. We seem to be able to read and interpret that which is predictable and familiar to us, but when it comes to interpreting the present time, we "hear and hear again, but do not understand; see and see again, but do not perceive" (Isa. 6:9; cf. Matt. 13:13–15).

To read the signs of the times is one of the most difficult theological tasks, yet it is a theological imperative. Too often we do not behold the announcement of God in our present reality. Rather, we cling to what we already know of God, to tired and weary theological frameworks that have lost their sense of timeliness, to religious truths that lull us to sleep rather than provoke us to wakefulness. Any sense of expectation, announcement, or the coming of the kingdom is lost to us. Knowing the ways and purposes of God becomes as customary and familiar as forecasting the weather, yet we are cautioned to "stay awake" lest we hear but do not hear, see but do not see. This vigilance does not come easily because it challenges theology to be observant and mindful — to "think again" — to be alert and attentive. We are called to think and act for these times, for this reality, in the face of "the joy and hope, grief and anguish of the people of our time, especially of those who are poor or afflicted . . . in deep solidarity with the human race and its history."

AS IT IS IN HEAVEN

"Is there a way," asks Emmanuel Levinas, "for the wisdom of heaven to return to earth?"[31] While it is crucial that practical theology attend to the concrete *conditions* of human existence, it must seek to read or interpret those conditions in the light of "the kingdom of heaven." What is the kingdom of heaven like? In many ways, the whole of the biblical tradition is an attempt to answer this question — or rather, to *provoke* this question — like the unsettling, demanding cries of the Hebrew prophets, or the disruptive parables of Jesus that keep turning things around, or the irritating lives of crazy saints with their impossible visions and out-of-place utopias.

When we pray, "Thy kingdom come," we are subjecting the *conditions* of human existence, "on earth," to the *unconditional* claims of God's word, "as it is in heaven." There are, for example, no conditions that limit or circumscribe the biblical message of mercy and justice, as though we could ever put up our feet and say, "No more is required of me." Each new age and every new generation must wrestle again with the question of what it means to act with justice and yet to love tenderly and be merciful.

The biblical message is not timeless (or "heavenly") in the sense that it has nothing to do with time or history. Rather, it is timeless in the sense that it proclaims a "surplus of love" or an "amazing grace" that knows no bounds, a love that refuses to be measured by the history of human events, but that continually bursts forth and breaks into human history as an immeasurable love that awakens, inspires, and agitates our lives.

Practical theology is an effort to always honor the appeal to human experience, drawing our attention to questions of history, culture, and society, urging us to respond to the real needs of our world, to the conditions of human existence, "on earth." This is perhaps what is meant by the word "practical." Yet it is practical *theology* — an effort to regain the transcendent appeal of God's word to humanity, an appeal that calls out to us and asks us to be people of God, people of faith, people of hope, people of justice and mercy — a people living and acting on earth, "as it is in heaven."

APPENDIX:
What Is Distinctive about Practical Theology?
Some Representative Quotes from Scholarship

St. Thomas University, Miami, recently launched a new doctoral degree in Practical Theology. To celebrate the event, I coordinated a Symposium on Practical Theology, bringing together some leading scholars in the field to discuss the shape and relevance of practical theology for the academy, the church, and society.[32] We began one of our discussions with the following meditative reading, which offers representative quotes concerning the distinctiveness of practical theology. I offer it here as an appendix to this introductory chapter.

• • •

The joy and hope, the grief and anguish of the people of our time, especially of those who are poor or afflicted in any way, are the joy and the hope, the grief and the anguish of the followers of Christ as well. Nothing that is genuinely human fails to find an echo in their hearts.... We must be aware of and understand the aspirations, the yearnings, and the often dramatic features of the world in which we live.... At all times the Church carries the responsibility of reading the signs of the times in the light of the Gospel.

(*Gaudium et spes*, "The Church in the Modern World," nos. 1, 4)

By Christian practices we mean things Christian people do together over time to address fundamental human needs in response to and in light of God's active presence for the life of the world.

(Craig Dykstra and Dorothy Bass)[33]

And when he saw the crowds he felt sorry for them because they were harassed and dejected, like sheep without a shepherd. Then he said to his disciples, "the harvest is rich but the laborers are few...."

(Matt. 9:36–37)

Practical theology is that theological discipline which is concerned with the Church's self-actualization here and now — both that which *is* and that which *ought to be*. This it does by means of *theological illumination* of the particular situation in which the Church must realize itself in all its dimensions.... *Everything* is its subject-matter.   (Karl Rahner)[34]

There is only the demand — the properly theological demand — that wherever and whoever the practical theologian is, he or she is bound by the very nature of the enterprise as theological to show how one interprets the tradition and how one interprets the present situation and how these two interpretations correlate: either as identities of meaning, analogies, or radical nonidentities.   (David Tracy)[35]

At its best, theology means figuring out how to bring faith and life together. The theological method I recommend is that people reflect on their lives from the perspective of faith, and on faith from the perspective of their lives. Quite simply, I encourage *bringing life to faith, and faith to life.*   (Thomas Groome)[36]

Practical theology is a place where religious belief, tradition, and practice meets contemporary experiences, questions, and actions and conducts a dialogue that is mutually enriching, intellectually critical, and practically transforming.   (James Woodward and Stephen Pattison)[37]

Seeking God's presence involves theological reflection, the artful discipline of putting our experience into conversation with the heritage of the Christian tradition. In this conversation we can be surprised and transformed by new angles of vision on our experience and acquire a deepened understanding and appreciation of our tradition. In this conversation we can find ourselves called to act in new courageous and compassionate ways.
            (Patricia O'Connell Killen and John de Beer)[38]

The underlying purpose of practical theological reflection is to sustain a disciplined conversation between a faith community's vision of the world as it should be and the often harsh realities of the world as it is, a conversation that leads to faithful and feasible action.
                          (Michael Cowan and Bernard Lee)[39]

You know how to interpret the appearance of earth and sky, but why do you not know how to interpret the present time?   (Luke 12:56)

We can no longer speak of culture and world events as areas *to which* theology is adapted and applied; culture and world events are *the very sources* of the theological enterprise, *along with and equal to* Scripture and tradition.   (Stephen Bevans)[40]

Knowledge emerges only through invention and reinvention, through the restless, impatient, continually hopeful inquiry people pursue in the world, with the world, and with each other. (Paulo Freire)[41]

A religious discourse with some chance of being honest will not move too far from the particular, with all its irresolution and resistance to systematizing: it will be trying to give shape to that response to the particular that is least evasive of its solid historical otherness *and* that is also rooted in the conviction that God is to be sought and listened for in all occasions. (Rowan Williams)[42]

My Father is working, and I am working still. (John 5:17)

To think and act practically in fresh and innovative ways may be the most complex thing that humans ever attempt. (Don Browning)[43]

When you try to tidy up unsystematized speech, you are likely to lose a great deal. . . . The meanings of the word "God" are to be discovered by watching what this community does — not only when it is consciously reflecting in conceptual ways, but when it is acting, educating, imagining, and worshiping. (Rowan Williams)[44]

To venture a theological life is *to live theologically*. It is not so much to ask about the ways that theology can be made practical; rather, it is to ask how the practices of my life can be made theological. (Terry Veling)[45]

Theology has to study its own workings, not in narcissism but in penitence. (Rowan Williams)[46]

Why do you call me, "Lord, Lord" and not do what I say? (Luke 6:46)

We do not have a plan of action to propose, but we do know that if we can develop a true spirituality of the sacredness of others, we will find a way of creating a truly sacred human family wherein no one will be forced to live as an unwelcome alien; no one will be ashamed of the color of their skin, the shape of their eyes, or the size of their bodies; no one will be denied the basic opportunities of life; and people, institutions, and governments will truly care for the welcome of every single person. Thus will society become the temple of the Living God. (Virgilio Elizondo)[47]

The respect for the stranger and the sanctification of the name of the Eternal are strangely equivalent. And all the rest is dead letter.

(Emmanuel Levinas)[48]

Any attempt to separate the love of God from the love of neighbor gives rise to attitudes which impoverish both.   (Gustavo Gutiérrez)[49]

Those who say, "I love God," and hate their brothers and sisters, are liars; for those who do not love a brother or a sister whom they have seen, cannot love God whom they have not seen.   (1 John 4:20–21)

We must take on the form of Christ, as Christ took on our own form.

(Robert Schreiter)[50]

For the desert monks, the question of how to bring one's life into conformity with Scripture was a burning question. They were convinced that only through *doing* what the text enjoined could one hope to gain any understanding of its meaning.   (Douglas Burton-Christie)[51]

In every age the community of faith must discover the shape of its ministry. We must discern how we are to be faithful to the gospel and effective in our mission: to celebrate God's saving presence and to contribute, by word and action and sacrament, to the fullness of this presence — the coming of the kingdom.   (Evelyn and James Whitehead)[52]

In this sense practical theology is not an occasional, problem-solving technique but an ongoing way of doing theology and living the Christian faith.

(Robert Kinast)[53]

Those who do what is true come to the light, so that it may be clearly seen that their deeds have been done in God.   (John 3:21)

TWO

Scripture and Tradition — Heaven's Door

PRACTICAL THEOLOGY AND THE ART OF INTERPRETATION

Most of us are aware today that our understandings and approaches to life are deeply shaped by our particular contexts — our cultural backgrounds, our social conditionings, our economic realities, our personal histories, and so on. This is a fairly commonplace truth in today's world, especially in today's globalized world, where we are increasingly exposed to a plurality of human ways of being-in-the-world. In other words, most of us are aware that the world around us is never simply "given," as though it came to us "pure and neat" without the important mediations of culture, language, and social location.

All this is to say that we live in the world as interpreters of the world, that we are always interpreting ourselves and the world around us, that to be human is to be an interpreter of life in all its rich distinctions and variations. The art of interpretation is a fundamental condition of human existence. As David Tracy notes: "Every time we act, deliberate, judge, understand, or even experience, we are interpreting. To understand at all is to interpret....Whether we know it or not, to be human is to be a skilled interpreter."[1]

To affirm that human beings are fundamentally "interpretive beings" is to affirm a positive creativity to human life. Indeed, from a theological point of view, it is to affirm that humanity shares in the creative goodness of divine life, that we share in God's own creative spirit in naming and shaping our world. Just as God continually brings forth existence in

23

generous creativity, so do we. A famous rabbinic text says that God smiles and takes delight in our interpretive abilities (Tractate *Bava Metzia* 59b). It is not difficult, for example, to marvel at the human spirit that interprets life through great works of poetry and art, through the slow incubation of intricate and often ancient cultural forms, through the deeply probing questions of inquiring minds that have shaped philosophy and science, through the great religious traditions of our world that have searched the wellsprings of compassion and moral goodness.

"To be human is to be a skilled interpreter." For all its creative capability and potential, interpretation nevertheless remains an "art" or a "skill" that needs to be nurtured and guided, for not every interpretation is a good interpretation. We can interpret well, or we can interpret poorly. Moreover, we often face *conflicting* interpretations that require of us considerable skills in discernment and decision. The question, therefore, is how do we become *good* interpreters — how do we become practiced in the skill and art of good interpretation?

A whole literature has devoted itself to this question, under the umbrella term of "hermeneutics."[2] Hermeneutics is concerned with the art of interpretation, and one of the first claims it makes is that interpretation is primarily concerned with the *event* of understanding. The question hermeneutics asks is: what does it mean to understand? — be it another person or my own self, a different culture or the culture in which I live, an ancient text or a contemporary poem, the memory of a sacred tradition or the urgency of a present question, an event in history or the dilemmas of current times, a previously held understanding or a newly emerging one, what has been given to us or what we must yet create, the urgency of the "here and now" or the urgency of what is "not yet" and "still coming."

In many ways, hermeneutics is concerned with mediating "competing claims" such as these — not in the sense of pitting one against the other, such that one wins out over the other — but in the sense that these competing claims bring to the fore a need to *decide* and to *choose*. If understanding is what hermeneutics seeks, it is equally insistent that any understanding (if it truly *is* an understanding) plays itself out in the choices and decisions we make — that it *affects* how we will be in the world — our values, our behaviors, our actions, our relationships with others. Otherwise, we could not really claim that we have understood at all. Any understanding that doesn't issue forth in changed or renewed behavior and action in the world isn't really understanding. In other words, understanding is never a purely theoretical or speculative exercise that stands aloof; rather, it always carries practical intent for the ways we live in the world.

It is perhaps not surprising that practical theology is interested in hermeneutics and the art of interpretation. It often speaks of two fundamentally interpretive acts that are central to theological activity — "searching the scriptures" and "reading the signs of the times." These are poetic descriptions that highlight the importance of interpretation as a crucial theological activity. "Reading" and "searching" are active, verb-like words of inquiry: seeking, attending, laboring, grappling, wondering, praying, probing, questioning, listening, responding, acting.

"Searching the scriptures" refers to the reading and studying of God's word. It means paying attention to the biblical testimony and the way this testimony has been lived and received across generations of people of faith. Searching the scriptures is an interpretive and communal exercise that links us with a rich tradition of faith, filled with commentary and teaching, liturgy and art, prophetic witness and saintly lives.

"Reading the signs of the times" is concerned with the way this tradition of faith opens onto our present reality. God's word is always a word addressed to us and for us — a word that calls forth our response. Reading the signs of the times means paying attention to God's concern for the world. It means listening and responding to the questions and issues that are circulating within our culture and society, within our own lives, within our parishes and congregations, our workplaces, our local neighborhoods.

A third complexity emerges when we begin to ask how these two interpretive acts are related to each other. Is my current reality the "lens" through which I search the scriptures, or does my searching of the scriptures provide the "lens" through which I view my current reality? How do these interpretations cultivate a faithful response to the world in which we live and the tradition in which we stand?

Rather than shy away from these complexities, practical theology prefers to highlight this interpretive activity as central to the theological enterprise. Indeed, it is the vital wellspring of its creativity, arising as it does from the three "constants" or "essentials" that have stirred the life of faith communities in every age: attention to their faith tradition, to their present experience, and to the way these two relate to each other and call forth response. In this chapter and the following two chapters, we explore each of these entwined threads of practical theology.

MORE THAN METHOD ALONE

Most disciplines in life are a mixture of method and artfulness. A parent or a teacher, for example, learns methods for good parenting or good pedagogy. Similarly, an artist learns different methods of brushstroke, or a poet different methods of word-craft. Musicians learn techniques for playing their instruments well, and mathematicians learn formulas for solving intricate equations. A chef learns about different recipes and ingredients, and a philosopher learns how to work with different theories and ideas. In other words, whether we speak of the sciences or the arts, certain methods in these various disciplines are integral to their practice.

However, we also know that the best practitioners of any discipline are those who develop a certain "intuition" or "naturalness" in the practice of their discipline that takes them beyond an attachment to "rules" or "methods" alone. They come to know their material or their subject matter so well that they develop an "intimacy" with its inner workings, and their initial schooling in the disciplined application of *method* is transformed into the wondrous creativity of *art*. Knowledge becomes a "wisdom," instruction becomes a "craft," and practice becomes — if not perfect — at least skillful and artful in its creativity and expression.

To call theology "practical" is to suggest, among other things, that it too is a *practice* that requires a transformation from the technique of a method into the artfulness of a craft. It means learning the *habitus* or essential "habits" or "practices" of theology that come from a disciplined "practical wisdom." In other words, at some point we must move beyond the world of methodological application into the riskier and yet more creative world of artfulness. A good practitioner of any discipline — be it a good teacher, a good physician, a good parent (or a good theologian) — is someone who has nurtured and developed one's skills through an attuned and artful "practical wisdom."

Hans-Georg Gadamer's major work on hermeneutics is titled *Truth and Method*. A key concern of this work is to reclaim the practice of interpretation as an *art concerned with truth* (and *beauty* and *goodness*), rather than simply a *method* concerned with determining or replicating a "correct" outcome or a "correct" reading.[3] As if reading a poem, for example, or a passage from scripture, could ever be reduced to a purely detached and unmoved theoretical investigation. As if the beauty of poetic truth could ever be distilled through the finely filtered controls of a methodological approach.

Moreover, when we consider that the *creativity* of human expression involves moving through and beyond methods and techniques, then surely we must also consider that the *reception* of a creative work also involves moving through and beyond methods and techniques. In other words, just as more is at stake in the *creative production* of a work than reliance on method alone, so too more is also at stake in the *interpretive reception* of a creative work than methodical concerns alone. The art of interpretation is intimately tied to the art of creativity, and this is as it should be, for the *creativity of a work* necessarily calls forth the *creativity of the interpreter.* Otherwise, the "work" would be relegated to the "dustbins" of history — neither creating nor eliciting any active historical engagement. Simply put, creative and inspired works demand creative and inspired interpretation.

There are some who worry about creative interpretation. It makes them nervous. Rather than an "art," they see the possibility of deception. Rather than creativity, they worry about "the truth." They think that interpretation will only lead to a confusion of multiple meanings devoid of any objective measures and criteria. If all is interpretable, then all is up for grabs, and "truth" becomes a confusion of endlessly contested meanings — plural and ambiguous, rather than clear and distinct. "Truth" becomes "many" and "relative," rather than "one" and "the same." Those who are nervous about interpretation feel that it only leads to confusion, ambiguity, and conflict. This seems to me like a valid concern. Indeed, why would we inquire into the art of interpretation except that we want to somehow avoid confusion and misunderstanding, and seek better ways of coming to *understanding* between us? However, as we know from our own daily interactions with the people and events of our lives, reaching shared understandings or finding the "truth of things" is a difficult task fraught with risk and complexity.

Gadamer is seeking to remind us that the human heart is always deeply involved and engaged in the art of interpretation, such that anyone who truly encounters a sacred or poetic word knows that little of its beauty or truth can be discovered by detached, methodological analysis alone. Truth's beauty and goodness is essentially creative in its expression and therefore needs an equally creative reception. Method only offers us a sense of "controlled" meaning, whereas the poetic word knows nothing of this cool and detached approach. Rather, what is required to hear the poetic word is a deeply felt movement of the heart — a *resonance* that responds rather than simply a method that controls.

Gadamer is at pains to suggest that we moderns have lost this sense of *interpretive resonance*, preferring instead the cool rationality of a detached, unencumbered, "enlightened" rationality. In other words, we moderns prefer an interpretive stance of rationally controlled distance, rather than an interpretive approach of heartfelt resonance. What is lost to us, according to Gadamer, is an appreciation of *tradition* as a deep font of *interpretive resonance*. If *resonance* with a work is crucial to the art of interpretation, then surely much is to be gained from the wisdom of past generations who have learned, over the years, to *attune* their hearts to the essential contours of a work. In other words, tradition is a font of patient and hard-won wisdom that *resounds* with intuitive sense — a deeply felt and historically gifted *resonance* with a work that we should mine as an interpretive resource rather eschew as a burden.

WHAT ENDURES?

Nothing lasts for long. Just this morning, I collected a week's worth of newspapers and dumped them in the recycling bin. All those headlines and attention-grabbing new stories, all the gossip and advertisements, all those specially packaged pages — sports, business, lifestyle, health, entertainment — all this seeming "stuff of life" simply dumped and disposed of. As though it counted for nothing, as though it simply came along and now it is gone.

While throwing out those newspapers, I found myself struck with the image of millions of people who are exposed, each day, to "the news." It is virtually a daily ritual of contemporary life — the morning newspaper, the drive-time news program on the radio, the evening news on television, the daily e-mail news alert. And along with the news, of course, comes all the trappings of the media — advertising, social gossip, "infotainment." In a twist on a well-known Gospel verse (Luke 4:4), I found myself wanting to say, "One does not live on the news alone."

"The news" is an image that bespeaks our fascination with current events. We are often captivated by the latest, the newest, the contemporary, the "now." The literature of hermeneutics, however, reminds us that we are radically historical beings, that we do not live simply in the present; rather, we are deeply shaped by history and tradition. One of the crucial questions raised by hermeneutics is: What is our relationship to the past? As we shall see, this question is not unconcerned with our present reality, but it is seeking to place our present within the broader context of the weight and influence of history and tradition. Hermeneutics reminds us that our interpretive frameworks reach far deeper and stretch far wider than the smaller slice of time that we call "contemporary."

This attention to the past is of great interest to the practical theologian. It would be wrong to assume that practical theology is only concerned with making theology relevant to contemporary situations. Rather, it is deeply rooted in a living, breathing tradition that binds people across centuries. To simply bypass this living tradition in the hope of arriving at a more applicable, relevant, or contemporary rendering of that tradition would be a grave mistake. Moreover, according to the insights of hermeneutics, it would also be a fairly "modern" mistake.

In *Truth and Method*, Gadamer paints a picture of the modern, enlightened mind-set that seeks to unshackle itself from past traditions in the desire to become free, autonomous, and critical thinkers — guided by reason and unburdened by past prejudices.[4] In this modern scenario, religious discourse is considered antiquated and trumped by a newfound confidence in humanity's ability to demystify religious truths, dethrone tradition's authority, and break free from the tutelage of the past. Whereas the ancients once considered theology the "queen of sciences," the language of secular modernity has now long held ascendancy, forcing religious language into the realms of purely private and subjective truth. It is "merely belief" and nowhere near the enlightened truth of our supposedly progressive, scientific, enlightened world of modernity — championing the causes of democracy and freedom, pluralism and tolerance, demystification and enlightenment, technology and progress. What was once a "royal discourse" has now become a "marginal discourse," of little or no account except that it may "resource" society with some moral values or provide a few humble souls with a sense of religious consolation in their difficult lives.[5]

As I threw out those newspapers, I found myself wondering about the modern scenario in which many of us find ourselves. I found myself wondering about what endures. Is there anything that marks my existence beyond the seeming day-to-day living of contemporary life? The newspapers — which became for me a symbolic conduit of our modern, informed, and supposedly progressive and liberal society — were in reality quite readily disposable. What, I wondered, is not so disposable? What would I not so readily throw away? What endures, and why does it endure? Here again, we are breaking upon the heart of a hermeneutical question — is there a quality to human existence that is more than the "daily news"? Is there a deeper memory that claims our existence, something that comes to us — in a long line of descendants — from a "past" that is less prone to evaporation? Is there, for example, a different type of "news" that I need to expose myself to — the "good news" of the Gospels, for example?

What is this "more than" that echoes in our hearts? What is this sense that something "more than" our contemporary lives claims and urges our attention? This question is itself both a hermeneutical question and a religious question. For the former, it draws our attention to our radically historical condition as human beings — that we exist in time and in history and, as such, we cannot too readily dispense with our "past" as a supposed burden of outmoded thinking. Rather, our past functions in human discourse much like it functions in our personal lives; it is our living memory. Imagine, for example, what your life would be like without memory. You would have no sense of who you are because you would have no sense of the important events, people, and connections that have shaped your life. Deprived of memory, you would simply be existing in the present, but you would have no way of understanding that present, because it would be divorced from the rich fabric of connection and meaning that memory provides you. Hermeneutics is striving to make a similar point, namely, that human beings live within important collective memories and traditions that serve as crucial and fundamental interpretive frameworks for our understanding and apprehension of life.

Similarly, our faith tradition serves as a reminder that there is more to my life than can be construed from the present alone. It hints or points to a memory that exceeds the simple renderings of present reality. This memory "stretches back" to a time that is not purely contemporaneous with the "current time." Rather, it holds the current time answerable to a longer view, a deeper trajectory, a wider frame of reference — almost, one might say, to "another time." In traditional religious language, we are brought before a "transcendence" that claims our attention as an "excedence" that stretches beyond our lives — that we stand within historical and religious traditions that far exceed our contemporary lives. Transcendence here is not an "otherworldly" realm — operating aside from or behind the scenes of history; rather, it is a desire that stretches our attention to that which exceeds our lives, to a tradition that is larger than (exceeds/transcends) this historical moment, to a wisdom that is older than the nineteenth, twentieth, or twenty-first centuries.

"Another time"? This is not an ahistorical sentiment. Rather, it is deeply historical. It points backward and forward at the same time. Even a casual reflection upon our lives will reveal how much of our "past" accompanies and shapes our present — that our past is not simply that which has been and is now gone; rather, it is very present to us in shaping our current responses to life. Similarly, our future is not simply a vacant "not yet" that is always deferred; rather, it too shapes our present reality by drawing us to pursue innovative and fresh possibilities of life inherent in any given situation.

"Another time" suggests both a deep remembering and an expectant hopefulness that is characteristic of the historically gifted human spirit. It is not just "this time" — rather, it is this time as shaped by the past and leaning into the future. It is "this time" (both memory-laden and future-expectant) that hermeneutics celebrates, and it is "this time" that religious tradition best exemplifies.

"HEAR, O ISRAEL"

One of the oldest and most concentrated statements in the sacred texts of Jewish literature is the *Shema*, "Hear, O Israel" (*Shema yisra'el;* Deut. 6:4). Against the clamor of human events, it draws our attention elsewhere. It carries no immediate message, except that we listen. Somewhere, way back when, an ancient people realized that their lives were not simply caught in a chain of events, nor less that their lives were simply autonomous and of their own making. Rather, they experienced a prior condition that required of them "to listen" — a condition of *being addressed*.

This condition of being addressed is crucial to hermeneutics. Indeed, there would be no need for interpretation at all if we did not first acknowledge that a word is being spoken to us. The interpretive question — "what is this word saying to me?" — can only be asked if I first acknowledge that I am being addressed. The first act of hermeneutics, therefore, is to listen, to hear the word. Whether it be my encounter with a sacred text, a poem, an artwork, or another person — I sense that something is claiming my attention, and I am drawn to interpret what is being said to me. Whatever "meaning" I may subsequently discover, its origin is not first *in myself*, but comes originally from *the speaking of another*.

What does it mean to truly hear a word? In many ways, this is the question hermeneutics asks. To truly hear a word requires a certain passivity and openness, a willingness to be spoken to, to be addressed. Otherwise, we may as well not listen at all. Moreover, nothing will be heard if it has to fight its way across the clamor of our cluttered minds, filled with so many ready-made opinions and prejudgments. Still less, nothing will be heard if our hearts are hardened and unreceptive.

When we truly listen to a word, we realize that something is being asked of us. Gadamer calls this "the priority of the question."[6] We hear the word as a question put to our lives. We realize that we didn't know something as well as we thought. There is yet more depth to be discovered, a deeper insight to be lived. We will feel something of the limits of our own horizons, as our own worldviews are stretched to accommodate different perspectives and new understandings. The way we live — the patterns of our lives, our actions and responses — are placed in question: "Are you sure this is the way to live, the way of life, the path you are called to follow?"

The question, however, is not one that we raise purely out of our own self-reflection. Rather, the question comes to us, is put to us, addresses our lives. Questions are rarely of our own making. Rather, they come to us as provocations that address our lives and invite our response. They are, if you like, out of our control, and that is precisely why a question is a question and not an answer that we already possess, or a certainty that we are already sure of.

I am all the time put in question, though typically I live out of my already well-formed answers. I know what it means to be a good spouse, a good parent, a good teacher, a good friend, a good neighbor, a good citizen, a good human being. And yet, in all of these contexts, there is a question constantly put to me: Do you really know? Or, are you that sure? Or, what are you missing or not seeing? What are you forgetting? How well are you listening and responding?

According to Gadamer, the "word" that speaks to me is like a "Thou" — it is like another person in my life. It is an awareness that I do not stand alone in the world, that my existence is not solitary; rather, I am all the time exposed to what is other than my own life. To hear a word means that I must listen to the other who speaks. It means "heeding" or "hearkening" to a voice that is not my own. It means paying attention to that which addresses my life as a "Thou":

> In human relations, the important thing is to experience the "Thou" truly as "Thou," i.e., not to overlook his claim and listen to what he has to say to us. To this end, openness is necessary.... Without this kind of openness to one another there is no genuine human relationship. Belonging together always also means being able to listen to one another.[7]

For theological hermeneutics, the act of listening is crucial. "Faith," says St. Paul, "comes through hearing" (Rom. 10:17). Although it evokes a certain passivity, it is a passivity that seeks to open one's mind and heart to the word of God. It is an attempt to create a "clearing" for God's word to be heard. It is receptivity and openness — an effort to expose oneself to a word that is *revelatory* — a word that speaks to our lives. It is perhaps not surprising that Jesus often framed his parables and teachings with a *Shema*-like phrase, "for those who are listening," for those "who have ears to hear."

THE GIFT OF TRADITION

If theology is anything, it is first and foremost the word of God addressed to our lives. It is first and foremost a *teaching*, a *commandment*, a *revelation*, a *deep well*, an *infinite* word, a *provocation*, an *announcement*, a *saying*, a speaking *to us* and *for* us — for our sake and for our salvation. It is a recognition that we exist within a vast discourse that is prompted by God's attention to humanity, that finds its origin in this first word of the *Shema* — "Listen!" "Hear!"

The *Shema* reminds us that a word spoken is no word unless it is heard. A word given is no word unless it is received. A word that teaches is no word unless it transforms. These two together — God's word to us, and the response it calls forth — form the heart of a living tradition. Theological hermeneutics begins in the recognition that we exist within a religious tradition that consists of founding texts — the scriptures — and the way these texts have been received and interpreted by communities of faith across time and history.

We sometimes think of tradition as tired and worn, old and dusty, but it is first and foremost a *gift*. Among other things, it is the gift of memory — a memory that is older and larger than my life. Tradition is not of my own making. It is not generated by my own resources. Rather, it is *given* to me. In this sense, it exists prior to my arrival on the scene. It is already "written" or inscribed, and it is given to me to read, to respond, to interpret, to listen to its voice.

I need not struggle alone through life, bravely and independently; rather, I have the gift of a tradition that is filled with the voices and wisdom of prophets and saints, thinkers and writers, texts and symbols, martyrs and mystics. All this is given to me, is older than me, will live long after me, endures, breathes, and offers itself. I can be brave and heroic and choose to think of my life as my own creation, or I can open my life to receive this *gift* of tradition.

Moreover, given that we live in a highly pluralistic and increasingly ambiguous world, tradition has the unique ability to concentrate our attention amidst the competing social environments and ideologies clamoring for our loyalty. To accept the gift of tradition is to privilege its teachings and way of life over and above other teachings and ways of life. Tradition would not be tradition, would not even be felt as a great gift in our life, except that we have given ourselves over to it. The very essence of belonging to a religious tradition is the radical decision to place our lives in its hands, to trust that it will not lead us astray, to wholeheartedly join our lives with its gift by giving ourselves over to its life.

The gift of tradition, however, is not something we admire and then place in a glass display case, or enshrine in a museum as an artifact of the past. Nor less is it a possession — something "we" own, something that belongs "to us" — something we hoist on a flagpole to which we pledge our allegiance and sing our anthems. Religious tradition has *nothing to do* with this puffed-up human pride, with collective identities and vain, human glories (even though we know that too often, this is exactly how religious traditions have functioned in our sadly distorted human affairs).

In speaking of religious tradition as a gift, we must not be lulled into thinking that it is given to us so that we can now "own" or "possess" it. Rather, it is given to be given, not to be owned. *Traditio* is giving, and *trans-dare* is the very process of continuing this giving. Rather than self-possession and clinging tight, tradition is more about giving over, offering, "handing on" with an open hand.

While it offers us words of life, these words are often difficult words that require *metanoia* or conversion. There would be little point, it seems to me, in receiving words that simply leave me "the same" — unchanged, un-affected, untouched, unmoved. "If we understand at all," writes Gadamer, "we understand differently."[8] Otherwise things just stay comfortably fa-miliar, routinized and conventional, and thereby of little concern. Only when we find our lives rubbing up against difficult truths will we even begin to approach new understanding. What tradition offers us are "words" that serve life, as, for example, when I find my cold and hard-ened heart opened up to forgive, or when my anger toward another is released into an ability to love. In many ways, my change of heart, my new attitude, my reassessment of my behavior, my different way of liv-ing, my renewed response to the call of justice and mercy — all this is the gift of tradition. These are amazing gifts, and they often come as great surprises as we stand amazed that love and forgiveness are actually possible, that they carry enormous redemptive power in our lives and in our world.

One of the most important elements of religious tradition, if it truly warrants this name, is that it is about the *dispossessed* and *our* disposses-sion. This is not to deny its healing and consolatory qualities. However, there is a fundamental work at the heart of the biblical and Christian tra-dition that is concerned with "turning our hearts" toward the love of God and neighbor. This work is not easily achieved in the human heart. Nor is it easily achieved in human society. The Catholic theologian Johannes-Baptist Metz calls religious tradition a "dangerous memory" that keeps us mindful of the suffering ones in history whose plight is usually forgotten or suppressed.[9] It is a "memory of suffering" (*memoria passionis*) that makes demands on us to be for "the orphan, the widow, and the stranger" which is, as Levinas reminds us, a constant biblical refrain. It is a memory that requires the conversion of the heart, the surrendering of our will, the letting go or emptying (*kenosis*) of our self-possession, the giving of our selves in service and love. This is a memory that endures through time and endangers the comfortable. It endangers those who sleep well at night; it endangers the self-righteous; it endangers every human urge to be at peace — to feel safe and secure in the comfort of our dwellings, where no more is required of me.

Although it seems a bold statement and open to misunderstanding, I think we can say that religious tradition is "not of this world." It is about a people whose memories are drawn to a more original vision. Utopian? Yes. Out of place? Yes. Not of this world? Yes. The kingdom of heaven? Yes. Where the downtrodden are set free? Yes. Where the ragged and browbeaten have priority seating? Yes. Where prostitutes and sinners are welcomed rather than shunned? Yes. Where the poor and the lowly are raised up? Yes. Where the one who serves is lauded over the master who rules? Yes. Where the peacemakers and the pure of heart are the blessed ones? Yes. Where justice flows like a running stream? Yes. Where mercy reaches from age to age? Yes, yes. Amen.

"Where are the philosophers now?" asks St. Paul. "Where are the scribes? Where are our thinkers today?" (1 Cor. 1:20).

The kingdom of heaven is a stunning announcement, bearing with it a divine unconditionality that defies the all-too-human practices of the world. St. Paul even goes so far as to say that it is a "madness" and a "foolishness" — a crazy love (1 Cor. 1:21–25). In this sense, we can say, along with Paul Ricoeur, that tradition carries a profound "surplus of meaning" that is continually proposing "new worlds" in front of us.[10] It is an "excess" — continually overflowing — and in this sense signals the "excedence" or the "more than" of God's infinite love. Far from being a stagnant force of inertia, it is a compelling and agitating announcement for those who have ears to hear.

Tradition calls out to us from the deep memory of the past, not to celebrate nostalgia or comforting doctrines, not to enshrine some truth in a timeless vault. It is no quaint or comforting reminiscence; rather it is the memory of a passionate people with deeply spiritual longings and burning hearts. Tradition is the collective and living memory of a people, but what they remember is not a "glorious past" to be revered and enshrined. Rather, they remember a time that has not yet arrived. Paradoxically, they carry and preserve the memory of a future that is yet to be, a time that is still coming, a promise that still beckons and asks us to respond.

Tradition carries the seeds of the future, because a truly living memory is also a living hope born of yearning and expectation. Indeed, the past survives and endures precisely because it leans into the future, precisely because it carries the promise of what could yet be, what is still coming. It is the passion and lifeblood of a praying, living, responding people. It is heaven's doorway.

THREE

On Earth —
Reading the Signs of the Times

AN OPEN BOOK

You cannot judge a book by its cover. Why? Because this would mean that you see it only as a *closed* book. You see only its cover, without exposing yourself to its real work that lay in wait for you. To be sure, the cover of a book is an invitation, but it is an invitation to take it into your life and read it. The real life of a book happens only in its opening, such that you are led to consider the new possibilities for life and learning that its words are proposing to you. A closed book is no book at all, for every book is meant to be *opened* — to be read, engaged, and taken into our life.

This is true of all classic texts, and it is especially true of the scriptures. In the Jewish tradition, the Torah — the divinely revealed "instruction" of sacred scripture — does not even take the form of a covered book. Rather, it takes the form of a scroll (*Sefer Torah*) whose continuous rolling pages are open and exposed, and impossible to close like the pages of a book. Moreover, the Talmud — the compendium of Jewish learning and commentary — has no page one. Every tractate of the Talmud begins on page two, so that you know from the very beginning that you are dealing with a book that is of divine origin — without beginning, and infinitely open — without end.

In the Christian tradition, the scriptures are usually placed on a lectern as an *open book*. This is a very symbolic gesture, and I have taken to practicing it myself. At home on my bookshelves are rows and rows of tidily shelved books, all lined up one against another with only their spines showing. However, I always clear a space on one of the shelves where I

38

place the scriptures as an open book. It is a wonderful sight, the sight of this open book — its pages looking out, its words exposed, its unfolded gaze that is like a beautiful invitation: "take and read." Amidst all those closed books lined up on my shelves, this one book stands in its rightly assumed posture — open and invitational. It reminds me that all life and learning is about this openness, this invitation, this desire to learn and to love.

I am also reminded of the poet Edmond Jabès, whose respect for the fundamental openness of texts was deeply shaped by his Jewish sensibility. The Jewish tradition uniquely combines the "written Torah" with the "oral Torah" of ever-expanding commentary and interpretation. The written text is never finally closed or sealed off, but continually opens onto newly emerging questions and concerns. "The open book," says Jabès, "occupies only a little space on the table, yet the space it engages is huge."[1] How true. The open book engages not only the space of its own times, its own questions, its own words. It also engages the "huge space" of a long line of descendants who — right up to our own day — continually bring their lives to this open text, searching its ever-renewing and ever-recurring meanings and implications for their lives.

Paul Ricoeur suggests that the scriptures have a "surplus of meaning." They can be read and interpreted over and over again without exhausting their significance. The appeal of the scriptures is not tied to one place and one time, but continually spills over with new insight for different people and different times.[2]

If we think of the scriptures as "timeless" texts, we must think of them as texts that *endure* because of their very ability to constantly engage time. This is a key hermeneutical insight. The "past," the testimony of the scriptures and the tradition in which we stand, is never sealed off from the present. It is no "once upon a time." Rather, it is a claim on my existence here and now — today — in this moment, in this place, in this time.

THE SIGNS OF THE TIMES

It is in the signs of life which happen to us that we are addressed by the living word of God. However, as Martin Buber notes, too often our hearts are hardened or dulled to hearing the word that cuts to real concerns:

Each of us is encased in an amour whose task is to ward off signs. Signs happen to us without respite, living means being addressed, we would only need to present ourselves and to perceive. But the risk is too dangerous for us...and from generation to generation we perfect the defense apparatus. All our knowledge assures us, "be calm, everything happens as it must happen, but nothing is directed at you, you are not meant; it is just 'the world,' you can experience it as you like, but whatever you make of it in yourself proceeds from you alone, nothing is required of you, you are not addressed, all is quiet."[3]

It is not difficult to hear echoes of Jesus and the prophet Isaiah in Buber's words:

> For the heart of this nation has grown coarse,
> their ears are dull of hearing,
> and they have shut their eyes,
> for they fear they should see with their eyes,
> hear with their ears,
> understand with their heart and be converted
> and healed by me. (Matt. 13:15; cf. Isa. 6:9–10)

There is little purpose in reading the scriptures, as a *living* address to our lives, if we are continually "warding off" the signs of the times that constantly *resound* with this address. Against our propensity to fall asleep in the drowsy calmness of our self-satisfied worlds, we are urged to "stay awake" lest we perceive but do not perceive, hear but do not hear (cf. Mark 13:33; Matt. 13:14).

When Pope John XXIII convened the Second Vatican Council, I have this image of him walking the great halls of Vatican antiquity, yet all the time hearing the echoes of Jesus' question: "How do you not know how to interpret the present time?" (Luke 12:56). John XXIII seemed to notice that the world was racing along, changing at a furious pace, and yet the church was failing to notice or to respond. Too wrapped up in itself, it seemed unable to cope with "the seriousness of the world."[4]

Vatican II marked a fundamental shift away from an insular, inward-looking church toward a church that is *open* to dialogue and engagement with the world. It represented a wonderful movement of renewal and "release" — freeing the scriptures and the great legacy of the Catholic-Christian faith tradition from its somewhat closed mustiness, as though the testimony of faith had for too long been sealed in old and tired tomes of formulated doctrine, treated "as read" — conclusive — rather than tapping its true resource as an "*open* book," with its unique capacity to face and engage the world in all its stunning "seriousness."

The seriousness of the world in which we live suggests, among other things, that we do not have another time to live the message of the gospel. We only have this time. The kingdom of God is "near at hand" (Matt. 3:2). "It is in the world of history that we accept or reject the word," says Gutiérrez. "The decision we make is heavy with consequences."[5] There is little in the gospel message that suggests deferral, or even less, resting in the comfort of well-worked doctrines that give the illusion of timeless sureties. Rather, the message of the gospel commands the most down-to-earth realism: "I was naked and you clothed me" (Matt. 25:35). The seriousness of the world — the seriousness of suffering and injustice — must claim our attention, must claim the work of our hearts and our hands.

"TOLLE, LEGE!" — "TAKE AND READ!"

In his *Confessions* (Book VIII, Ch. 12), St. Augustine tells the story of how he felt weighed down by his own sinfulness, and how impossible it seemed for him to break free of this weight. He writes:

> I felt that I was still the captive of my sins, and in my misery I kept crying "How long shall I go on saying 'tomorrow, tomorrow'? Why not now?"...I was asking myself these questions, weeping all the while with the most bitter sorrow in my heart, when all at once I heard the sing-song voice of a child in a nearby house..."take it and read, take it and read." [*"tolle, lege; tolle, lege"*][6]

Augustine immediately went to where he had left his Bible lying open, picked it up, and began to read a verse from St. Paul. At that moment, he says, "It was as though the light of confidence flooded into my heart and all the darkness of doubt was dispelled."

What verse did Augustine read from St. Paul that so transformed him? Well, I read the verse but I confess that it didn't strike me with the same transformative "shock of recognition" with which it obviously struck Augustine. Yet that is beside the point. I am not here to relive Augustine's life. I must come to my own "confession," to bear witness with my own life, to read the scriptures as an *address to me* — in this time and in this place — and this is perhaps one of the main points of Augustine's story. His confession, his testimony, is surely a great teaching and inspiration to us, but if we think that it can now "save us" from having to deal with our own troubled times, our own weeping and sinfulness, our own need to listen to the scriptures and have them address and transform our lives, then we will have surely missed Augustine's testimony altogether.

To stand within a tradition of faith is to acknowledge that I am implicated as one who is chosen to respond. According to Martin Buber, the life of faith means acknowledging that "in each instance a word demanding an answer has happened to me." We may call this speaking to us the word that "says something *to* me, addresses something to me, speaks something that enters my own life." In order to signal its infinite capacity to be "ever-present-everywhere," we may also call this speaking to us the word of God, "for nothing can refuse to be the vessel of the Word."[7] After all, it was the simple playing and singing of a child that led Augustine to open the scriptures.

Like Augustine, Buber is urging us to "take and read." We are being asked to notice and pay attention to the living word of God — a word that is always open and never closed, a word that is always a "saying" to us — here and now — not a closed word, a word already "said." The word of God is unique in this regard, for it resists being put down, closed, filed on a bookshelf, and treated "as read." Rather, "the word of God is something alive and active" (Heb. 4:12). From Augustine in the fourth century to Buber in the twentieth century, the word of God is forever open, forever awaiting and provoking fresh readings, new appropriations, real and concrete connections to life as it is lived.

"EXPLAIN ME!"

When we open the scriptures, we are seeking to understand what they are saying to us. In the Christian tradition, theology is often spoken of as "faith seeking understanding." In the Jewish tradition, this seeking is referred to as *midrash* — to search, to inquire into the meaning of a text.[8]

Every encounter with the word of God is led by the simple demand: "Explain me!" Or, if you like, "Read me, listen to my words, tell me what I am saying to you." This is a crucial interpretive moment as an imperative given in the present. "What am I saying to you today?" This question lends to the scriptures their wonderful open quality. For there are no readers of the scriptures who can exempt themselves from this question, as though they already knew the meaning, as though they already understood, as though the scriptures had nothing more to say to them — in which case, they may as well close the book and consign it to their bookshelves along with the many other "already read" books.

As soon as we hear this demand, "Explain me," our own lives are instantly "brought into play."[9] They come into play because they are put in question by the text, which asks of us, "What am I saying *to you?*" What is the text saying, for example, when we read in Mark's Gospel: "You know that among the pagans their so-called rulers lord it over them, and their great men make their authority felt. This is not to happen among you" (10:42)? Is this text simply about another time, another place, another audience? Can we read it and simply bracket or exempt our own lives from its meaning and its message? Or, in trying to understand it, must we not hear it as a *saying to us* that questions our current lives, here and now, in this time and place? Will not this text bring into play or bring into question the various ways that authority is practiced in my own life (all the times I try to make my authority felt), and the various ways that authority is practiced in the church, in my workplace, in society?

The interpretive demand — "explain me" — clearly places the practice of interpretation in our hands. It is up to us to interpret the meaning of the text. However, we should notice that this task is *given to us by the text*, not by our own authority. Even though we are the ones who must interpret, we do not have the upper hand. We do not rule over the text. Rather, when the text asks us to interpret what it is saying, it is *at the same time interpreting our own lives* — placing our own lives in question — as if the text were raising interpretive questions of us: "Why do you like to make your authority felt?" As if the text were trying to understand us: "Why do you need to lord it over others?" As if *we* were the puzzle and the question that needs to be explained and interpreted, much more than the text. This is where the true rub of hermeneutics happens.

THE EVENT OF UNDERSTANDING

Hermeneutics — the art of interpretation — is concerned with the event of understanding. For understanding to *happen* at all, it must necessarily have this *eventlike* quality — otherwise, it is not really understanding, but simply something I have *already* known, *already* understood, *already* assimilated. Understanding is an *event* — a *happening* — more than it is something that I already possess. Who among us can say that they have no need for further understanding? Those who say that they "have it" or are "in possession of it" are those who are furthest from it. Yet those who recognize that *faith* is not *possessing* but *seeking* understanding are those who grow in grace and wisdom. The wise person is "full of understanding" because they continually seek it, unlike those who smugly proclaim their possession of it.

For understanding to truly warrant its name, it must necessarily be something that *strikes me now*. A popular way of naming this hermeneutical quality of understanding is when we speak of the "aha" moment. "Aha — *now* I understand!" Understanding — if it truly warrants this name — is always a present event, a happening, an occurrence, something that comes to us and suddenly impacts us — "aha!" In traditional theological language, this event is *revelatory*. A word is spoken to us, something is said to us, and like St. Augustine, we are transformed. I begin to understand something differently, with new eyes, with a changed perspective, with a renewed heart. Or, as Gadamer says, "It is enough to say that we understand in a *different* way, *if we understand at all*."[10]

This is the eventlike quality that hermeneutics seeks to highlight and celebrate as a pivotal moment of all interpretation. To be skilled in the art of interpretation is to be alert to this moment, to be expectant, hopeful, waiting, open — ready for that moment when a true revelation happens. Whether it be the sacred scriptures, or the sacredness of a poem, or a song, or the speaking of another person, the moment of understanding always shares this same quality of revelation. If I understand at all, I understand differently.

Moreover, for understanding to truly warrant its name, it must be something that affects the way I live. No real understanding takes place unless it touches life in all its concreteness and particularity. According to Gadamer, the event of understanding can never be separated from the event of *applicacio* ("application") in our current situation. The text, "if it is to be understood properly — i.e., according to the claim it makes — must be understood at every moment, in every concrete situation, in a new and different way. Understanding is always application."[11] A text's meaning is never simply given "back then" but only becomes meaningful when its message can be restated or represented for us today. "Is this not true of every text," writes Gadamer, "that it must be understood in terms of what it says? Does this not mean that it always needs to be restated? And does not this restatement always take place through its being related to the present?"[12] Only when the meaning of a text becomes a concern for us today — affecting our values, our behaviors, our actions, our relationships — only then, can we say that the event of understanding is actually under way.

A PROPOSED WORLD

Paul Ricoeur suggests that the sacred texts and classic testimonies of a faith tradition are primarily concerned with offering us a "proposed world which I could inhabit," not simply a mirror of the world as it is.[13] He is reminding us that the work of interpretation is primarily led by the "proposal of the text." The text is offering a message or a meaning — a proposal — for us to consider. This is what matters to a text. This is its "subject matter." This is what it is "about" — a "proposed world which I could inhabit" — and this is what interpretation seeks to understand.

In other words, what matters to a text matters little unless it also matters to me. For interpretation to happen at all, the concern of the text must also become my concern. It is only at this point that interpretation comes into play, when I am led to consider what the text is saying as a possibility for my own life. If nothing of what the text says is of concern to me, then it hasn't really said anything at all (and there would be no need for interpretation). Only when *what it says* is also a *concern for me* does interpretation come into play. Otherwise, we would only be dealing with a "dead" text, with no future beyond it. All good interpretation is oriented by this futurity — the "proposed world I could inhabit." Everything of creative interpretation happens *in front of the text* as each new generation — right up to our own generation and our own times — feels that something here matters, and is able to make the matter and concern of the text the matter and concern of their own lives.

If we ask, "Where does interpretation lead us?" or "What is its goal?" or "To what end and for what purpose?" — Ricoeur suggests that it is finally concerned with opening the horizons of our hearts and minds toward a new understanding, a new possibility, a new way of living in the world. To interpret or understand a text is not just to understand something back there and back then. Rather, the path of interpretation always stretches out in front of us, such that we are led to consider how our ways in the world could be made different, made new, transformed by a possibility that exceeds the way things are. Interpretation happens when the subject matter of the text (what it is about) becomes the subject matter of our own lives (and what we could also be "about"). Ricoeur writes:

> The "matter of the text" and what I call the world of the work . . . is not *behind* the text . . . but *in front of* it, as that which the work unfolds, discovers, reveals. Henceforth, to understand is *to understand oneself in front of the text.* It is not a question of imposing upon the text our finite capacity of understanding, but of exposing ourselves to the text and receiving from it an enlarged self. . . .[14]

Ricoeur goes on to say that in seeking to understand a text, it is not we who possess the "key." Rather, it is the text that possesses the key that unlocks our own narrow worlds and opens our horizons to newer and wider understandings and possibilities. It is the text that is revelatory and inspired and that stirs our imaginations. As David Tracy suggests, if "the text is a genuinely classic one, my present horizon of understanding should always be provoked, challenged, transformed. In encountering a classic we are compelled to believe . . . *that something else might be the case than is the case.*"[15]

As a teacher, Jesus spent a long time trying to get his listeners to dwell differently in the world, to see the world differently, to live according to God's ways — not according to the ways of the world, that is, the accustomed and predictable ways that are all too human. For example, in Luke's Gospel Jesus says, "When you give a luncheon or a dinner, do not invite your friends or your brothers or your relatives or rich neighbors, in case they may invite you in return, and you will be repaid" (14:12). If our hospitality extends only to the intimate circle of our family and friends, then we are only doing what most people do. We are not extending our lives much further than the conventional ways of the world, whereby we offer friendship to those who we know will offer us friendship in return. Jesus' teaching, however, seeks to offer us a *proposed world that we could inhabit:* "When you give a banquet, invite the poor, the crippled, the lame, and the blind. And you will be blessed, because they cannot repay you..." (14:13–14). The kingdom of God is concerned with friendship and hospitality to those who are not normally "our friends," to those who are not part of our "circle," to those who have no means of returning our hospitality — and this is the true test of what hospitality means. Otherwise, it is simply loving those who love us, which is all too easy, all too human.

Like many of the teachings of scripture, the "path" of this text stretches out in front of us and opens onto the kingdom of heaven. However, at the same time, everything of this text's subject matter (what it is about) is finally concerned with our own lives and how we could be living here today — "on earth."

If we can speak of the biblical and Christian tradition as "heaven's doorway," it is nevertheless a door that we must pass through, that *we must enter.* When Ricoeur suggests that all good interpretation is finally taken up with the question of a "proposed world that I could inhabit," he is suggesting that interpretation ultimately leads to this "open door." The question hermeneutics asks, therefore, is "can I enter"? Can I move from the world I currently inhabit to a new world that I *could* inhabit? Am I open to a different way of dwelling in the world?

Rather than simply reflecting the world as it is, the biblical and Christian tradition offers us possibilities for the "world as it could be." The "world as it is" is often quite routinized and conventional, and its path is crowded and wide. As such, we do not consider it or think about it too much because we are simply caught up in its jostling and numbing normalcy. It simply churns along day by day and, like any other day, there is not too much that captures our attention.

The scriptures, however, seek to move our hearts according to the ways of God. They seek to align our lives according to the kingdom of heaven. They awaken our imaginations. They disturb our routines. They offer us a "proposed world" — not simply the world as it is — but the world as it could be, "on earth as it is in heaven."

"Where your treasure is, there your heart will be also" (Matt. 6:21). We only have to stand in line at a supermarket checkout to notice what the world treasures. If we are wondering what "worldliness" means, then we only have to notice all those magazines that are well positioned on their racks — waiting for us like great temptations — with their covers celebrating fame, fortune, and the "good life." If we are wondering what worldliness means, it means being lured by the things of the world, of which Jesus said, "Lead us not into temptation" (Matt. 6:13). The wilderness of Jesus' temptations, when he faced "all the kingdoms of the world" (Luke 4:5), remain surprisingly on par with much of the wilderness of our own times. The vacuous allure of those supermarket magazines is just as barren as the desert of Jesus' temptations. In this sense, little has changed. Our yearnings and our desire are constantly being eroded, worn-down, or co-opted by the ways of the world, and yet — as the popular saying goes — all that glitters is not gold.

The kingdom of heaven, however, glitters differently. As one of Jesus' parables suggests, should we capture even a glimpse of the kingdom's sparkle, we would "sell all and buy the field" (Matt. 13:44). We would realize how much we have been "duped" by the world's glitter that is like "fools' gold." According to the Gospels, many of the signs of modern life simply urge us to "store up treasures for yourself on earth" (Matt. 6:19). While they seem deceptively real and of crucial concern (the new car, the new cell phone, the new credit card, the new look, and so on), they are destined to pass away. They will consume our hearts only to be consumed themselves "by moth and woodworm." The temptations of the world are all around us, whereas the path to the kingdom of heaven is very narrow, "and only a few find it" (Matt. 7:14).

Perhaps this is why the early followers of Jesus were called people of "the Way." The real life of the kingdom of heaven happens only when its path is opened, such that we are led to consider its proposal for dwelling differently in the world — "on earth as it is in heaven." The door to the kingdom of heaven is always a door that opens onto our lives and onto the world that is groaning and suffering and not yet healed, a world caught up in too much "worldliness" and too little "heavenliness." As Abraham Heschel suggests, the scriptures are not primarily concerned with "worldly concerns"; rather, they are concerned with "God's concerns." This is *not* to suggest that we should have no concern for the world, as if God's concerns lay elsewhere (where?). Rather, it means that our concerns are more deeply shaped by the proposals of God rather than the proposals of the world. It means that our focus or attention shifts from "what man does with his ultimate concern" to *"what man does with God's concern."* It means that we view the world with divine concern rather than with worldly concern. As Heschel notes, unless we share the concerns of God, "We know nothing about the living God."[16]

GOD'S CONCERNS

What, then, we may well ask, are the concerns of God? For a start, let us say that God is not concerned with God's own self. It amazes me how much theological ink has been spilled in trying to determine who God is, as though God were completely enraptured in his own being, which would say little about God's "concern" other than that he is self-obsessed. Why do we too readily take it upon ourselves to say who God is, when this is a question that rarely troubles God? And if it is a question that rarely troubles God, why should it trouble us so much? Why are we so often preoccupied with naming and defining God, as though God were a being that spends most of his time looking in a mirror? As though it were necessary for us to help God work out his identity?

When Moses inquired into God's identity, God simply dismissed his question as somewhat pointless, as if to say: "Don't trouble yourself. I certainly don't." Yet we've been troubling ourselves ever since, not satisfied with God's lack of self-concern: "I am who I am" (Exod. 3:14), which means (among other things) that "I don't really worry too much about who I am. It doesn't really concern me too much. I am who I am." Moses learns that God is the one whose awareness is never a solipsistic self-awareness, but an awareness that is "well aware of their sufferings" (3:7). God is encountered as the one who notices an enslaved people's misery, who witnesses their oppression, who hears their cries and takes heed of their appeals. And then God says to Moses to tell the people that "I Am has sent me to you" (3:14). Rather than being drawn into the mystery of a nameless God, Moses is drawn into the mystery of *the one who sends.* God's name, "for all time" (3:15), is the one who *sends me to you.*

When I pause briefly to reflect on this strange name of God — the one who sends me to you — I find myself thinking about all those times I've encountered a person who reaches out to me in love, or all those times when someone has released me from the burden of my sin by offering forgiveness. On occasions like this, I feel as though God has sent this person into my life, to offer me the gift (the grace) of God's love and forgiveness. Or when I witness the life of a saintly person who gives of themselves with generosity and compassion, who cares for the poor or who struggles for justice, I find it easy to say of that person's life, "surely they have been *sent by God,*" which means they are *of God* or *from God.*

God is the one who sends, and the saintly person or prophetic figure is the one who bears the name of God—who gives witness to God—as the one who has sent them. This leads me to ask of my own life: Am I living in a way that is *of God* and *from God?* Am I living in such a way that another person can say of me, "Surely God has sent you into my life today"? Have I shown mercy to another? Have I been gracious and compassionate in my actions? Have I worked for the justice of those who have no justice?

What interests God is whether we share her interests, whether we share her concerns, whether we share her life, whether we see things the way she sees things, whether we value the things she values, whether we want to be "like God" and the way God acts in the world. Indeed, this is how we ultimately "get to know God" — and this is not unlike how we get to know anyone—by sharing their life, learning more about what makes them tick, discovering the things they value, feeling their passions, sharing their concerns — this is how we know who they are — and it is no less with God.

In her book *The Silent Cry,* Dorothee Soelle offers the testimony of a medieval woman mystic, Mechthild von Hackeborn, whose vision of God was not an ecstatic-erotic fusion, but the receiving of God's "senses" and God's "heart."

> She once begged the Lord to give her something that would always cause her to remember him. Thereupon she received from the Lord this answer: "See, I give you my eyes, that you may see all things with them, and my ears, that you may hear all things with them; my mouth I also give you, so that all you have to say, whether in speech, prayer, or song, you may say through it. I give you my heart, that through it you may think everything and may love me and all things

for my sake." In these words God drew this soul entirely into him and united it in such a way that it seemed to her that she saw with God's eyes, and heard with his ears, and spoke with his mouth, and felt that she had no heart than the heart of God.[17]

When I first encountered Catherine Mowry LaCugna's book *God for Us*, not only was I struck by the title, I was also struck by the very simple and yet beautiful proposal of her work: *the mystery of God and the mystery of salvation are inseparable.* According to LaCugna, we cannot speak of God *in se* without speaking of God *pro nobis*.[18] In other words, it makes no theological sense to speak of God in God's own self without speaking of God's heart, God's concern, God's love. It makes no sense to speak of God unless we are at the same time speaking of God who is *for us* . . . for our sake and for our salvation. Theology's greatest temptation is to be concerned only with God, whereas it should always be concerned with God's concern. God's "being" is always "being-for-us," rather than a "being-locked-in-self-identity."

Knowing God's "essence" as some sort of distilled, unaffected, "pure" God is to miss God's essence all together. What is essential to God is not God. Now *that* is a "mystical" statement — not unlike Meister Eckhart's prayer, "God, free me of God." Concern for God can easily become ego-driven concern, which is of little concern to God. If God becomes simply a mirror of my own introspection, a capital "Meaning" for my life, then I am probably caught in the realms of religious idolatry, and will have missed God all together.

Contrary to popular conceptions, the "mystic" is not so much one who strives to reach God as a summative, mystical goal of their lives. Rather, the mystic is one who gradually discovers, along with St. John, that "God is love" (1 John 4:8). God's essentiality — what is "essential to God" — is found in God's heart, God's care, God's love, God's concern, God's attentiveness. St. John's hymn to God's love is one of the most beautiful and tender passages of scripture. "My dear people," he says, "let us love one another, since love comes *from* God, and everyone who loves is begotten *of* God and knows God" (1 John 4:7). However, the high point of St. John's hymn — the truly mystical point — is when he asks us to consider the love of which he speaks. "This is the love I mean," he says, "*not our love* for God, but God's love *for us* . . ." (4:10). *Pro nobis.*

TODAY

I would like to conclude this chapter with two stories that are told concerning the coming of the Messiah. "Take and read." Both stories speak of the one who is anointed by God, who is of God and from God. Both speak of the Messiah who is here among us, bearing the name of God, "the one who sends." One text is from Matthew's Gospel, and the other is from the Talmud. Both are ancient texts, and both call out to us today, in our times, "Explain me!" . . .

• • •

Now when Jesus had finished instructing his twelve disciples, he went on from there to teach and proclaim his message in the cities.

When John heard in prison what the Messiah was doing, he sent word by his disciples and said to him, "Are you the one who is to come, or are we to wait for another?"

Jesus answered them, "Go and tell John what you hear and see: the blind receive their sight, the lame walk, the lepers are cleansed, the deaf hear, the dead are raised, and the poor have good news brought to them. And blessed is anyone who takes no offense at me." (Matt. 11:1–6)

• • •

Rabbi Joshua ben Levi once met with Elijah the prophet and in the course of their conversation he asked, "When will the Messiah come?"

"Why don't you go and ask him yourself?" said Elijah.

"Where can I find him?" the rabbi wanted to know.

"You will find him sitting at the gates of Rome," answered Elijah.

"And how will I recognize him?" Rabbi Joshua asked.

"You will see him among the poor, the afflicted and the diseased, binding up their wounds. However, while all the others bind an entire area covering several wounds with one bandage, the Messiah dresses each wound separately."

With this information Rabbi Joshua took himself off to Rome, and there at the gates of the city he saw the Messiah attending to the poor and the sick, just as Elijah had described.

"Peace to you, my master and teacher," said Joshua.

"Peace to you, son of Levi," answered the Messiah.

"Master, when will you come to redeem us?" the rabbi asked.

"I will come today," the Messiah answered.

Rabbi Joshua ben Levi returned home, and soon afterwards he again met with Elijah the prophet.

"Did you speak with Messiah?" the prophet asked.

"I did," replied the rabbi. And he reported on the conversation. But then he added, "The Messiah lied to me. He promised that he would come 'today'; but he didn't come."

The prophet answered, "What he meant was 'today' if the people would but hearken to God's voice." (*San.* 98a)[19]

FOUR

Between Heaven and Earth

The Life of Faith for the Life of the World

MILLIONS OF MOMENTS OF ENCOUNTER

The task of practical theology, according to a widely accepted working definition, is "to establish mutually critical correlations between an interpretation of the Christian tradition and an interpretation of the contemporary situation."[1] The art of interpretation is crucial, as Don Browning suggests, "because the practical theologian never has access to either the raw, uninterpreted Christian fact or the unbiased and uninterpreted reality of ordinary experience. This is why practical theology must be seen as first of all an interpretive or hermeneutical task."[2]

To speak of a conversation between heaven and earth is a poetic way of naming this essential task of practical theology — to read and interpret the signs of God in the midst of the signs of life. Every age has grappled with this task of theology — to bring the life of faith to the life of the world, to discern the ways of God for the sake of the coming of God's kingdom, "on earth as it is in heaven."

An image often associated with hermeneutics is that of a text and a reader. Yet W. Dow Edgerton suggests that hermeneutics also speaks of a third "hidden presence." We see a reader and a text — we see only two — but "between the two, there is a third." According to Edgerton, the question hermeneutics asks is, "Who is the third?" In other words, what happens between a text and a reader, what transpires between them? Hermeneutics is concerned with questions and possibilities "about the interpreter, about the text, about their relationship."[3]

Perhaps the key word here is "between." It evokes a profound sensibility for the dialogical quality of life. "All real living is meeting," says Martin Buber.[4] It is an encounter between two: "Spirit is not in the *I*, but between *I* and *Thou*."[5] Whether we speak of love, or understanding, or forgiveness, or peace — these cannot happen except that they happen between us, except that they become a matter of concern for both of us. "This between," writes Gadamer, "is the true locus of hermeneutics."[6]

Gadamer suggests that the relationship between a text and a reader is like a conversation that takes place in the to-and-fro dialogue of question and answer, speaking and listening, address and response.[7] "Text" and "reader" are metaphors that need not be identified in all cases with written expression. An important claim of hermeneutics is that we are always interpreting — or entering into conversation — not only with texts, but with the people, life, and events of the world around us. Like Buber, Gadamer sees this conversational or dialogical structure as integral to life. The art of interpretation happens between I and Thou, between one person and another, between text and reader, past and present, present and future, memory and promise, questioning and answering, listening and responding, reflecting and acting.

The "space of the between" is notoriously difficult to pin down. It is the meeting or encounter of life itself. It is impossible, for example, for me to define my relationship with Mary, even though we have been married for many years. Rather, our relationship is made up of millions of moments of encounter between us. The same holds true when we speak of a people's relationship to their faith tradition. It consists of millions of moments of encounter. It happens in the "between," in the to-and-fro of the encounter between God and humanity, between the life of faith and the life of the world.

In the same way that we cannot too mechanically define a method of relationship or prescribe a method of "encounter," so too we cannot too mechanically define a method of practical theology. However, we can learn something of its *artfulness*. We can watch what happens, for example, when we are engaged in practices of interpretation. We can try to discern "movements" of interpretation that are integral to its workings. In what follows, I would like to distill some of these crucial movements as guidelines for good interpretive practice. While I am writing about them

sequentially, it is important to keep in mind that these are not methodological steps that one follows like a recipe. Rather, they are interconnected
movements that are all the time affecting each other.

MOVEMENTS OF INTERPRETATION

What are you *saying* to me?

Interpretation begins, if it begins anywhere, with the question: "What
are you saying to me?" Without this question, there would be no need
for interpretation at all. It may seem unusual to begin with this rather
obvious question to describe an interpretive encounter. However, the art
of interpretation is often doomed at the start because we fail to notice
the importance of this question. Nothing is more certain to prevent a
conversation or close down interpretive understanding than a hardness of
heart that refuses to listen.

"What are you saying to me?" is therefore a crucial question that signals
my willingness to listen to you, to take your words seriously. It directs
my attention *to you* and allows your words to speak *to me*. Interpretation
cannot happen without this fundamental openness toward another that
speaks to me and addresses my life.

But I say this to you who are listening . . .

Such begins one of Jesus' teachings or sayings in the Gospel of Luke
(6:27–35). In the very opening of the text, we realize that we are being
addressed. Whenever we interpret, we must necessarily be willing to hear.
Moreover, the words that are spoken are not spoken to anyone or everyone.
Rather, they are addressed "to you who are listening" — to this people in
this time and this place. Their address is quite singular in "singling out"
this particular reader or community of readers in this particular time and
place. Interpretation always means that I am implicated, that the text
is speaking *to me, to this community, here and now, today*. If the art of
interpretation is a dialogical event, then *I am required*. This means that
I cannot excuse myself from the interpretive encounter. Rather, my own
situation and context must be brought into play as the only real arena in
which any text can speak.

My experience is placed in question.

But I say this to you who are listening: Love your enemies, do good to those who hate you, bless those who curse you, pray for those who abuse you. If anyone strikes you on the cheek, offer the other also; and from anyone who takes away your coat, do not withhold even your shirt. Give to everyone who begs from you; and if anyone takes away your goods, do not ask for them again.

This is a very difficult saying. All my familiar concepts are placed at risk; all the ways I usually make sense of the world are called into question. I feel as though something within me is being stripped away or laid bare. The text exposes me to myself, as if it were reflecting some part of me that I can hardly recognize. According to Gadamer, this exposure is a pivotal movement in the art of interpretation. It is the experience of "being pulled up short by the text."[8] The text lays claim to me in a way that I may never be able to finally settle or resolve, but which nevertheless strikes me as something essential that I can no longer renounce or do away with.

While it is crucial that we hear a text according to our own experience and in the context of our own lives, we cannot simply stay within the realm of "my experience." To do so would simply leave me locked into my own familiar world, rather than exposed to a world of new and sometimes uncanny possibilities that stretch far beyond my current understandings or expectations. For example, while it is true — as every teacher knows — that the best learning happens when it engages the experience of students, it is also true that no learning happens if it doesn't provoke or widen the experience of students into new learning and deeper understandings.

Little would happen in the art of interpretation if something of my own experience were not placed in question or, as Gadamer says, "put at risk."[9] If I enter an interpretive encounter only to come out of the process unchanged and unaffected, then it would be difficult to say that any interpretation has occurred. Interpretation is an *event* that always *affects* my understanding, or it is no event at all.

"Every experience worthy of its name," writes Gadamer, "thwarts an expectation."[10] Gadamer is suggesting that we can only call something an "experience" when *what happens* has a quality of unexpectedness or surprise. Experience that is "worthy of its name" can never be reduced to that which is expected or foreseeable in advance. In order to deserve the name "experience," something happens or we discover something that we did not expect, and our familiar world of understanding is disturbed or surprised. Without this quality of surprise or transformative effect, we could not use the word "experience"; rather, we could only speak of something that is routinely familiar and in this sense quite uneventful, predictable, and expected.

We often equate the word "life" with the word "experience." This is evident, for example, when we intuitively affirm the deep connection that exists between the wisdom of experience and the wisdom of life. We know that the experienced person is someone who has gleaned or accrued a measure of wisdom through life experiences. However, what we too often miss is the process by which the "person of experience" becomes the "person of wisdom." We would be wrong to assume, for example, that the experienced person is the one who always knows "what is around the corner," as though wisdom simply meant knowing what to expect. Rather, the person of experience and wisdom is the person who is able to respond to life precisely when the way ahead is uncertain and uncharted. As Gadamer suggests, the experienced person is someone who knows that "experience always thwarts an expectation." The experienced person is someone who knows that life will always surprise, that life can never be tamed, that *creativity* and *risk* are essential to every encounter with life, that no amount of knowledge can tame the inexorable demands of being human. In other words, the experienced person does not *rely on accustomed or programmable responses;* rather, the experienced person knows that there is always more to life than meets the eye, that life itself always exceeds our grasp, that wisdom is not found through our measure of conceptual control, but through our measure of openness to that which always exceeds and surprises our current take on things.

A crucial element of interpretive experience is that it calls forth a re-interpretation or reassessment of my situation in ways that *open* me to new understandings and new behaviors in my life and in the world. It is only through this breakdown of my prior understanding that any possibility of a breakthrough into new understanding can occur. While this may sound like a negative requirement, it can also be viewed as a positive process of *releasing* me from past positions and frameworks that have held me captive for too long, or limited me from truly *experiencing* new insight and recognition. In biblical terms, the heart of the hermeneutical experience requires a "change of heart," a *metanoia* that stirs up our lives, turning our lives around, as though plunging us into the tumbling waters of repentance and conversion.

What is this text asking of me?

Do to others as you would have them do to you.

Most of us know this saying as the "golden rule" that is an ethical benchmark in virtually every religious tradition. However, it is strange the way this typical standard of love suddenly appears in the middle of this text. It seems out of place, because the previous verses, and the ones that follow, seem to be questioning even this standard of love, calling into question this sense of love's equivalence, whereby we simply love others as we want them to love us. Luke's text places in question this notion that love is a reciprocal measure, rather than a love that is *immeasurable* — loving even those who do not return love, loving even those who are our "enemies."

If you love those who love you, what credit is that to you? For even sinners love those who love them. If you do good to those who do good to you, what credit is that to you? For even sinners do the same. If you lend to those from whom you hope to receive, what credit is that to you? Even sinners lend to sinners, to receive as much again. But love your enemies, do good, and lend, expecting nothing in return. Your reward will be great, and you will be children of the Most High; for he is kind to the ungrateful and the wicked.

It is obvious that this text is asking questions of us. However, we should notice the types of questions it asks. It does not, for example, question *that* we love; rather, it questions the *way* we love. It assumes that most people want to love, but it questions our understanding and practices of love. It holds a mirror to ourselves and our ways of acting in the world, and asks us to consider what we see. It holds our typical understanding of the word "love" to the very flame of this word, testing it to see if it really is love. If we cannot love our enemies, or if we cannot give to another without expecting something in return, then in what sense can we say that we are loving? Aren't we, rather, just caught up in games of calculation and exchange, whereby love is measured and meted out to those who we know will love us in return? And if this is the way we love, is it really love?

The matter of concern

It is typically *only when we hear the question of the text* that we will even begin to approach its subject matter, that is, what *matters* to the text. The subject matter, however, is no matter at all unless we are drawn into its question, unless we ourselves are led to take up and consider the *matter of concern* that it raises.

I have come to appreciate the importance of hearing the question as one of the most crucial movements of hermeneutics. Gadamer calls this the "priority of the question."[11] In the art of interpretation, it is the question that has priority and leads the way. What a strange thing, that interpretation should be primarily concerned with "hearing a question" rather than with "finding an answer." However, Gadamer is seeking to remind us that we do not come to new understanding so much by coming to answers, as we do by hearing questions that present themselves to us. To enter the realm of the question is to recognize that we do not know, and to expect the unexpected. To enter the realm of the question is to allow our familiar worlds to be provoked by an unfamiliarity, a strangeness, a "lure" that hooks us and begins to reel us in. "A question presses itself on us," says Gadamer, "and we can no longer avoid it and persist in our accustomed opinion."[12] The question brings us into the open — into a less guarded or defensive space — but this openness allows the subject matter to emerge or break through and claim our attention.

Whenever I am engaged in a conversation that matters, I try to remember that "the question has priority." When Gadamer suggests that the question has priority, he is saying that what must *lead* every conversation is not so much our ready-made answers, but rather a *listening for the question that matters*. If I only let my preformed opinions or ready-made answers lead the conversation, then I may as well be talking to myself, because everything I say will only lead back to me and to what I already know. If interpretation means anything at all, it must surely mean trying to understand a voice that is other than my own.

Whether between "text" and "reader" or between "I and thou," it is all too easy in an interpretive encounter for our own preformed answers to lead the conversation rather than a *question* that is as yet unanswered or unmet. It is all too easy to talk and talk and talk—while all the time the question is completely missed, such that both partners come away less the wiser about the matter of concern and only more assured of their own position (which, in my experience, is more likely to lead to an argument or a debate rather than a conversation).

The priority of good conversation is with the question or the issue-at-hand that can only arise as both partners earnestly seek it and listen for it, letting it emerge such that it leads the way and makes an answer or a new understanding possible. Interpretive dialogue does not simply mean that "I understand you" or that "you understand me"; rather, it means that *I and you come to an understanding together* as we consider the subject matter that is a matter of concern between us. In other words, it is the subject matter that we are seeking to understand, not simply each other. It is the subject matter that must "lead the conversation," rather than "the will of either partner."[13] A conversation is not led by me or my opinions alone, nor is it led by you or your opinions alone. "The partners conversing," says Gadamer, "are far less the leaders than the led...."[14] What *leads* a conversation is the subject matter that arises between us as we listen for the question or the issue at hand, guiding us toward a newly found understanding that is always a *shared understanding between us.*

When the question arrives, then the subject matter arrives, and when the subject matter arrives, then — and only then — is the art of interpretation fully under way. "The heart of dialogue," says Edmond Jabès, "beats with questions."[15]

> *If you love those who love you...?*
> *If you do good to those who do good to you...?*
> *If you lend to those from whom you hope to receive...?*
>
> *Is this love?*
>
> *If anyone strikes you on the cheek, offer the other also.*
> *If anyone takes your coat, do not withhold your shirt.*
> *If anyone takes away your goods, do not ask for them back.*
>
> *Is this justice?*

What do you say? How will you choose to respond?

The tension between acting according to the ways of love and acting according to the ways of justice are constant in my life. Hardly a week goes by where I do not feel the need to make a decision and choose a direction that is not affected by the demands of love and the demands of justice. I may never be able to fully answer or resolve this question, but I am always provoked to make a response.

According to Gadamer, the real "rub" of hermeneutics happens when the question of the text finally becomes a matter of concern to me, and I am led to answer or respond to it. This is not so much a "final" movement of interpretation, as if I first inquire into the meaning of the text and then decide how I will respond. Rather, the moment of *applicacio* ("application") — what the text means for my life or for this community of readers today — *is* the very moment of understanding or interpreting the text. Gadamer writes:

> The interpreter dealing with a traditionary text tries to apply it to himself. But this does not mean that the text is given for him as something universal, that he first understands it per se, and then afterward uses it for particular applications. Rather, the interpreter seeks no more than to understand the text — i.e., to understand what it says, what constitutes the text's meaning and significance. In order to understand that, he must not try to disregard himself and his particular hermeneutical situation. He must relate the text to this situation if he wants to understand at all.[16]

By opening up a question, the text invites my own questioning: "What does this mean in my life? How should I respond to this text? What is it asking me to do?" Moreover, I will be led to consider the context and conditions in which my own response is situated. The unique demands of my concrete situation will, if you like, talk back to the text, bringing forth its own particular questions and dilemmas.

What is happening in the world today, in my society, in my workplace, in my church or family, or in the culture at large, that requires me to "love my enemy"?

What does it mean to call another person an "enemy"? When I call someone an enemy, haven't I already killed any possibility for love, and made it all the more likely that I will deride or attack them?

Am I acting justly toward another? What does it mean to act justly and yet tenderly as well? Could it be that an "excess of justice" — lacking in love or mercy — is dangerously close to becoming an injustice? On the other hand, is it possible that an "excess of love" could ever jeopardize or fail the demands of justice? Isn't it, rather, that the practices of love and mercy keep justice from becoming unjust, such that the conditions of justice are always tested against the infinite demands of unconditional love?

Do I act as most sinners do, loving only those who love me? And if I am a sinner, won't I always be dependent on the mercy and forgiveness of another? Isn't it the case that we are always responsible to each other and for each other, and therefore we are always in debt, and therefore always in need of asking for the forgiveness of our debts — even as we forgive the debts of others?

Our response to these questions, and the decisions and actions they call forth, will necessarily vary according to the particular demands and needs of each changing situation. According to Gadamer, it is only when "the world of the text" enters a conversation with "the world of the reader" that interpretation attains its genuine effectiveness and productivity in the world. It is only when the saying of the text and the response of my life "fuses" that the real chemistry of interpretation happens.[17]

LEARNING FROM THE RABBIS

In undertaking my own search into the interpretive art of practical theology, I have found myself surprisingly attracted to the richness of the rabbinic tradition. I recall one snowy evening in Boston, some years ago, when I read the following words from the Jewish poet Edmond Jabés:

"Ah, who will ever count the centuries examined in the margins of our books?" wrote Reb Amit ...

I myself have tried, in the margin of tradition and through words, to find again my fountainhead.[18]

I remember how much these words stood out for me. I was immediately struck with the image of "the margins," which suggests an interpretive link between a people bound in time and history, caught, like every living person, in the throws of practical human existence, yet also bound to their tradition, to that living conversation that endures through generations of prayerful reading and attentive response.

Jabès offers us an image of a people who, over centuries and centuries, live with such a deep attachment and attentiveness to their religious tradition that they return to it over and over again, as one returns to a fountain or to a well. "Turn it and turn it," the Mishnah says, "in it all things can be found" (*Pirkei Avos* 5:26). Page after page, day after day, through long nights and difficult questions, across the centuries, the Jewish people bring their lives to these ancient sources, weaving their own voices into the texts they are reading. Jabès offers another beautiful image:

To be in the book. To figure in the book of questions, to be part of it. To be responsible for a word or a sentence, a stanza or a chapter.

To be able to say: "I am in the book. The book is my world, my country, my roof, and my riddle. The book is my breath and my rest."

I get up with the page that is turned. I lie down with the page put down. To be able to reply: "I belong to the race of words, which homes are built with" — when I know full well that this answer is still another question, that this home is constantly threatened.

I will evoke the book and provoke the questions.[19]

In speaking of "the book," Jabès is evoking a deeply felt sense of belonging to a tradition into which his own life is inexorably bound. He realizes that he is part of the Jewish story and the Jewish experience, that he lives within its pages, that he is "in the book." It is a place of belonging, "my roof" and "my rest," yet it is also an unsettling experience of questioning and being questioned.

The "book" is by no means a closed, settled, and completed text. Indeed, Jabès's major seven-volume work is called *The Book of Questions*. The story is unfinished, and the book is like a "riddle" or a place of questions that continually calls forth new responses and new writing. "We always start out from a written text and come back to the text to be written," says

Jabès.[20] To be "in the book" is to be responsible for its ongoing story, "for a word or a sentence, a stanza or a chapter."

I find this metaphor of the book very helpful in exploring the relationship of a people to their religious tradition. Even though I am drawing upon the Jewish tradition, I do not find it difficult to relate the image of the "book" to my own Catholic tradition, which has also consistently affirmed the value of tradition and commentary as deep sources of God's revelation in history.[21]

The metaphor of the book is particularly interesting when we consider that a book can actually mean two things to us — it can mean *something that we read* and it can also mean *something that we write*. Indeed, Jabès suggests that the book is always both:

> *"What book do you mean?"*
> *"I mean the book within the book."*
> *"Is there another book hidden in what I read?"*
> *"The book you are writing."*
> — *Reb Haod*[22]

Though seemingly enigmatic, Jabès is referring to the unique ability of the Jewish tradition to speak of the book as both something that we *read* and something that we *write*, and that these two approaches are intimately related. Both approaches to the book are essential to the life and vitality of tradition — to "take it and read it," and "to write it and prolong it." Indeed, it is impossible for the rabbis to read the pages of tradition without at the same time writing their commentary. Hidden within the story they are reading is the story they are writing. The very act of reading the book allows its story to generate ongoing life and creativity, such that the story of the book is prolonged and kept alive and active. It is the very reading of the book that generates the creativity of interpretation and commentary, such that we can say, paradoxically, that the book is indeed both something that we read *and* something that we write.

In the Jewish tradition, the book is always twofold. It is indeed God's Word, but it is also the people's response to God's Word. The book is indeed written and given to be read. There is always a normative quality or a "deep story" that marks every religious tradition. The rabbis refer to this as the "Written Torah." In the Written Torah, God has given and intended all, such that everything is filled with divine intention and meaning.

However, because the Written Torah is the Word of God — filled with infinite meaning — it necessarily calls forth interpretation and commentary. The rabbis refer to this interpretive responsibility as "Oral Torah." The following parable attempts to reveal the relationship between the Written and the Oral Torah, suggesting that the only responsible way to read a book is to take responsibility for its words, or as Jabès says, "to be responsible for a word or a sentence or a stanza or a chapter."

What is the difference between the Written and the Oral Law? To what can it be compared? To a king of flesh and blood who had two servants and loved them both with a perfect love. He gave each of them a measure of wheat and each a bundle of flax. What did the wise servant do? He took the flax and spun cloth. He took the wheat and made flour. He cleaned the flour and ground, kneaded and baked it, and set it on top of the table. Then he spread the cloth over it until the king would come.

The foolish servant, however, did nothing at all. After some time, the king returned from a journey and came into his house. He said to his servants: my sons, bring me what I gave you. One servant showed the wheat still in the box with the bundle of flax upon it. Alas for his shame, alas for his disgrace!

When the Holy One, blessed be He, gave the Torah to Israel, he gave it only in the form of wheat — for us to make flour from it, and flax — to make a garment from it. (*Seder Eliyahu Zuta*, chapter 2)[23]

The parable suggests that interpretation is always a productive and creative craft that shapes "garments from flax" and creates "bread from wheat." The rabbis are suggesting that interpretation actively weaves, shapes, and "makes" the text: "the text is experienced only in the activity of production."[24] As Ricoeur reminds us, interpretation does not so much unveil established meanings "behind the text"; rather, it produces new meanings "in front of the text."[25]

Some readers may notice the similarity between this rabbinic parable and the Gospel "parable of the talents" (Matt. 25:14–30). However, there is another saying of Jesus that is perhaps closer in meaning:

Every scribe who has been trained for the kingdom of heaven is like the master of a household who brings out of his treasure what is new and what is old. (Matt. 13:52)

This is not unlike Gadamer's insistence that the interpreter is always mediating the wisdom of the text with the unique claims of their own present experience, in which "the old and the new combine into something of living value."[26]

IN THE MARGINS OF THE BOOK

The place where the "reading of the book" and the "writing of the book" happens is "in the margins of the book."[27] The margins represent the vital space between text and reader. If we think, for example, of any book that truly engages us — a book we read well — we typically read it "in the margins." (At least, this is what I typically do when I am reading — always with pen in hand, ready to write!) It is in the margins of the text that I scribble the response of my own reading in the form of commentary and question. It is in the margins that I am most deeply involved and engaged with the text — reading it — but also creating it and bringing it to life.

This image of "the margins" is starkly evident when we look at a page of Talmud. For those of you who have never seen a page of Talmud, I would encourage you to someday take a look at this most amazing page. It is quite a wonder and a testimony to interpretive genius and creativity. It is a page that is swarming with writing and commentary. It is a page that is completely overtaken by the expansiveness of the margins.

The roots of the Talmud go back to the Bible, the Word of God, which was communicated to the people of Israel at Sinai through the mediation of Moses, and amplified later through the teachings of the prophets. With the destruction of the Temple in 70 c.e., the rabbis emerged as a distinct group of teachers who sought to preserve the life of Israel in the wake of this disastrous event. They considered the Pharisees their intellectual and spiritual forebears, who had already begun the process of reinterpreting or extending the holiness of the Temple into the ordinary and daily events of people's lives.[28]

The rabbis believed that ultimate authority could not be found in fixed texts but only in a living interpretation of those texts. There is no question that the texts are sacred; however, given the finitude of the human condition and the pressures of new historical situations, these sacred texts must also be carefully interpreted as deep sources of wisdom for encountering daily dilemmas. Much of this teaching, which was mostly oral, was eventually recorded and redacted, and ultimately what resulted was the Talmud — a vast encyclopedia of teachings and spiraling commentaries. The Talmud seeks "to preserve the record of earlier generations studying their own tradition and provide materials for later generations wishing to do the same."[29] In many ways, it is a quintessential expression of practical theology. "The Talmud applies the Bible's basic teachings on the human condition to its own age; it offers procedures for dealing with problems that challenged the Jews in the new historical situations they faced."[30]

In *The People of the Book*, Samuel Heilman provides a rich account of the time-honored Jewish practice of *lernen*, "the eternal review and ritualized study of sacred Jewish texts."[31] Heilman describes the Talmudic study circle (*shiur*) as a place of communal, interactional drama through which *lerners* play the game of interpretation, taking their cue from the Talmud, which itself is a book of interacting, circling commentaries in the ever-expanding margins of the book:

Both literally and in effect, the Talmudic page is framed by commentaries: Rashi on the inside margin, his successors the Tosafists on the outside....

These commentaries in turn may be reframed by later commentaries which have been added to the outer margins of the page.... With each new edition of Talmud, the publishers may add more commentaries or new appendices — new interpretive keys....

Passing through layer upon layer of interpretation, the *lerners* bring themselves, their ethos and world view to bear upon the subject and animate the whole.... As the folio of Talmud is characterized by commentary, replies, response, questioning, debate, information exchange, digression, narrative, and repeated recountings, so the *shiur* is marked by keys of all of these.... The conversations during *lernen* are always something different from the written page, patterned by it but not exactly the same....

So complicated does the process — the *lernen* game — become that one would have trouble determining where the written page leaves off and oral commentary and reframing begins.[32]

I sense that something in my own Catholic tradition shares the spirit of this vibrant interpretive activity. I recently came across this rather lively image of St. Thomas Aquinas:

One imagines his study filled with books. As Thomas writes (or dictates) each article of the *Summa* one can see Scripture at his right hand, Augustine's great corpus at his left, Aristotle's philosophy on a table nearby, the works of the Fathers piled up on the floor, and the questions and perplexities of the monks he taught and lived with written on scraps of parchment and arranged in the order of topics as he would tackle them. One sees secretaries scurrying to find the precise wording of the citations he has requested, and copyists awaiting the finished manuscript. And one can hear the clucking of those who criticized the new synthesis of truth and knowledge as it appeared.[33]

In many ways, there is a kinship between this interpretive activity of Aquinas and the interpretive activity of the rabbis. Aquinas has the scriptures "at his right hand." They represent his primary text, the normative story. Yet he is also relying on past commentary, and so he has Augustine's work at his left hand. Augustine's "great corpus" has now become part of the story, and so too have all the commentaries of the Fathers, "piled up on the floor" around him. In other words, like the Talmudic page described above, Aquinas's work is "framed by commentaries" which have now become authoritative texts themselves, incorporated into the very heart of the tradition.

However, Aquinas isn't simply "rehashing" these texts. Rather, he himself is offering a new commentary. "On a table nearby" is the philosophy of Aristotle. "On a table nearby" is perhaps suggestive that while Aristotle's work is proximate to Aquinas's new interpretive venture, the works of Aristotle are nevertheless a "strange" or "new" voice that have not yet gained the same credibility or authority as Aquinas's other sources. In many ways, Aquinas is crafting his commentary by creatively playing with "the old" and "the new" — with the scriptures, Augustine, and the Fathers all around him, but also with Aristotle, that "pagan philosopher," daringly positioned on a "table nearby."

Lastly, we should notice that all of this is taking place amidst "scraps of parchment" that represent the urgent questions and concerns of the monks he is teaching and living with. All these pressing and unanswered questions are crucial to Aquinas's interpretive work. These questions are like "scraps" and remnant pieces — not yet ordered or systematized — and yet Aquinas takes them with utmost seriousness. They are central in forming and shaping the new commentary he is crafting — a commentary that will, as we now know, outlive him and become itself a new and enduring voice in the pages of tradition.

Aquinas, who is now considered one of the great doctors of the church, was initially engaged, much like the rabbis, in the practice of commentary and interpretation "in the margins of tradition." What interests me here is the need to rescue the term "marginal" from its negative connotations as "on the outside," "separatist," or "insignificant." Margin space, which we typically think of as narrow, insignificant space, is actually a vital interpretive edge that enlivens the pages of tradition. The margins represent the very space upon which the book's life is dependent. It is in the margins of commentary and interpretation that the book either spills its borders to enlarge and expand itself, or shrinks into virtual nonexistence through lack of provocation, questioning, commentary. It is in the margins that the book will either become a book of great size or a book of little measure. The success of the book depends largely on how much its margins are filled with commentary, question, and response; in other words, how much it provokes interpretive reading and writing among communities of interpretation.

HOUSES OF PRAYER AND STUDY

It may seem that images of reading and interpreting, studying and writing, questioning and commenting, are more suited to "academic" pursuits rather than the pursuits of "pastoral" or "practical" theology. However, I would like to suggest that these images bring us into the heart of practical theology's concern with the creative interplay that results when a community reads-prays-studies-interprets its faith tradition in dialogue with an equally attentive reading of the events-needs-questions-concerns of its own current reality.

According to David Tracy, the modern age has suffered a "fatal separation" between "theory" and "practice."[34] We are unsure how to bring these two back together again in a healthy relationship. We typically consider "theory" as somewhat speculative, and "practice" as something that "puts theory into action." We often equate the word "study," for example, with theoretical pursuits that are separate from "practice." In contrast to this modern scenario, Ivan Illich notes that the ancient Latin meanings of the word "study" denote "affection," "friendliness," "devotion to another's welfare," "sympathy," "desire," "pleasure or interest felt in something."[35] Prior to modernity's fatal separation between theory and practice, the art of reading-studying-praying-interpreting the sacred texts of tradition was essentially linked with the art and practice of living the Christian life, in all its concrete forms and conditions. The exercises of prayer, study, and service were not divorced from the living questions, concerns, and pastoral needs of the day.[36]

Study was not an abstract exercise divorced from life. As Tracy notes, this mentality would have been quite foreign to "the ancients," who felt deeply "the magnetic pull of the Good, and thereby of God."[37] Many of the monastic, medieval schools and the great scholastic thinkers such as Aquinas displayed little sense of the debilitating division between the "theoretical" and the "practical." Indeed, they would have found such a separation not only strange but self-destructive ("fatal"). In his study of Aquinas, for example, Marie-Dominique Chenu makes it plain that Aquinas never functioned as "an ivory tower theologian working in isolation from the burning questions of the people around him." Rather, "all of St. Thomas's writings were shaped by pressing academic, social, and pastoral concerns."[38] As Jean Leclercq so eloquently reminds us, what impassioned many of the ancients was the intimate link between "the love of learning and the desire for God," rather than their separation.[39]

The Jewish tradition also preserves this link between the "house of study" (*Bet ha-Midrash*) and the "house of prayer" (*Bet ha-Tefillah*). According to the rabbis, the essential marks of the house of prayer and study are devotion to scripture and its Talmudic interpretation, devotion to prayer and to God's Name, and devotion to our fellow human beings. "You need these all year," suggests one of the sages, "but never more than now." And again, "You are not required to complete the task, yet neither are you free to withdraw from it" (*Pirkei Avos*, 2:21).

For most of my adult life, I have been a member (along with my family) of small Christian communities. I like to consider these small communities as "houses of prayer and study," "houses of hospitality and service" (sometimes referred to as "house churches"). Where does practical theology happen today? Certainly, I think it should be happening more and more in our parishes and congregations, in our schools and universities, in our religious institutions and social involvements. Yet I also think it should be happening more and more among intentional gatherings of small Christian communities — among people of faith who devote themselves to prayer, study, and service — whereby we desire God with all our hearts and minds and deeds.

Jabès begins his first volume of *The Book of Questions* with the scene of rabbis going into the house of study:

> "What is going on behind this door?"
> "A book is shedding its leaves. . . ."
> "I saw rabbis go in."
> "They are privileged readers. They come in small groups to give us their comments."
> "Have they read the book?"
> "They are reading it."[40]

Christian communities have much to learn from this ancient practice of rabbis gathering around an open book. For these sage interpreters, "what matters is that they belong to the Book, and through the Book they belong together. The Book is the world and the world is the Book; to live is to interpret, and to interpret is to live. But they can only do it together, not alone."[41] The Mishnah says: "If two sit together and words of Torah are between them, the Divine Presence rests between them" (*Pirkei Avos*, 3:3). The Gospel says, "Where two or three are gathered in my name, I am there among them" (Matt. 18:20).

In my experience of belonging to small Christian communities, I have always sensed that this represents a time and a space that is marked with an essential quality. This is conversation that matters. It is where people are bound together to speak of experiences that count, questions that weigh, issues that matter. The conversation is characterized by stories, commentaries, questions, digressions, needs, responses, actions, and reflections. This is where the *interpretive edge* of small Christian communities takes on most of its creative power and energy. We begin to see that these communities are reading their questions and writing their commentary in the margins of the book, between the claims of tradition and the claims of new, contemporary situations. This suggests a profoundly communal activity in discerning the way forward through deliberation, conversation, and decision making in specific, local, concrete situations among communities of interpreters. "It becomes all the more imperative," writes Richard Bernstein, "to try again and again to foster and nurture those forms of communal life in which dialogue, conversation, practical discourse, and judgment are concretely embodied in our everyday practices."[42]

"You must believe in the book," says Jabès, "in order to write it." To believe in the "story of God" is to write it, to live it, and to enact it in the story of our own lives. Each generation must take this task to hand, reading and interpreting the signs of God for the life of the world, continuing to write the story of God into the story of life. "The time of writing," says Jabès, "is the time of this faith."[43]

PART TWO

MAY YOUR NAME
BE HELD HOLY

FIVE

"We Will Do and We Will Hear"

I am writing on the eve of the festival *Shavuot*, in which the Jewish people celebrate "the giving of the Torah." I am also writing in the midst of a sultry thunderstorm in South Florida, which provides a good backdrop to the dramatic events of Mount Sinai:

> On the morning of the third day there was thunder and lightning, as well as a thick cloud on the mountain, and a blast of a trumpet so loud that all the people who were in the camp trembled. Moses brought the people out of the camp to meet God. They took their stand at the foot of the mountain. Now Mount Sinai was wrapped in smoke, because the Lord had descended upon it in fire; the smoke went up like the smoke of a kiln, while the whole mountain shook violently. (Exod. 19:16–18)

The people panic and beg Moses to ascend the mountain and accept the teachings on their behalf. When Moses comes down from the mountain, the people respond: "we will do, and we will obey" (Exod. 24:7).

This is a celebrated verse in Jewish tradition, especially because of its strange inversion. "We will do" (*na'aseh*) is followed by "we will obey" (*nishma*), where *nishma* means both "obey" and "hear." Similarly, in Latin, obedience comes from the root *audire*, which means "to listen." What could it mean to say "We will do" before saying "we will hear"?

The relationship between "hearing" and "doing" is an important question for practical theology. It is typically addressed as a question concerning the relationship between "theory" and "practice." Practical theology suggests that we normally give priority to theory over practice, that we typically place "hearing" before "doing." In the following chart, for example, all the words associated with "to hear" are given primacy over all the words associated with "to do." We work out our theory before we put it into practice. We think before we act. We engage in reflection and discernment before we respond or make a commitment. The normal ordering is that "we hear" before "we do," and not the other way around.

To hear:	*To do:*
Theory	Practice
Reflection	Action
Knowing	Doing
Thinking	Acting
Discernment	Commitment
Listening	Responding
Hearing	Answering

The verse, "We will do and we will hear," puzzles us because it jars our normal ordering of the relationship between theory and practice. Placing doing before hearing creates a dissonance within us. How can doing come before hearing? Surely we must first hear or know what we are to do, before we can do it? Surely we must first "work it out" (theorize) before we can put it into practice (application)? Surely we must first understand something before we can act on it?

"We will do and will we hear" overturns the primacy we typically give to theory over practice. In a well-known passage from the Talmud, the Israelites are rewarded for doing *before* hearing, for acting even before they have understood, and each Israelite receives two crowns — one for *doing*, and the other for *hearing:*

> Rav Simai taught: When the Israelites committed themselves to doing [*na'aseh* — "we will do"] *before* hearing [*nishma* — "we will hear"], 600,000 angels came down and attached two crowns to each Israelite, one for the *doing*, and the other for the *hearing*. (Tractate *Shabbath*, 88a)[1]

"We will do and we will hear" is a strange teaching, especially for a tradition that is founded upon the *Shema:* "Hear Israel..." which is directly followed by, "You shall love..." (Deut. 6:4–5). The first word is "hear," which is then followed by what we must do, "you shall."

"We will do and we will hear" is therefore quite a puzzling verse because of its strange reversal, and as Emmanuel Levinas says, the rabbis "keep being astonished by it."[2] They are astonished by this "error in logic" that is nevertheless full of "merit which consists in acting before understanding."[3] Our task in this chapter is to explore this strange "error" that places doing before hearing, practice before theory, acting before knowing, and to see what merit it holds for us.

THE SECURITY OF KNOWING

"Every philosophy seeks truth," Levinas says in a wonderfully plain statement.[4] It begins in a search that takes us out of our familiar world, toward a truth that is unknown. If we already knew the truth, we would not seek it. So our search takes us outside of ourselves, toward a truth that is other than what I know, other than me, toward "another region, toward a beyond."[5] We are, as Levinas says, "turned toward the 'elsewhere' and the 'otherwise' and the 'other'."[6] We are led by a desire to seek truth, even if truth is something we can never fully attain and, thereby, always "infinite," "beyond," "more than me."

Every philosophy seeks truth, yet Levinas suggests that its search is also motivated by another factor: it also wants to *know* the truth. Our *search* for truth can all too easily be tempted by the need to *possess* truth, to make it *my own*, something I can now claim that *I know* as a truth *belonging to me*. In other words, the search for truth is often tamed or domesticated — no longer infinite in its horizon — but reduced to my own horizon of knowing. Truth is scaled down to coincide with myself, such that anything strange or different or other is now secured, safely incorporated into my own world of knowing, brought home to me and made comfortably "the same." Knowledge becomes *self-knowledge*, rather than a response to the call of the other, and it is this movement of philosophy that worries Levinas, the movement toward knowledge that assimilates and appropriates truth to our own familiar designs and frameworks.

Knowing, in other words, becomes a way of securing ourselves in the world. We treasure our ability to know and give it pride of place —

it grants us our *reason for being* — or, in that now-popular phrase of Descartes, "I think, therefore I am."

However, I am more than a self who simply thinks. I also act. Life is something that is lived, not just something we think about. We *do* life. We engage life through our actions. So, in some respects, that puzzling verse that begins with "we will do" seems right in the priority it gives to acting *before* knowing.

And yet, in his commentary on this verse, Levinas suggests that our actions nevertheless remain "tempted" by knowledge, by the need to know *before* we act. There is a certain security in knowing that safeguards the risk of acting. Before we act, we subject our actions to knowledge. "We want to know before we do."[7] Our priority lies with the temptation of knowledge that offers us a reasonable base from which to secure our actions and to lessen the risk — to first "work it out" before we put it into practice, to first understand something before we act on it, to know before we do.

Our actions "arise only after calculation, after a careful weighing of the pros and cons."[8] We want to take the risk of acting, but only if we can be sure! Thinking comes first. Knowing takes precedence. Only when we can act within a certain security of knowing beforehand will we finally commit to the task of doing. To suggest otherwise, to place doing before hearing, is often considered imprudent and unreasonable. "Any act not preceded by knowledge," Levinas says, "is considered in an unfavorable light."[9] It is considered as either naïve or foolish, or even crazy and mad.

"Think before you act," goes the popular saying. Maybe Descartes is right; we are thinkers first and foremost, before we are doers.

THE RISK OF ACTING

I recall my days as a graduate student when I took a class in the "sociology of knowledge" at Harvard University, and I still remember the professor's opening words: "The search for truth," he said, "is a privilege of leisure that most people in the world do not enjoy." Knowledge is often a luxury that affords us a time of leisure. Action, however, is a point of urgency.

This reminds me of a line from Kierkegaard: "The instant of decision is a madness."[10] Before we decide, we typically engage in a "careful weighing of the pros and cons." We subject our action to the counsel of knowledge, to what we can reasonably discern beforehand. However, we cannot stay forever in this realm of knowledge that is always a prelude, always a *before* "we will do." At some point we have to decide and to act. No amount of prior deliberation (knowing *before* we act) will save us from finally stepping into the realm of action that is fraught with uncertainty, and without the guarantees of knowing in advance, beforehand. Eventually we must forego the temptation to knowledge and succumb to a certain madness of acting without knowing.

Think of Abraham, for example, whom St. Paul calls "the ancestor of all who believe" (Rom. 4:11). He is perhaps the exemplary figure of doing before hearing. Even before the book of Genesis tells us that he "believed" (Gen. 15:6), we are told first that he "went forth" (Gen. 12:4). God said to Abraham: "Go from your country and your kindred and your father's house to the land I will show you" (Gen. 12:1). So Abraham departed, "toward another region, toward a beyond" (recalling Levinas's words). He left, "not knowing where he was going" (Heb. 11:8). He had no clear indication of where the journey would lead. There was not even the suggestion that he might eventually return to his familiar home. There was no certainty, no knowing. Just "Go, leave, do it!" *"Vayomer hashem el-Avram lech-lecha..."* — "The Lord said to Abram, 'Get thee out, Go forth...'" As Rabbi Barry Leff says:

> Everyone, at some time or another in their life, has had to pick up and leave, if not physically, as in to go off to college, at least metaphorically, as in deciding to jump into the uncharted territory of getting married. Everyone sees their life in some way as a journey, and at some point something or someone comes along which gets them to move in a different direction.[11]

We do not always act purely or solely on the basis of what we know. Perhaps this is our first clue into the strange verse that says, "we will do" before "we will hear." Often in the course of life, we take decisive steps or actions before we know, sometimes even without knowing, without any guarantees or certainties. If we had to wait until we knew everything before we acted, we probably wouldn't act at all; we would be paralyzed by uncertainty.

When Kierkegaard speaks of a "madness" that accompanies every decision to act, he is probably alluding to his famous "leap of faith." Whereas knowledge tempts us into thinking that we can act securely and on a firm basis, faith asks us to act without knowing all the ins and outs or reasons why, without having any prior certitudes. Faith asks us to trust — go, leave, take the step, do it.

Saying "we will do" before "we will hear" is perhaps telling us that we often have to act on faith before we know all the reasons why. And even though St. Anselm says that theology is faith seeking understanding, he also says that we must first have faith *before* we can understand: "I do not seek to understand so that I may believe, but I believe so that I may understand."[12] Or as Augustine says, "Unless you believe, you will not understand."[13] This same thought has found its way into the works of the controversial French philosopher Jacques Derrida, who nevertheless says, *"Je ne sais pas. Il faut croire."* "I do not know. One has to believe."[14]

THE TEST OF FAITH

We can approach the verse "we will do and we will hear" from yet another angle. It is, after all, a diamondlike phrase that can be turned this way or that to catch its various rays of light. Indeed, the rabbis recommend this "turning" of a verse, because we are dealing with the Torah, with God's infinite word: "Turn it and turn it; in it all things can be found" (*Pirkei Avos* 5:26).

What happens if we turn this verse such that it angles its light toward me? Such that it might read, "I do, therefore, I hear" (which carries a different tone to Descartes's "I think, therefore, I am."). Put another way, what happens if we take this verse and read it as a verse referring to my own life:

> *Look at the way I live,*
> *and you will see what I therefore hear and understand.*
> *Look at what I do,*
> *and you will see what I truly know and believe; you will see my faith.*

Put this way, referring to me, this verse takes on a fearful tone — as though it were a judgment that is suddenly measuring me, rather than a judgment of my own knowledge by which I measure everything and everybody else. The "plank" is now squarely in my own "eye" (see Matt. 7:1–5). Indeed, St. Augustine suggests that often the truth is not only that which enlightens me; it can also be that which accuses me (*"veritas redarguens,"* in *Confessions*, Book 10, 23). It can often arrive as a truth that strikes me with a great blow, rather than with a flash of enlightenment. We rarely choose this type of truth; rather, it befalls us.

"You will know them by their fruits" (Matt. 7:20). Isn't this the true test of faith? In other words, our lives are meant to bear witness, as if saying: "Look at my life, at the way I live, and you will see a testimony to faith. Look at my life, at the integrity of my words and actions, and you will see a witness to truth. Look at my life, at what I do, and you will see a mirror of goodness. Look at my life, at the way it is patterned, and you will see an exemplar of God."

"Look at what I do.... Look at my life ... and you will see my faith ... you will see what I know and believe ... you will see a witness to divine life." This is the severest of criteria, pointing directly at me — a scrutiny from which I am never released. In everything I do, in all my actions, I am always held answerable. "Each of us is guilty before everyone and for everyone, and I more than the others," which is a phrase from Dostoyevsky's *Brothers Karamazov* (Book 6, 2) that Levinas is fond of quoting.[15]

To say that we are all guilty is perhaps another way of saying that our lives are constantly put in question, as though someone said to us: "Well, you may believe it, you may know it, but do you really live it?" Or: "That is fine in theory, but how are you putting that into practice? Show me where you are doing it." In other words, *action* is a very daunting and severe criterion — I will always fall short of living a completely responsive and responsible life; and quite inescapable — I can never put up my feet and say, "No more is required of me."

Many of the rabbinic and Gospel parables suggest that the Torah or God's word is more concerned with what we do and how we live, rather than with what we know or what we believe. The following two parables (the first from the rabbinic tradition, the second from the Gospels) serve as an example:

A person who knows a great deal but does not do very much — what is this person like? To a tree with many branches but only a few roots: the wind will come and pluck it up and turn it over onto its face. But the person who does many good deeds, even without knowing a great deal — what is this person like? To a tree with few branches but many roots: all the winds in the world cannot move it from its place. (*Pirkei Avos*, "Ethics of the Fathers," 3:22)

Everyone who listens to these words of mine and acts on them will be like a sensible man who built his house on rock. Rain came down, floods rose, gales blew and hurled themselves against that house, and it did not fall: it was founded on rock. But everyone who listens to these words of mine and does not act on them will be like a stupid man who built his house on sand. Rain came down, floods rose, gales blew and struck that house, and it fell; and what a fall it had! (Matt. 7:24–27)

These two parables suggest that simply "hearing" or "knowing" is not enough. It is not our knowledge or our beliefs on their own that anchor or secure our lives. They can all too easily be swept away and collapse if they are not rooted or founded in action. It is our deeds that offer the deepest roots, our actions that provide the true foundation — not simply our knowing.

According to Abraham Heschel, the realm of faith asks us to "take a *leap of action* rather than a *leap of thought*."[16] A person of faith is asked "to do more than he understands in order to understand more than he does." "We will do" claims priority because our *doing* leads to *knowing*, rather than the other way around. "Right living is a way to right thinking."[17] Doing leads to faith. "We do not have faith because of deeds," Heschel says; rather "we may attain faith through sacred deeds."[18] In the Christian tradition, it is the letter of St. James that offers us the classic example:

Take the case, my brothers, of someone who has never done a single good act but claims that he has faith. Will that faith save him? If one of the brothers or one of the sisters is in need of clothes and has not enough food to live on, and one of you says to them, "I wish you well; keep yourself warm and eat plenty," without giving them these bare necessities of life, then what good is that? Faith is like that: if good works do not go with it, it is quite dead. (James 2:14–18)

THE ANSWERABLE LIFE

In his posthumous work *Toward a Philosophy of the Act* (found in a damp and rat-infested attic), the Russian writer Mikhail Bakhtin says that each and every human life is an "answerable life" without any "alibi."[19] I cannot ask someone else to answer for my life. I have no "alibi" that can come to my defense. I cannot evade "the answerable act or deed" of my own life — no one can answer for me or take my place. Only I can respond to another, and this is what constitutes the singularity of my unique place in existence, and the unique vocation or answerability of my life. In other words, I am required.

The biblical phrase that Levinas evokes to call to mind this answerability is the prophetic response to the call of God, "Here I am" (*hineni*). Here I am, for you. "To *be* is to *stand for*," Heschel says.[20] The meaning of my life, what it signifies or stands for, is to be for you. The self ("I am") is positioned as a responsive, answering self ("Here I am"). "The word *I* means *here I am*," writes Levinas.[21] The priority is not with the *I* constituting itself, but with the call of the other who asks after me. It is this call that comes first, that is always prior, that is always before me, and constitutes my identity as a response-ability and answer-ability. Levinas is converting the "I think, therefore, I am" of modern, Western thought into the "here I am" of biblical, prophetic response. This is the election of the *I* as chosen and responsible before the face of God and neighbor. "I am," says Levinas, "as if I had been chosen."[22]

"We will do" is not the doing of an autonomous and self-sufficient subject; rather it is the doing of an answering and responding subject. It is not a doing based on my own self-choosing; rather it is my being chosen to respond to the call of the other. It is not a doing based in power and control; rather it is a doing based in service and hospitality. It is not a self-made doing in which I accomplish the project of my life; rather it is a responsive doing in which I answer with my life.

Karol Wojtyla (John Paul II) suggests, in ways similar to Levinas and Bakhtin, that the answerable life is what constitutes our very personhood. The key thesis of his book *The Acting Person* is that "action *reveals* the person."[23] The way people live, the commitments they make, the actions they take, the way they answer with their life, "gives us the best insight into the inherent essence of the person and allows us to understand the person most fully." Action "constitutes the specific moment whereby the person is revealed."[24] Or as Heschel says, "The deed is the distillation of the self."[25]

"We will do" *before* "we will hear" — why does "doing" come first? Perhaps this verse is trying to remind us that life is encountered first and foremost in action, rather than in thought. Bernard Lee, for example, suggests that classical theology typically gives pride of place to reason. It "presupposes that reason is what is most definingly human about us, the finest exercise of which constitutes human fulfillment." Practical theology, however, is an attempt to give priority to "we will do" — to human action, and "presupposes that historical agency is what is most definingly human about us, the finest exercise of which constitutes human fulfillment."[26] "Action," says Lee, "names the whole process of living together in a world. Everything that belongs to being in the world with others from life to death is action."[27] Our relationship with God is more than a contemplated act; it is a performed deed. "Human action (living) that cleaves with God's action (living) is the end of human life."[28]

It is interesting to note that every statement of the Nicene and Apostles' Creeds begins with "We believe" or "I believe." It is also interesting to note that much of Western philosophy has centered itself around questions of ontology (what is being?) or questions of epistemology (what is thinking?) and how these two — thinking and being — belong together. The Jewish tradition, however, begins with "we will do." Its theology is patterned more by commandment and response, rather than by belief and assent. It gives a priority to the question, "What must I do?" or "What is required of me?" rather than "What should I believe?" or "What should I know?"

The priority of the performed deed, of response, of giving an answer with my life, is at the core of Judaism. Central to Judaism's way of life are the *mitzvot* — the commandments of God, and our response to the divine call by way of action. Practical theology is inherent in the Jewish tradition, and exposure of Christianity to its Jewish matrix is a crucial way for helping retrieve the practical sensibilities of theology. Perhaps no one has taught me this more than the works of Abraham Heschel, who refers to Judaism as a "science of deeds."[29] In the last chapter of his slim and yet beautifully written volume *Who Is Man?* Heschel recasts and transforms the language of modernity and autonomy into the language of biblical commandment and prophetic response. Following are some brief and yet exemplary selections that speak to us about the "answerable life":[30]

How to live

Modern thinking has often lost its way by separating the problem of truth from the problem of living.... Reflection alone will not procure self-understanding. The human situation is disclosed in the thick of living. The deed is the distillation of the self....

Where does man come upon himself most directly? Is it in abstract self-consciousness, in the generality of "knowing that I am," of "knowing that I think"? Man encounters himself, he is surprised to know himself, in the words he utters, in the deeds he does, and above all in living as an answer." (94)

Being-challenged-in-the-world

Human living is not simply being here and now, being around, a matter of fact; it is being in dilemma, being cross-examined, called upon to answer.

Human living is being-challenged-in-the-world, not simply being-in-the-world. The world forces itself upon me, and there is no escape from it. Man is continuously exposed to it.... He cannot evade the world. It is as if the world were involved in man, had a stake in man. (104)

Requiredness

Significant living is an attempt to adjust to what is expected and required of being human. This sense of requiredness is as essential to being human as the capacity for reasoning.... The sense of requiredness is not an afterthought; it is given with being human; not added to it but rooted in it. (106)

Indebtedness

Here is a basic difference between the Greek and the biblical conception of man. To the Greek mind, man is above all a rational being; rationality makes him compatible with the cosmos. To the biblical mind, man is above all a commanded being, a being of whom demands are made. The central problem is not: What is being? But rather: What is required of me? (107)

This is the most important experience in the life of every human being: something is asked of me.... There is a calling, a demanding, a waiting, an expectation. There is a question that follows me wherever I turn: What is expected of me? What is demanded of me?...We know ourselves as exposed, challenged, judged, encountered. (108)

Indebetdness is given with our very being. It is not derived from conceptions; it lives in us as an awareness before it is conceptualized or clarified in content. It means having a task, being called. It experiences living as receiving, not only as taking. Its content is gratitude for a gift received. (108)

I am commanded — therefore I am

Do I exist as a human being? My answer is: *I am commanded — therefore I am.*

There is a built-in *sense of indebtedness in the consciousness of man,* an awareness of *owing gratitude,* of being *called upon* at certain moments to reciprocate, to answer, to live in a way which is compatible with the grandeur and mystery of living. (111)

"Thou art" precedes "I am." (98)

"I DO"

In most wedding ceremonies, two people dedicate their lives to each other in an exchange of vows and reply, "I do." This "I do" is also used in swearing-in ceremonies of various kinds, including those of public office. "Do you promise to love, to uphold, to serve...?" "Yes. I do." Such are fundamental acts of answerability.

This "I do" is perhaps another clue into the verse that says "we will do" before "we will hear." Perhaps saying "I do" *at the very beginning* is a way of saying "I promise" or "I will," even before I know. Perhaps covenantal relationships all require this "I do" as their very foundation. *Before* anything can get under way, "I do" must be said from the very beginning.

I do. I promise in advance. I give my word. This is my answer. Before I hear or understand, before I know what lies ahead, I say "I do" — to you, to the future, to what is coming — none of which I can ever know in advance. According to Jacques Derrida, the act of promising is the original act that begins everything, that gets everything under way:

When I say "yes" to the other, in the form of a promise or an oath, the "yes" must be absolutely inaugural....I say "yes" as a starting-point. Nothing precedes the "yes." The "yes" is the moment of institution, of the origin: it is absolutely originary.[31]

Everything *begins* with this "yes, I will" — this answering promise. It is the very basis of faith and hope, of love and fidelity. "Yes, I will" is always first and foremost, before all else. Nothing would move or live or have its being without this originary "yes." Indeed, John Caputo calls this "yes" an "amen" which is like the infinite and ever-renewing affirmation of the world by God, whose "let there be" is a perennially creative event that affirms and sustains all creation. The best way to think of "yes" is "to think of a great and sweeping "amen!"[32] To say "yes" is to "choose life" and to say "I do," to say "amen" to life, to you, to the future.

The Jewish philosopher Hannah Arendt sees this ability to say "I do" as one of the most creative and sustaining acts of human life. Human action that is life-giving shares in the creative action of God, who is continually "bringing forth" and sustaining life and existence. Every act that serves life is an act of "bringing forth," of pledging oneself to the coming of something new, to the promise of new life:

Without action, without the capacity to start something new and thus articulate the new beginning that comes into the world with the birth of each human being, the life of man, spent between birth and death, would indeed be doomed beyond salvation.... Action, with all its uncertainties, is like an ever-present reminder that men, though they must die, are not born in order to die but in order to begin something new. *Initium ut esset homo creatus est* — "that there be a beginning man was created," said Augustine. With the creation of man, the principle of beginning came into the world....[33]

"I promise, I am here *for you*," is one of our most fundamental human acts. "Binding ourselves through promises," says Arendt, is the only way we can sustain our life together. "Without being bound to the fulfillment of promises, each of us would be condemned helplessly and without direction in the darkness of his own lonely heart."[34] The act of promising invests the future with hope. Promising looks forward as a commitment to the future and to each other.

Arendt knows, however, that we live in a world of broken promises, that our social and interpersonal relationships are wounded and frail and in need of healing and repair. For this reason, she suggests that acts of promising must also be accompanied by acts of forgiveness.

Promising and forgiving belong together, go hand in hand, because we often fail in our promises, and forgiveness allows us to begin again, to renew the covenantal relations between us. "Without being forgiven," writes Arendt, without being "released from the consequences of what we have done, our capacity to act would, as it were, be confined to one single deed from which we could never recover; we would remain the victims of its consequences forever...."[35]

To promise and to forgive are the threads that keep us woven and bound to each other. We need to keep saying "I do." We need to keep promising, over and over again. And because we know our human frailty, we also need to keep forgiving, over and over again. "How often should I forgive?" Peter asks Jesus, "As many as seven times?" "Not seven times," Jesus replies, "but seventy-seven times" (Matt. 18:21–22). In other words, all the time, because we are constantly failing each other.

Trespassing is a daily occurrence in life and needs acts of forgiveness in order to make it possible for the promise of life to go on. Rather than clinging tight to past hurts and injuries, forgiveness offers us the promise of a new future, a new beginning. Forgiveness sets us free from the burden of sin and starts up a new chain of events. "Go, and sin no more" (John 8:11). By constantly releasing us from the burden of what we have done to one another, acts of forgiveness break the cycles of violence and vengeance, of death and destruction. Only in this way can we "choose life" rather than always "keeping score."[36]

There is a very tender and moving scene recorded in the Gospel of John when the risen Jesus, after having cooked breakfast for the disciples, turns to Peter and asks him if he loves him. Peter, as we know, had denied Jesus three times and totally abandoned him. However, Jesus does not condemn Peter. He has already forgiven him and he knows that Peter loves him, and he provides an opportunity for love to be renewed and the promise restored.

When they had finished breakfast, Jesus said to Simon Peter, "Simon son of John, do you love me more than these?" He said to him, "Yes,

Lord; you know that I love you." Jesus said to him, "Feed my lambs." A second time he said to him, "Simon son of John, do you love me?" He said to him, "Yes, Lord; you know that I love you." Jesus said to him, "Tend my sheep." He said to him the third time, "Simon son of John, do you love me?" Peter felt hurt because he said to him the third time, "Do you love me?" And he said to him, "Lord, you know everything; you know that I love you." Jesus said to him, "Feed my sheep." (John 21:15–17)

Peter, who knows what it is to break promises, who once "wept bitterly," is called to care for the small and struggling community, to "feed my lambs." Jesus entrusts this vocation to Peter because he knows that humility and a truly repentant heart are among the best qualifications for pastoral leadership.[37]

Do you love me? Yes. I do.

DOING THE WORD

When I was a Golda Meir Fellow at the Hebrew University of Jerusalem, I had the great privilege of studying Torah with Professor Michael Rosenak.[38] One of the things I learned from the rabbinic tradition was that as the rabbis searched for the meaning of a text, they were always drawn to finding its *ethical* message. Even when the ethical message was not immediately apparent to them, they would stay with the text, "turning it and turning it," until its ethical import twisted free. The meaning of a text was primarily about *the way one should live*. God's word, the Torah, is something *to live, to do*, and such was the purpose of study and prayer, to bring our lives into alignment with the teachings and commandments of Torah.

In a wonderful book titled *The Word in the Desert*, Douglas Burton-Christie shows how this concern for living or *doing* the word was central to the ancient asceticism of early Christian monasticism.[39] This tradition took shape in the fourth century among the desert fathers and mothers of Egypt. Interestingly, he notes that the roots of this monastic tradition were deeply influenced by "the life of the early Church, particularly in areas with a strong Jewish influence" (39). Many of the collected *Sayings* of these holy men and women make frequent allusion to "keeping the commandments" or "fulfilling the commandments" or "doing what is written" as the essential key to spiritual growth (151).

The *Sayings* are typically framed in the context of a dialogue between a monk and an elder: "Abba, give me a *word*." The meaning of the *word*, however, is never left to pure speculation, but is always tied to the question of how one should live: "Abba, what should I do?" (134). "The questioners wanted to know," writes Burton-Christie, "what they were to *do*, how they were to *act*." He continues:

> Their questions took various forms: "What should I do?" "How should a person behave?" "How should we conduct ourselves?" "What good work should I do that I might live in it?" These practical questions reveal the kinds of concerns the monks brought to the elders. They sought not so much ideas about the spiritual life narrowly conceived, but rather a new way to live. (150)

This concern for the speaking word carried an eventlike quality that closely resembled the Hebrew *dabar*, as "a deed or an 'event' which is announced by a word, expressing the close correlation between life and action" (77). Those who came to the elders seeking a *word* were not seeking an "extended spiritual discourse" or "general, universal prescriptions." Rather, they were seeking "concrete and precise keys" to help them unlock the very real difficulties and practical concerns of their lives. For these desert-dwelling monks, the best way to "unleash the power of the word" was not to focus on its theoretical meaning, but to focus attention on the "earthly" and "practical demands of their life" (157). Burton-Christie writes:

> Because the desert fathers held integrity of words and life to be so important, the question of how to bring one's life into conformity with Scripture became a burning question. They were convinced that only through *doing* what the text enjoined could one hope to gain any understanding of its meaning. (135)

More than a merely contemplated act, it was the performed deed that counts. "The elders made it abundantly clear," says Burton-Christie, "that their words were spoken only for the sake of being taken up and integrated into the hearts, minds, and actions of those who received them" (134). Of the numerous and telling stories that fill the pages of Burton-Christie's book, the following is but one striking example:

> We can gain further insight into this practical orientation by examining the attitude of Abba Pambo toward Scripture: Pambo was... reticent to speak about Scripture: "If he was asked to interpret part of the Scriptures he would not reply immediately, but he would say *he did not know* that saying. If he was asked again, he would say no more." We hear elsewhere that the reason for Pambo's silence before Scripture had to do with his strong conviction that words without practice were useless. Early in his monastic career, he went to one of his elders to learn a psalm. Having heard the first verse of Psalm 38 ("I said I will take heed to thy way, that I offend not with my tongue"), he departed without staying to hear the second verse. He said to himself: "This one will suffice, if I can practically acquire it." More than six months passed before he returned to consult the elder again. When he did so, the old man reproved Pambo for staying away for so long. But Pambo told him that the reason for his long absence was that he had been fully occupied with the verse he had been given. Even now, he said, "he had not yet learned to practice the verse of the Psalm." Many years later, Pambo was asked by one of his companions whether he had finally mastered the verse. He responded, "I have scarcely succeeded in accomplishing it during nineteen years." Such honesty and humility served as an example for anyone who wished to unlock the mysteries of Scripture: no amount of speculation and conversation about the text was as valuable as a silent and earnest effort to realize in one's life the meaning of even a single verse. (156)

WE WILL DO *AND WE WILL HEAR*

According to Levinas, "We will do and we will hear" means that "one accepts the Torah before one knows it."[40] In a similar way, the story of Abba Pambo tells us that he accepts the verse given him, not because he knows it; rather, he says, "I do not know that saying." He accepts the verse by trying to live it in his life, by "doing the word," so that he might one day come to know it and understand it.

Rabbi Barry Leff suggests that it is only by keeping God's commandments, by accepting them and doing them, that we are able to better hear and understand their meaning and their wisdom for life. He offers the example of observing Shabbat:

> We will do and we will understand. This is a very profound teaching. I could give a dozen brilliant sermons about why it is a wonderful thing to observe Shabbat, and someone who has never tried it would still not get what Shabbat is about. To understand Shabbat, you simply have to do it.... Taking 25 hours out of a busy life, and spending it doing nothing but being with friends and family, eating good meals, drinking wine, singing, hanging out, is incredibly restorative. Not to run around from here to there, not to watch TV, not to run errands, not to do the laundry, but to simply BE, and be with each other, is an incredible experience. But to appreciate it requires a "leap of action" — a willingness to try it and experience it, and understand what it's about later.[41]

To do before we understand means that it is through our doing that we are led to deeper understanding. As we do, we hear or we learn. As I teach, for example, I learn more and more what it means to be a good teacher. As I parent, I learn more and more what it means to be a good parent. As I write this book, as I do the writing, I begin to better understand or "hear" what I am writing about. As I practice forgiveness, I begin to understand more deeply what forgiveness is. As we follow the ways of God, we become more and more like the people of God.

The Israelites were rewarded for doing before understanding, yet they nevertheless received *two crowns* — "one for the doing *and one for the hearing.*" Doing without hearing is just thoughtless "activity." In the Jewish tradition, right action is always accompanied by *kavanah.*[42] *Kavanah* is attentiveness, acting purposefully, being aware of what we are doing, reflecting upon and learning from our doing. Any good artisan or practitioner knows what *kavanah* means. It is no mere external performance or blind obedience. It is not a "mechanical act" but an "artistic act." Who could imagine poets or musicians who do not write or compose with their heart or teachers who do not care for their students, or parents who lack attentiveness to their children, or ministering persons who do not discern or pray?

Along with our deeds, "God asks for the heart," Heschel says, "for insight, not only for obedience; for understanding and knowledge of God, not only for acceptance."[43] "You shall love the Lord your God with all your heart, and with all your soul, and with all your strength, and with all your mind..." (Luke 10:25; cf. Deut. 6:4–5). Jesus often supplemented his teachings with references to the person's "heart," to *kavanah:*

> The good person out of the good treasure of the heart produces good, and the evil person out of evil treasure produces evil; for it is out of the abundance of the heart that the mouth speaks. (Luke 8:15)
> This people honors me with their lips, but their hearts are far from me. (Matt. 15:8; cf. Isa. 29:13)

Kavanah means that while we are living and acting on earth, we should keep our hearts turned toward heaven and attentive to the ways of God. "But strive first for the kingdom of heaven," Jesus says (Matt. 6:33). "For where your treasure is, there your heart will also be" (Luke 12:34). "We have learned," the rabbis say, that "it matters not whether one does much or little, if only he directs his heart to heaven" (Tractate *Berakhot*, 17a).[44] Action is not action without love, action is not action without faith and concern, action is not action without thoughtfulness and understanding, without reflection and contemplation, without the involvement of the heart.

When the Holy Spirit came upon Mary to announce the birth of her child, she responded, "Here I am, the servant of the Lord; let it be with me according to your word" (Luke 1:38). She said "yes" at the very beginning. Later, the Gospel tells us, "Mary treasured all these words and pondered them in her heart" (Luke 2:19).

BINDING HEAVEN AND EARTH

> Truly I tell you, whatever you bind on earth will be bound in heaven, and whatever you loose on earth will be loosed in heaven. (Matt. 18:18)

Commentary

According to Abraham Heschel (1907–1972):

It is in *deeds* that man becomes aware of what life really is, of his power to harm and to hurt, to wreck and to ruin; of his ability to derive joy and to bestow it upon others; to relieve or to increase his own and other people's tensions.... The deed is the test, the trial, and the risk. What we perform may seem slight, but the aftermath is immense. An individual's misdeed can be the beginning of a nation's disaster. The sun goes down, but the deed goes on. Darkness is over all we have done. If man were to survey at a glance all he has done in the course of his life, what would he feel? He would be terrified at the extent of his own power.... Even a single deed generates an endless set of effects.... Gazing soberly at the world man is often overcome with a fear of action, a fear that, without knowledge of God's ways, turns to despair.[45]

According to the Trappist monk Thomas Merton (1915–1968):

Here was [my] will...ready to generate tremendous immanent powers of light or darkness, peace or conflict, order or confusion, love or sin. The bias which my will was to acquire from the circumstance of its acts would eventually be the direction of my whole being towards happiness or misery, life or death, heaven or hell.

More than that: since no man ever can, or could, live by himself and for himself alone, the destinies of thousands of other people were bound to be affected, some remotely, but some very near-at-hand, by my own choices and decisions and desires, as my own life would also be formed and modified according to theirs. I was entering into a moral universe in which I would be related to every other living being, and in which whole masses of us, as thick as swarming bees, would drag one another along towards some common end of good or evil, peace or war.[46]

According to Rabbi Hayyim Volozhiner (1759–1821):

Let nobody in Israel — God forbid! — ask himself: "What am I, and what can my humble acts achieve in the world?" Let him rather understand this, that he may know it and fix it in his thoughts: not one detail of his acts, of his words and of his thoughts is ever lost. Each one leads back to its origin, where it takes effect in the height of heights.... The man of intelligence who understands this in its truth will be fearful of heart and will tremble as he thinks how far his bad acts reach and what corruption and destruction even a small misdeed can cause. (*Nefesh ha'Hayyim*, or "The Soul of Life")[47]

Our actions and words are not performed or spoken into a vacuum or a void. They can do good or harm; they bear responsibility; they carry the weight of life and death, good and evil. We can serve or hinder the association of God with the world. The rabbis offer a commentary on a verse from Isaiah 43:12: "You are my witnesses, says the Lord, and I am God." According to the rabbis this means, "When you are my witnesses I am God, but when you are not my witnesses I am not God" (*Sifre Deut.*, 346).[48] "We will do." "Here I am." "We will hear." It is the answering and promising life that testifies to God's living presence in our midst, that binds heaven and earth.

S I X

"Ecce Homo"

The Human Person: Holy and Like No Other

Several years ago, I spent a year with my family living in Jerusalem. During this time, I was a Golda Meir Fellow at the Hebrew University of Jerusalem. My wife, Mary, worked for the Sisters of Sion, a Catholic women's religious order committed to Jewish-Christian dialogue. Their community in Jerusalem served as an educational center and house of hospitality called *Ecce Homo*. The reference is from St. John's Gospel, when Pilate brings Jesus before the crowd and says, "Behold the man" (John 19:6). The trial of Jesus is one of the "stations of the cross" along the *Via Dolorosa* ("way of suffering") in Jerusalem's Old City. Each time I visited *Ecce Homo* and passed the chapel's statue of the man sentenced to death, I found myself wondering: does this scene of a lone and condemned figure represent the trial of God, or the trial of humanity?

I thought of the time when I met Cantor Deutsch, a regular speaker at an annual Holocaust seminar sponsored by the Temple Emmanuel Synagogue in Sydney. Cantor Deutsch, who for more than thirty years has served the synagogue with his passionate and beautiful voice, is a survivor of the Nazi atrocities. Each time he spoke to the seminar of his trauma, tears inevitably welled in his eyes, as though his memory only needed the slightest prompting and he was there again, reliving those unlivable days. Somewhat clumsily, we asked him: "What is the hardest thing in recalling this time?" "How have you kept going?" "What of your belief in God?" His response always stayed with me. He said that the hardest thing is not so much trying to maintain his faith and belief in God. What is even more difficult and unbelievable, he said, is trying to fathom how one human being could perform such acts of cruelty and violence toward another human being. How can human beings do this to each other? This is the question that still haunts him ever since those horrific days, that still visits him in the middle of the night, that still leaves him pained and disbelieving.

Cantor Deutsch struggles more with a disbelief in humanity than with a disbelief in God. He struggles more with our culpability rather than with God's, with our inhumanity rather than with God's divinity. How is it possible that human beings — that is, people who are supposedly persons, people who supposedly have hearts and souls — can inflict such violence and hatred on another person, another soul, another human being? How can they not see that they are killing not just "anyone," but rather another *person* who is like themselves? How can humans do this to each other? This is the unbelievable question that rises above us and continually demands our answer and our response.

THE "NONPERSON"

Gustavo Gutiérrez maintains that human beings are most prone to inflicting violence upon other persons precisely when the other person is considered as anything but human — indeed, as a "nonperson."[1] It is easier to kill or disregard a nonperson than it is a person. History abounds with examples. For Gutiérrez, it is the history of his own people in Latin America. One of the most poignant videos I show in my class is a reenactment of an actual debate that took place in the sixteenth century — known as the "Valladolid Controversy" — in which the ecclesial authorities of Spain sought to determine whether or not the indigenous people of the "new world" were persons or were of an inferior class.[2] On one side of the debate stood a Dominican friar, Bartolomé de Las Casas, who argued that the Indians were indeed persons, and therefore deserved human respect and dignity. On the other side of the debate stood a Jesuit priest, Professor Sepúlveda, who argued that the Indians were not persons and could therefore be rightfully subjugated and treated as slaves. During the course of the debate, a surprise announcement is made — an Indian family has been brought to Spain, and are presented to the court as "specimens" to be tried and examined, so as to better determine whether or not they are human beings, or whether they are of a category other than human.

While we may consider this debate scandalous to our modern and enlightened sensibilities, Gutiérrez suggests that this trial of the sixteenth century is still playing itself out today, as many peoples of the world find their very existence as persons placed in question. "The majority of peoples today are still nonpersons," says Gutiérrez, "they are not considered as human persons."[3] In other words, we are still — in our very own times — debating the question of "who is a person?" I am often reminded, for example, of a striking image from a civil rights march of the 1960s, where African American men are walking down the streets with placards declaring, "I am a man!" Behold!

I also remember my first foray into feminist literature when I encountered the searing indictment of ingrained patriarchal structures that suppress women's voices and women's experience — unaccounted for and unacknowledged — as though they too were not persons or fully recognized human beings. As I read the voices of these women — their protest, their poetry, their forgotten and reclaimed stories — I heard again the voice of those who cry out and say, "Behold!"

All our ills, it seems to me, all our trials, are indeed trials of humanity — and whether or not we will, one day, finally recognize and affirm the fundamental dignity of each and every human person, or whether we will continue to "depersonalize" and "dehumanize" our fellow human beings.

A student in my class recently told a story from his past when, as a young person, he was living as a gang member on the streets of New York. One night he broke into an apartment, but immediately on entering he saw a picture of a grandmother with her family around her. The picture was inscribed with a prayer, asking for God's blessing and protection on her family and her home. He stopped in his tracks, stunned by the picture, and thought of his own mother, and how she too constantly prayed for him (like St. Augustine's mother, Monica!). He saw the face of this grandmother; he saw her children and her children's children; he saw the sign of the cross and the prayer for protection — and at that moment he decided he could no longer do violence to another human being. He crawled back out the window, empty-handed, to face the ire of his fellow gang members, and, as he says in his own words, on that night he became "a new man."

Of all the trials we face, the greatest is that which accuses us of our "crimes against humanity." And that trial — which is not simply a question of "to be or not to be," but rather, to be human or not to be human — is also the trial or travail of God who has risked God's very self in the form of vulnerable humanity. *Ecce Homo.*

HUMANITAS

At the conclusion of his splendid series of lectures offered at Stanford University in 1963 and published under the title *Who Is Man?* the Jewish theologian Abraham Heschel writes:

> Who is the human person? *A being in travail with God's dreams and designs*, with God's dream of a world redeemed, of reconciliation of heaven and earth, of a humanity which is living truly in God's image, reflecting God's wisdom, justice, and compassion. God's dream is not to be alone, to have humanity as a partner in the drama of continuous creation. By whatever we do, by every act we carry out, we either advance or obstruct the drama of redemption; we either reduce or enhance the power of evil.[4]

The great philosopher of dialogue Martin Buber always insisted that the relation to a human being is the proper metaphor for the relation to God.[5] "I consider the human person to be the irremovable central place of the struggle between the world's movement away from God and its movement towards God."[6] We cannot speak of God without speaking of humanity. We cannot speak of our relation to God without speaking of our relation to one another. We cannot love God unless we love our brother and sister. *Divinitas* can never be separated from *humanitas.*

Reflecting on our language about God, Rowan Williams suggests that "whatever else is to be said, whatever further shifts and developments our language about God undergoes, this at least remains: God is not to be spoken of without humanity."[7] He then goes on to raise an interesting question: What *kind* of humanity do we speak of when we speak of God? To speak of God is never simply to respond to the question of God's meaning and existence, as if God existed in a realm isolated and apart from us. Rather, to speak of God is at the same time to inquire into humanity. The significance of our language about God is its significance or its referral to humanity. As David Tracy notes, "There is no theology which is not also an anthropology," such that "the doctrines of God and the human rise and fall together."[8] Indeed, Abraham Heschel goes so far as to say that the "Bible is primarily not man's vision of God but God's vision of man. The Bible is not man's theology but God's anthropology."[9] In other words, the primary reference of biblical language (what it "signifies" or "points to") is not so much a vision of God (as though it were speaking only of God), but a vision of humanity's well-being as intended by God.

When held in God's vision, as created and formed by God, the human person is no longer just anyone or everyone; rather, the human person has ultimate *significance* or an ultimate *reference* — the very referral or recommendation of God. In other words, one way of understanding the biblical tradition is to understand it as "letters of recommendation" on behalf of humanity, as though God were saying, "My name refers to this person. This is my recommendation, and I entrust this person to you."

As someone who has long survived on "letters of recommendation" written on my behalf, I do not find this metaphor too far-fetched. A great proportion of my life has been dependent on those who have signed their name on my behalf. I have always lived as a beneficiary of another's dedication, and could never imagine myself surviving without this extension of grace and goodness. When the biblical tradition speaks of a "covenant," I know well what this means — that my life depends at every moment on the fidelity of another who takes my life into account, and who therefore brings my life into existence. My existence is never simply of my own making. Rather, I am brought into being and created — by you, by God.

All this teaches me that my existence and the existence of every human person is dependent on our dedication to each other. In the biblical tradition, God always lends his good name to those who are often without name or voice, to those whose existence is disregarded. A constant theme of the biblical prophets is that if we want to honor God's name, we should realize that God's name *refers-to* or *stands-for* the one who is often disregarded and who lacks significance. While we may "stretch out our hands" and "multiply our prayers," God will not listen unless we "cease to do evil, learn to do good, search for justice, help the oppressed, be just to the orphan, plead for the widow" (Isa. 1:15–17). Gutiérrez captures the starkness of the prophets' message:

> Whenever one tries to justify the failure to love the poor and the oppressed by claiming that one is worshipping, one is in fact doing evil. God is not bound to accept our religious works; if they are not inspired by the desire for life and justice, God is not present in them.[10]

HOLY AND LIKE NO OTHER

One of the greatest trials of humanity must surely be to remember our humanity and to dedicate ourselves — not just to humanity in general — rather, to the unique singularity and dignity of each and every person. The singular cannot be generalized. If we want to call to mind what is essential to humanity, we cannot speak of it "in general," because the essence of the human person is no generality but rather the unrepeatable and irreplaceable — this one, this human person, like no other.

Primo Levi, a survivor of the Nazi concentration camps, knows well the death that descends upon humanity when the human person is forgotten and obliterated. In a poem titled "Shemà," he suggests that it is as difficult — maybe even more difficult — to remember that each person is a person as it is to remember that God is God. Just as the *Shema* reminds us that God is "one" (*ehad*) and like no other, we should also remember that each and every person, who is made in God's image, is "one" and like no other — that no other one exists like this one (note: *Ehad* means "unique" or "only," like the etymology of the English word "only" is "one-ly"[11]).

> You who live secure
> In your warm houses,
> Who return at evening to find
> Hot food and friendly faces:
>
>> Consider whether this is a man,
>> Who labors in mud
>> Who knows no peace
>> Who fights for a crust of bread
>> Who dies at a yes or a no.

Consider whether this is a woman,
Without hair or name
With no more strength to remember
Eyes empty and womb cold
As a frog in winter.

Consider that this has been:
I commend these words to you.
Engrave them on your hearts
When you are in your house, when you walk on your way,
When you go to bed, when you rise.
Repeat them to your children.
Or may your house crumble,
Disease render you powerless,
Your offspring avert their faces from you.[12]

If the *Shema* ("Hear!") claims our dedication to the irreplaceability of God who is holy and like no other, then surely it also claims our dedication to the irreplaceability of each person who is also holy and like no other, made in God's image. If we consider God, Levi suggests, we must also consider the one "who labors in mud . . . who knows no peace . . . who fights for a crust of bread . . . who dies at a yes or a no." *Ecce Homo.* We must remember that this one, like God, is a holy existence, singularly unique and irreplaceable. And if we forget, if we cannot hear or if we refuse to listen, then death will surely visit us — our house will crumble, disease will set in, and our very future will be cut off from us.

We must engrave upon our hearts and repeat to our children: each person's existence is as holy and irreplaceable as the very holiness and irreplaceability of God. For what else could it possibly mean when, in the Jewish tradition, it is said that "*adam* was created singly to teach you that the one who destroys a single soul is, in the eyes of Torah, as one who destroyed a whole world. And the one who saves a single soul is as one who saved an entire world" (Tractate *Sanhedrin* 4:5). And what else could it possibly mean when, in the Christian tradition, the ultimate trial or judgment of God takes place under the following condition: "I tell you solemnly, in so far as you did this to *one of the least . . .* you did it to me" (Matt. 25:40).

PERSONALITY

In his beautifully meditative book *The Embers and the Stars: A Philosophical Inquiry into the Moral Sense of Nature*, Erazim Kohák asks us to consider:

Shall we conceive of the world around us and of ourselves in it as *personal*, a meaningful whole...bearing goodness — or shall we conceive of it and treat it, together with ourselves, as *impersonal*, a chance aggregate of matter propelled by a blind force...? That answered, all else follows.[13]

According to Nikolai Berdyaev, the human person is never "mere existence." Rather, the human person is unique *person-ality*, of which he writes:

Personality is like nothing else in the world, there is nothing with which it can be compared, nothing which can be placed on a level with it. When a person enters the world, a unique and unrepeatable personality, then the world process is broken into and compelled to change its course.... Personality finds no place in the continuous complex process of world life, it cannot be a moment or an element in the evolution of the world. Personality presupposes interruption; it is inexplicable by any sort of uninterruption; it is inexplicable by any sort of uninterrupted continuity.... Personality is a break through, a breaking in upon this world; it is the introduction of something new.[14]

My son Asher just arrived home from school, bursting onto the scene, interrupting me, interrupting the flow of my existence and the writing I had set out to do. No mere existence, rather, Asher arrives on the scene as an interruption of existence — interrupting the flow of time and the chain of words — a unique personality that compels my attention and a change of course in the otherwise uninterrupted events of my afternoon. And how strange that I as a parent of four children should nevertheless notice once again (though all too rarely) the unique personality that shines forth from Asher — like no other. Yet perhaps not so strange, as most parents I know speak of the wonderment they feel as they behold each of their children's unique personality, a personality that stands out even against the shared patterns of their common family environment.

According to Berdyaev, personality "is like nothing else in the world." Personality, however, is not meant to suggest a crass humanism where "Man is the measure," as though life were tailor-made to our own designs, fashioned to our own self-fulfilling projects. Nor less is personality meant to suggest the simply private realm of my own existence, with all the connotations of subjectivism and individualism — the "unencumbered self" — independent, self-reliant, and unconstrained. Rather, personality is meant to suggest that categories of respect and responsibility for each other and for the world in which we live — moral and interpersonal categories of love, care, and goodness — lie at the very heart of life. "The terms or poles of a *practical* relationship are persons," says Enrique Dussel.[15] Or as Gutiérrez says, biblical language "situates us in the context of a relation between persons and not between things and concepts."[16] This is what Berdyaev means by personality.

When he refers to "the world process," he is referring to all the various factors that condition human existence. Each one of us is caught in the flow of historical time, situated within the world and shaped by society and culture. We all exist within a complex web of social processes that condition our lives — the law, the media, political and economic arrangements, social norms, and so on. All these "world processes" mark our existence with an almost indelible ink, as though our lives were inescapably etched and inscribed.

However, to acknowledge our conditioned nature as human beings is not all that can be said. If it were, then human personality would simply evaporate. Berdyaev insists that human personality can never be reduced to its conditioning environs, to "the continuous complex process of world life." Rather, human personality also opens onto the unconditional, "breaking in upon the world," such that in the life of the human person "the form of unconditioned being is reflected."[17] He writes:

> In human personality there is much that is generic, belonging to the human race, much which belongs to history, tradition, society, class, family, much that is hereditary and imitative, much that is "common." But it is precisely this which is not "personal" in personality. That which is "personal" is original. ... Personality is the exception, not the rule. The secret of the existence of personality lies in its

absolute irreplaceability, its happening but once, its uniqueness, its incomparableness.[18]

For the past four or five years, I have lived under the very unusual condition of being legally defined as an "alien," as a foreigner living in a country other than "my own" (where, presumably, I "rightfully" belong). And yet here I am, an alien "stealing" existence in another country, stealing what does not belong to me. Living with an alien status means I can never presume to "rightfully exist" unless the law allows me a "permissible existence." I have never before had to constantly justify my existence "before the law."[19] Rather, I have typically lived with the taken-for-granted assumption that I am not an alien, but a human person, and that I therefore have a rightful existence rather than a merely provisional existence. Living with an alien status means I can never presume that my human existence (to reside, to work, to dwell) is actually guaranteed or secured.

The only other time I have strongly felt this mark of "alienation" on my existence was during a period of unemployment in my life. Standing week after week on those unemployment lines, I always felt that I was being "processed" by a system that left me feeling humiliated and less than human.

Such are the ways of the world, the "world processes." "Personality," however, "is like nothing else in the world, there is nothing with which it can be compared." And yet, we judge and compare all the time, continually weighing the worth of a person, sometimes even considering that a person's existence is barely worth any weight at all. Even though we speak of a person's "inalienable rights," human personality can never be taken for granted. Consider the following testimony from a Mexican immigrant, and "consider whether this is a man":

> When I first crossed the border . . . I didn't have a problem. I jumped the fence and made a run for it, and the Border Patrol didn't catch me. My brother was with me, but he was not so lucky; they apprehended him soon after he got over. Then I was alone. And I didn't know what to do, so I figured I would call my family and let them know what was happening. But I didn't have any money, so I begged some people on the streets for some change. And this was the worst part. Each person I asked on the streets turned away from me, rejected me, called me names, and even threatened to call the

Border Patrol on me, and all I wanted to do was contact my family! I mean, I know what it is like to go three days without food. I know what it is like to hide yourself as a stowaway in the lower baggage compartment of a bus. I know what it is like to endure the freezing temperatures of the mountains. But the worst kind of suffering is to experience these kinds of rejections, when people treated me like I was dirt, like I was only a dog. It made me feel so totally humiliated, like I wasn't worth anything. I felt about as low as any human being can feel on earth.[20]

According to this testimony, the most difficult of trials is to be rejected as a human person. This is "the worst kind of suffering." "Each person turned away from me...rejected me...called me names...treated me like I was dirt...like I was only a dog." No one on those crowded streets was able to really respond to the humanity of this person, to "behold the man," to act humanely, to *be* human, to recognize the absolute dignity of human personality, to realize, as Berdyaev suggests, that the human face "is the most amazing thing in the life of the world; another world shines through it. It is the entrance of personality into the world process, with its uniqueness, its singleness, its unrepeatability."[21]

I still recall my younger days as a student of philosophy, when I learned that the etymology of the word "existence" means "to stand out." "Existence," in other words, is always *exceptional* rather than generic — it "stands out" and "it matters" — your existence, my existence, the existence of a tree, the blooming of a flower, the birth of a child. Personality resists being absorbed into the flow of world processes, but rather interrupts or "stands out" with a dazzling brilliance of singular expression. It seems to me that nothing better honors "existence" (life) than to say that it "stands out" — that it matters and has unique "personality" such that each and every living being is a splendor of incomparable wonder.

"Personality is the exception, not the rule," Berdyaev says. Personality is a mark of the exceptional, rather than the rule or the norm. This is potentially a great blow to our legal system, which prides itself on the rule of law. And yet, the rule of law would not be worth its salt if it treated all cases "the same," and in so doing failed to take each singular case as a case that stands unique in its exceptional and untested claim.

Unless the law can deal with the singular and the exceptional, then it is dangerously close to becoming a tyranny.[22]
"The Sabbath was made for humankind, and not humankind for the Sabbath" (Mark 2:27). This is a key principle in both the Jewish and Christian traditions. Like a good rabbi, like a person well-schooled in the Torah, Jesus was always sensitive to the exception before the law. Jesus often gave preference to the errant one, rather than to the righteous or law-abiding one. He preferred the exceptional one rather than the well-placed or well-positioned one (see Matt. 18:12–14; Luke 18:9–14). He often came to the defense of the one accused before the law, as with that exceptional story of the woman "caught in adultery" (John 8:1–11). Even when thronged by the crowds, he never failed to notice the one who *stands out*, the one shunned by the crowds, rejected and silenced, pleading and begging, if not for some loose change, then at least for some merciful recognition:

> As he left Jericho with his disciples and a large crowd, Bartimaeus (that is, the son of Timaeus), a blind beggar, was sitting at the side of the road. When he heard that it was Jesus of Nazareth, he began to shout and to say, "Son of David, Jesus, have pity on me." And many of them scolded him and told him to keep quiet, but he only shouted all the louder, "Son of David, have pity on me." Jesus stopped and said, "Call him here." So they called the blind man. "Courage," they said, "get up; he is calling you." So throwing off his cloak, he jumped up and went to Jesus. Then Jesus spoke, "What do you want me to do for you?" (Mark 10:46–51)

This concern and regard for the unique face of the other goes to the heart of the prophetic and ethical message of Jesus' life and teaching. His service to others (he came "to serve, not to be served" — Matt. 20:28) was deeply shaped by the Hebraic concern for hospitality to the displaced and oppressed, to the "stranger, the widow, and the orphan." His table companionship — "he welcomes sinners and eats with them" (Luke 15:2) — encapsulates the heart of his hospitality. Jesus did not subsume people into the larger system (the "world process"), or leave them sitting at the side of the road while the crowds simply passed by. According to John Caputo, the *basileia* preached by Jesus is a "kingdom of singularities" built on love and attentiveness and relationship to one another:

What better embodiment of such a "kingdom of singularities" than the biblical kingdom itself, where God has counted every tear, numbered every hair on our heads, where God knows every secret nestled in someone's heart, where every least little nobody in the kingdom is precious beyond measure . . . which is the only measure of love. . . . In short, where every other is wholly other?[23]

In the same way that God is turned toward humanity, or in Edward Schillebeeckx's wonderful phrase, "bent on humanity," so too we need to be turned toward each other. In the Jewish tradition this turning is called *teshuva* or repentance ("Turn!" "Repent!"), which is similar to *metanoia* or conversion in the Christian tradition.

For practical theology, *divinitas* can never be separated from *humanitas*, but must always be related in their mutual concern. Here is perhaps a good definition of practical theology from Abraham Heschel: "Concern for the human person as held in God's vision and anticipation, on the one hand, and, on the other, a regard for the human person's concrete situation, are the two terms of this relationship."[24] Or as Schillebeeckx says, the "essence of the gospel is that humanity's affair is God's affair and God's affair must become humanity's affair."[25]

THE *IMAGO DEI*

"That which is personal is original," says Berdyaev, which is to say that human personality is not interchangeable, but rather incomparable and unique. Berdyaev calls this the "secret of existence" that belongs to each and every person. It is an absolute secret, because no human personality can ever be fully known by systems of thought, or subsumed by social processes, or reduced to any other form of contingency or conditioning. It is in this sense that we can say that the human person is the very "site" of transcendence. The "world processes" that condition our life together — our social arrangements, economic systems, political institutions, and so on — do not exist for their own sake, but are always held accountable to the more original and unconditional claims of human personality and human dignity.[26]

The biblical tradition relates the originality of human personality to the originality of divine personality. The human person is "like no other" because each person is "made in the image of God" (Gen. 1:27). Human originality is found in divine resemblance. You are holy and like no other because you are in the image of God who is holy and like no other.

The absolute dignity of the human person is the foundational principle of all Catholic social teaching, repeated over and over again, such that, if this were not first affirmed, everything else ventured would crumble like a house of cards. It is the "secret of existence," and some writers have even suggested that it is a secret that has been kept hidden for too long.[27] The sanctity of the human person resembles the very sanctity of God; the originality of the human person resembles the originality of God; the transcendence of the human person resembles the transcendence of God. This is encapsulated in the U.S. Catholic Bishops' pastoral letter, *Economic Justice for All:*

> We believe the person is sacred — the clearest reflection of God among us.... Human personhood must be respected with a reverence that is religious. When we deal with each other, we should do so with the sense of awe that arises in the presence of something holy and sacred. (13, 28)

This is not mere humanism — a self-congratulatory "religion of Man rather than God," which hardly inspires confidence when we consider all the suffering that we, as human beings, are capable of inflicting upon each other. Rather, this is a humanism based on the unconditional love of God, of which Edward Schillebeeckx says: "Is there another humanism which is not cruel and is more universal than the love of God for humankind: of a God concerned for humankind, who wants 'people of God' who are themselves concerned for humankind?"[28]

"The great symbol of the human as *imago Dei* is the one permissible image of God that is not an idolatry."[29] This is a simple and yet increasingly stunning thought for me. The one image of God that will never lead me into idolatry is the human person. The human person! Those that I come across every single waking day of my life — on buses and trains, in the streets, at work, on television — everywhere, everyday, the image of God is before me. When I wake in the morning, I open my eyes almost immediately upon the faces of life around me. Yet I rarely notice that these faces represent the most tangible and accessible image of God available to me, that the *humanum* represents the *foundational* symbol of

the Holy. Then, in the morning newspaper, the pages are filled with stories about human life — tragedies and conflicts and political debates grab
the front page. And I feel as though I am facing the *humanum*, in this
world, as the arena where the fate of the *imago Dei* is being determined
for good or for ill. If humanity is made in the image of God, then this
sacred image is being polished or defaced every day in our society and
relationships. And not only the *humanum*, but all of God's creation, for
our relationship to each other is also bound to our relationship with all
living creatures. Schillebeeckx urges us to consider

> that [we] have often hidden, spat upon and even mutilated the face
> of God's humanity and his care for all his creatures, down to the
> least of them. Where it is not God himself, but religion, science or
> some worldly power that is made absolute, not only human beings
> but also the "image of God" are sullied: the *ecce homo* on the cross,
> and on the many crosses which have been erected and continue to be
> erected, and also the *ecce natura* as the polluted world of creation —
> in animals and plants and the basic elements of life.[30]

To disparage the human person or any living creature is to make a
mockery of God, rather than to respect the image of God. The Hebrew
prophets constantly rallied against idolatry and the false worship of God
(see Jer. 7:1–7; Isa. 58:1–12; Ezek. 36; Amos 5:21–24). They always spoke
in the name of the living God who is concerned for creation and for the
welfare and *shalom* of human persons.

I recall attending a Passover celebration with a family in Jerusalem.
One of the readings during the meal was the following passage from the
Psalms, which made quite an impression on me:

> Their idols are silver and gold,
>   the work of human hands.
> They have mouths but do not speak,
>   eyes but do not see.
> They have ears but do not hear,
>   noses but do not smell.
> They have hands but do not feel,
>   feet but do not walk,
>   and no sound rises from their throats.

Their makers shall be like them,
all who trust in them. (Ps. 115:4–8)

God is not to be identified with dead and lifeless things, with idols that have no soul, no sense of the human, no living *personality.* God is not a faceless, impersonal God, but the God who is face-to-face, the God of the living.

"I AND THOU"

According to Martin Buber, the human person meets me as a "Thou" who is always a holy existence that stands in a personal relation to me, who has eyes that see, a mouth that speaks, hands that feel. I am never "just me." You are also there — a gaze that looks upon me, a voice that speaks to me, a presence that touches my life.

The meaning of existence is never the meaning of my life alone. You are always there. You exist and "stand out." There is always "I and Thou," and whatever happens in life, happens *between* us. There is no love, unless it happens between us. There is no forgiveness, unless it happens between us. There is no justice, unless it happens between us. Nothing moves between heaven and earth, unless it moves between us. Humanity "is the knot in which heaven and earth are interlaced," Abraham Heschel says.[31]

Buber speaks of our age as suffering an "eclipse of God,"[32] in which the modern world has become overshadowed by "dead and lifeless things," what Buber calls the world of the "I-It," the world of measurement and calculation, of profit and success, of progress and overcoming — a world that no longer knows how to relate to God's living presence, to the signs of life that continually remind us that we are personal, living, relational beings. We have blocked the light of heaven through our unrelenting obsession with the "I" — "I think, I will, I want, I can, I am." Reducing all meaning to my self, we are left only with "I-Me," and rarely exposed to the call of transcendence, to the call of the other in my life.

We have blocked the light of heaven, a light that shines in every face, in every "thou," a light that continually opens me to the vocational quality of life — that life is all the time speaking and calling out to me, that I am continually exposed to the wonder and the call of a real, vital, and living presence that claims my attention, my response, and my engagement. You are there. "Hallowed be your name." And yet, too often, I do not reverence you or respond to you — to your beauty in creation, or to the words you are speaking to me, or to the suffering you are going through, or to your nearness that I take for granted, or to your memory that you entrust to me. Do not forget. Do this in memory of me.

In his introduction to the theology of Gustavo Gutiérrez, James Nick-oloff offers this beautiful testimony, which I quote at length, because it seems to speak to Buber's "eclipsed thou," but, no less, also to the promise of a "light that shines in the dark, a light that darkness could not overpower" (John 1:5):

> Signs of the new era and the new world emerging from the old abound for those who have eyes to see. *Compassion* is necessary in any truly revolutionary project because cruelty only destroys. *Love* alone makes communion possible in a multicultural society.... Love is not a flight from history but the power that gives meaning and vitality to political commitment. *Memory* of the past with its joys and sufferings is not simple nostalgia but the source of renewal and subversion. *Repentance* (by those who wrong others) and *forgiveness* (by those who are wronged) together open the way to renewed relationship and life. *Music and beauty* nourish and express joy. Simple *kindness* saves through its power to refresh those who are tired. Finally, *suffering* accepted in order to end suffering is redemptive. Compassion, love, memory, repentance and forgiveness, music and beauty, gentle kindness, and redemptive suffering: these are the means by which a new era in human history comes to be and the signs of its coming. In theological language they are the sacraments of God's reign.[33]

Well, all I can say is, "Amen. Thy Kingdom come."

SEVEN

"Can the Wisdom of Heaven Return to Earth?"

With the appearance of the human — and this is my entire philosophy — there is something more important than my life, and that is
the life of the other. — Emmanuel Levinas

Emmanuel Levinas is well known in academic circles and is often
hailed as one of the most important philosophers and religious thinkers
of the twentieth century. His work has significantly influenced many
"postmodern" thinkers such as Jacques Derrida, Maurice Blanchot, Luce
Irigaray, Paul Ricoeur, and others. He has also influenced Jewish and
Christian leaders and thinkers, such as Pope John Paul II. However, his
thinking is not generally well known to a broader audience.

If practical theology is called to be of service to humanity, then there is
much that it can learn from Levinas's work. Everything in his work points
to God or, as he might prefer to say, approaches God, and yet everything
in his work is about *us* — about our humanity and the relations between
us. This strikes me as entirely resonant with practical theology's concerns
to mediate the love and wisdom of God with the joys and sufferings of
humanity. "Is there a way," asks Levinas, "for the wisdom of heaven to
return to earth?"[1]

LEVINAS'S LIFE

Levinas was born in 1906 to Jewish parents in Lithuania. His father owned
a bookshop, and he was introduced to the great classics of Russian literature (such as Dostoyevsky and Tolstoy). He also learned to read the

115

Bible in its original Hebrew and grew up in a climate of enlightened Jewish orthodoxy. In 1923 he moved to France and studied philosophy under Husserl and Heidegger, whose works he is credited for introducing to French thought. However, he remained marginal to the French philosophical scene until the publication of his first major work, *Totality and Infinity*, in 1961.[2]

Levinas lost his parents, brothers, and parents-in-law in the Nazi genocide. As a French army officer, he was spared deportation to the concentration camps and placed in a prisoner of war labor camp. He recounts a story from this period about a friendly dog. When returning to the camp after a day of labor, he and his fellow prisoners would face the glares and insults of the villagers and prison guards, who saw them as nothing more than dirty *Juden*. A little dog, however, befriended them. "When we used to come back from work," Levinas says, "he welcomed us, jumping up and down. . . . This dog evidently took us for human beings."[3] Amidst the hatred and condemnation of people, it was this friendly dog that helped them to remember that they were, indeed, human beings.

During this time in the prison camp Levinas began one of his earliest works, *Existence and Existents*, "written down for the most part in captivity."[4] In this work, he reflects on the terrifying impersonality and anonymity of "being," as though nothing in the grand sweep of *existence* really cared about a personal and individual *existent*. It was as though he felt chained and imprisoned in a world of cold indifference and disregard, a world without weight or responsibility. He referred to this dread-filled experience simply as "there is."[5] Nothing matters, nothing calls, nothing answers, nothing counts. There is. Nothing other.

Levinas's wife and daughter were able to escape the Nazi death machine through the help of his lifelong friend Maurice Blanchot, and "found refuge and protection among the nuns of St. Vincent de Paul."[6] Though he writes rarely of these horrific times, the memory of the Shoah has always accompanied his thinking. "It is dominated," he says, "by the presentiment and the memory of the Nazi horror."[7] He dedicated his second major work, *Otherwise Than Being or Beyond Essence*, to the memory of the victims of Nazism and to "the millions on millions of all confessions and all nations, victims of the same hatred of the other man," along with a Hebrew dedication to his lost family members, "that their souls may be kept in the bundle of life."

Aside from his philosophical corpus, Levinas also wrote widely on Jewish themes, including various collections of his own Talmudic commentaries. He credits his Talmudic learning to an enigmatic and mysterious teacher, Rav Shoshani, a genius and master of Talmud who also influenced Elie Wiesel in the postwar years, but of whom little is known.[8] Levinas died on December 25, 1995. Paul Ricoeur and Jacques Derrida offered eulogies to their venerated friend, to this man of "question-prayers."[9]

A SURVIVOR'S QUESTION

Levinas is a survivor. He survived the death of millions. He survived what his friend Blanchot calls the "countless cry...the utter-burn where all history took fire."[10] He survived the death of his mother, his father, his brothers, his wife's parents. He survived, and yet deeply inscribed within his thought, there lies the penultimate question that plagues virtually every survivor: What right have I to survive, to live, when so many have died?[11]

In his philosophical writings, Levinas transforms this question of survival into the very question of *being*. The burden of survival — what right do I have *to be, to live* — becomes the very burden of *being:* How is *being* justified?[12]

Levinas then takes this question of *being* and makes it an *ethical* question at the very outset.[13] It now becomes: What right do I have to be *in the face of the other person's suffering and death?* This is Levinas's primary question.

The burden of survival and the question of *being* could only be answered for Levinas when, as he says, "the burning of *my* suffering and the anguish of *my* death were able to be transfigured into the dread and concern for the *other man.*"[14] For Levinas, existence *for itself* is not the ultimate meaning; rather, it is existence *for the other.* The only justification for surviving, for living, for *being* is when the anxiety over my own life and death are transfigured into concern for the life and death of my neighbor. This is Levinas's primary response to his question. This is his subject matter, what matters most to him.

In raising this concern for "my neighbor," Levinas often speaks of the "face of the other." In language resonant with the Hebrew scriptures, he refers to the other as "the Most-High" to evoke the other's transcendence and eminence, yet he also speaks of the other's lowliness and destitution —

"the stranger, the widow, and the orphan." The other is both the "Most High," the Holy One, and the face of the neighbor — the stranger and the poor one. When speaking to Christian audiences, he often refers to chapter 25 of Matthew's Gospel, of which he says:

> The relation to God is presented there as a relation to another person. It is not a metaphor; in the other, there is a real presence of God. In my relation to the other, I hear the word of God. It is not a metaphor. It is not only extremely important; it is literally true. I'm not saying that the other is God, but that in his or her face I hear the word of God.[15]

To help us explore the main contours of Levinas's work, the remainder of this chapter is divided into two main sections. "Theology's About-Face" suggests a link between practical theology and the ethical concerns of Levinas's writing, particularly around his notion of responsibility for the face of the other as presented in his first major work, *Totality and Infinity.* The second section, "Being Faced," echoes themes from Levinas's second major work, *Otherwise Than Being or Beyond Essence,* in which the other looks upon me or regards me, without giving me any chance to escape.[16] Levinas makes a stunning contribution to the concerns of practical theology by keeping the face of the human other at the center of his concern, and refusing to allow this human face to be swallowed up by speculative theories or grand schemas of meaning.

THEOLOGY'S ABOUT-FACE

Back in 1974, when liberation theology was bursting onto the scene, Gustavo Gutiérrez wrote: "Rediscovering the other means entering his own world. It also means a break with ours. The world of inward-looking absorption with self . . . is not only interior but is socio-culturally conditioned. To enter the world of the other . . . with the actual demands involved . . . is to begin . . . a process of conversion."[17]

I find these words of Gutiérrez, written more than thirty years ago, strikingly resonant with what has come to be known today as our postmodern situation. Where should theology turn in its conversation with the cultural "mood" of postmodernity? According to David Tracy, it should turn around, and face the other:

The turn to the other is the quintessential turn of postmodernity itself. It is that turn, above all, that defines the intellectual as well as the ethical meaning of postmodernity. The other and the different come forward now as central intellectual categories across the major disciplines, including theology.... Part of that return to otherness...is the return of biblical Judaism and Christianity to undo the complacencies of modernity, including modern theology.[18]

One of the reasons Levinas wants to refocus our attention toward the face of the other is his concern that we have enclosed ourselves in a world of "immanence." In other words, we have reduced everything to our being-in-the-world, and we no longer know how to speak of transcendence — the desire of infinity, the voice of otherness, the God of revelation who addresses our lives. He wants to speak against the complacencies of an age that thinks itself free of everything that is other than itself and beyond the embarrassment of a relationship with an unknown God.

Levinas introduces his volume *Of God Who Comes to Mind* with a question like this: How can we speak of God "without striking a blow against the absoluteness that his word seems to signify?" How can we speak of "the infinity or alterity or novelty of the absolute" without giving it back into immanence? In other words, if we bring God too quickly and too readily into the ambit of our understanding and our grasp, don't we thereby miss God altogether, the God of transcendence and otherness? It seems then, that speaking of God requires "impossible requirements!"[19] For if we want to respect the "purity" and absoluteness of God's revelation, if we want to expose ourselves to the transcendence of God's word, if we want this word to come to us with a "power of speech" that addresses our lives, it must, somehow, be a word that comes "from on high" — a revelation that is nowhere already known by us, that is nowhere the same as us, that is not a knowledge we already possess or a god already within us. Otherwise, how could we speak of *revelation?*

In "Revelation in the Jewish Tradition,"[20] Levinas begins with a similar question: How do we connect the world we inhabit with something that is no longer of this world? How can we make sense of the exteriority of the truths and signs of revelation? How do we speak of an otherness that comes "from outside," from somewhere else? How is this thinkable? Truths from outside? From somewhere else? From where?

Haven't sociologists told us that our truths are the products of our own social constructions of reality? Haven't psychologists reminded us that many of our truths are reflections or projections of our own inner desires and conflicts? Wasn't it Heidegger who revealed that all our knowing reflects the ontological condition of being-in-the-world? And hasn't postmodernism (or at least, a certain type of postmodernism) confidently pronounced that there are no metanarratives, that there is "nothing outside the text"?

All this, for Levinas, is so much immanence, and it only serves to dull the voice of revelation, of that which comes from outside, from somewhere else, from somewhere otherwise, from beyond being. In the midst of "the magnificent funeral celebrations held in honour of a dead god,"[21] Levinas arrives with news that turns everyone's head, that leaves everyone somewhat stunned, for all of sudden, here is a philosopher who dares speak again of revelation, of truths from outside, of an Other that is "otherwise than being."

Levinas begins his first major work, *Totality and Infinity*, with the statement: "The true life is absent" (*TI*, 33). Isn't this something we all experience? At rock bottom, don't we always feel an "absence," or as Augustine said, a "restlessness," that we never seem to find the perfect match between our desires and their fulfillment, that we always experience a basic uneasiness in life, never a sense of total well-being and peace? Somehow, we always feel a separation, a gap, a rift, a rupture, never a feeling of completeness, harmony, perfect unity, communion — never a feeling of "totality," rather, always a feeling of "infinity" — of desires that are infinite, questions that always open out endlessly, yearnings that are never quenched. For Levinas, this experience is a first indicator of an otherness that we are always turned toward, of an "elsewhere" and an "otherwise," of a fundamental movement "from an 'at home' which we inhabit, toward an alien outside-of-oneself, toward a yonder" (*TI*, 33).

In the Greek philosophical tradition, this experience has generated whole systems of thought that attempt to close this gap, that have sought to correlate the structures of our thinking (epistemology) with the structures of being (ontology). It is the destiny of knowledge to search out and adhere to being, and it is the destiny of being to disclose itself to be known. The two (knowledge and being) share a common destiny, are entwined, are a harmonious whole, and are both fully present because always present to each other. As Levinas says, the whole trajectory of Greek philosophy is its "equation of truth with an *intelligibility of presence*... an intelligibility that considers truth to be that which is present or copresent, that which can be gathered or synchronized into a totality that we would call the world or *cosmos*."[22]

In contrast to this search for harmony, unity, and presence, Levinas prefers to speak of that "which cuts through and perforates the totality of presence and points towards the absolutely other."[23] He prefers to stay with the experience of rupture, because this experience opens us to the address of the other — that which speaks from outside, that which refuses to be tamed and domesticated into our harmonious worlds of rest and repose. Indeed, the philosopher's desire to get a good night's sleep where all is well in the world, a drowsy self-satisfied presence where there is no interruptive other, where everything is unified into a comfortable Sameness — this experience is contrasted by Levinas with the state of "vigilant insomnia" where the other haunts our ontological existence and keeps us awake, keeps us vulnerable and exposed to the revelation of God.[24]

In comparing the Greek tradition of speculative contemplation with the biblical tradition of revelation, Levinas says:

[For the Greek tradition], the opposites of repose — worry, questioning, seeking, Desire — are all taken to be a waste of repose, an absence of response, a privation, a pure insufficiency of identity, a mark of self-inequality. We have wondered whether the Revelation might not lead us to precisely this idea of inequality, difference, and irreducible alterity which is "uncontainable...," a mode of thought which is not knowledge but which, exceeding knowledge, is in relation with the Infinite or God.... Perhaps the attitudes of seeking, desiring and questioning do not represent the emptiness of need but the explosion of the "more within the less...."[25]

And again:

Should we not go beyond the consciousness which is equal to itself, seeking always to assimilate the Other, and emphasize instead the act of deference to the other in his alterity, which can only come about through the awakening of the Same — drowsy in his identity — by the Other?[26]

Levinas disturbs our quest for a self-satisfied harmony and wholeness. He is trying to wake us up, lest we fall asleep in our own drowsy, comfortable worlds. Attitudes of "seeking, desiring and questioning," rather than "rest and repose," provide the best environment for the revelation of the other. "Within the vision I am developing," he writes, "human emotion and spirituality begin in the for-the-other, in being affected by the other."[27] In this sense, Levinas doesn't have a lot of time for the peace and serenity of contemplation or mysticism — at least not with the "cheap" kind, where everything is played out in the depths of my self. "The mystical event," he says, "is always very suspect to me, unless it is a metaphor of something else, of a perfect accord with Him."[28] According to Levinas, losing myself in prayer and contemplation, being absorbed into the mystery, entering the space of mystical tranquility — this is the last thing revelation is meant to do. Union with God is not a mystical fusion; rather it is an "accord" with God's will. The other is always the prophetic voice of revelation, not the disclosive voice of being. God is otherwise than being, not the ground of being. And our problem is not so much that we have been forgetful of being; our problem is rather that we have been forgetful of the other. He writes:

> Ethical responsibility is . . . a *wakefulness* precisely because it is a perpetual duty of vigilance and effort that can never slumber. Ontology as a state of affairs can afford to sleep. But love cannot sleep, can never be peaceful or permanent. Love is the incessant watching over the other; it can never be satisfied or contented with the bourgeois ideal of love as domestic comfort.[29]

Much of today's "popular spirituality" goes in search of something that will give our lives a deeper sense of meaning, that will fulfill our desires and yearnings, that will absorb our fragmented, isolated selves into a larger, more integrated whole. For Levinas, this is reflective of an existential need that is too tied to the self and what the self lacks, rather than a Desire that reaches beyond the self toward the Other.[30] To be an "I," to secure my identity, to feel my own authentic subjectivity — this, for Levinas, will only lead us circling back into the Same. The subject is always trying to secure its identity in terms of itself.

According to Levinas, however, we need to start elsewhere, outside our selves, "outside the subject."[31] This strikes me as an amazing thought, particularly for our Western culture that is so dominated by a quest for my own self-authenticity, that so highly prizes the autonomous, free, self-sufficient individual. Our "enlightened" culture is often suspicious of anything that might impose itself on our lives or threaten our individual freedom. We like to stay in "control" of the world as critical, independent, self-empowered subjects. I have noticed in my own teaching, when dealing with Levinas's texts, that our class often bristles in the face of the priority Levinas gives to responsibility rather than freedom, obligation rather than choice, self-giving rather than self-agency, passivity rather than assertiveness, "exterior-to-me" rather than "interior-to-me." We bristle because Levinas rubs against our cultural habits. In effect, we find ourselves protesting, "What about me?"

What, then, does Levinas propose? What I find rather startling is his ability to speak in the name of the absolutely transcendent, the infinitely other, yet to do so by speaking of a very simple, concrete relation: that of the face-to-face (*TI*, 185–219). Every face we encounter is a face of otherness. Every face says, "I am other to you." Every face says, "I am not you." Every face says: "Don't kill me; don't absorb me into your world; don't obliterate me by making me the same as you. I am other. I am different. I am not you."

It is important to note that Levinas is talking here about the naked face, the face that is not masked by the whole social apparatus of roles and status. Rather, this is the naked face that stands before me, completely exposed, completely vulnerable, infinitely other, absolutely singular. "The skin of the face is the most naked, most destitute . . . there is an essential poverty in the face."[32] The face is the face of You, and you are vulnerable and dependent on me. Yet you also face me with an "uprightness" — face-to-face. The unique, singular face stands opposed to the indifference of "impersonal, anonymous Being." Rather, the face is "expression" — it is not just "something" that I look upon, that I hold in my gaze. The face "faces" me, and this "toward me" is both a profound appeal against my indifference to your naked vulnerability, and an accusation that prohibits my violence toward you. The face of the other "is a double expression of weakness and demand." The face is both "lordship and that which is without defense." "Exposed in its nudity," it is also "the supreme authority that commands...the face is the site of the word of God."[33]

The face of the other breaks into my world and calls out to me. I am not an *I* unto myself, but an *I* standing before the other. The other calls forth my response, commands my attention, refuses to be ignored, makes a claim on my existence, tells me I am responsible. And this always. I will never be freed from the face of the other. So much so, that Levinas says we are always held "hostage" to the other, that we are never released from the other's speaking to us and calling forth our response. "It is impossible to evade the appeal of the neighbor, to move away" (*OBBE*, 128). The other says, "I am here" — and appeals to us, commands us: "thou shalt not kill," which is one of the Commandments that Levinas often cites.

What matters for Levinas is not so much the question of meaning in life, but the question of ethics or holiness: "The concern for the other," he says, "breaks the concern for the self. This is what I call holiness."[34] What matters is not so much our separation from God and the desire for mystical participation; rather, what matters is our disregard for each other, and the desire for sociality, for ethical responsibility. What matters is not so much the declaration of my existence that says, "Here I am," but the "Here I am" that is the response of my existence to the call of the other.

According to Levinas, the "Here I am" is testimony itself to the revelation that comes from outside, from elsewhere, from otherwise than my being.[35] Wherever we find people saying "Here I am" — not as an assertion or declaration of their existence, but as a response — then we are witnessing a testimony to the voice of the Other that calls from beyond. For Levinas, this is Revelation, and this is "how God comes to mind":[36]

> We said right at the beginning: the subject of our enquiry is the very fact of Revelation, and the relation it establishes with exteriority. This exteriority...cannot be transformed into a content with interiority; it remains "uncontainable," infinite, and yet the relation is maintained. The path I am led to follow, in solving the paradox of Revelation, is one that claims we may find a model for this relation in the attitude of nonindifference towards the Other, in the responsibility towards him; and that it is precisely through this relation that a person becomes his "self," designated without any possibility of

escape, chosen, unique, not interchangeable, and — in this sense —
free. Ethics provides the model worthy of transcendence and it is as
an ethical kerygma that the Bible is Revelation.[37]

To turn around, to face the other, this is the conversion required of
theology. As David Tracy notes, "surely, on the central question of transcendence, this ethical route to the Absolute Other only by way of the
interrelationships of human others is Levinas's most original, and daring,
and for Jewish and Christian theology, both promising... and controversial move."[38] There are some that might question whether Levinas is
merely "reducing" religion to ethics. Yet this is a question that probably
troubles the "theologically comfortable" more than those who know what
is at stake in the world of real historical pain and suffering. The initial
reception of liberation theology, for example, was dogged by the accusation that it was a "political reduction of the Gospel."[39] Yet liberation
theology has continually insisted that the truth of theology will always be
judged by the practice of ethical action and the demands of justice and
mercy. "Any attempt," Gutiérrez says, "to separate the love of God from
the love of neighbor gives rise to attitudes which impoverish the one or
the other."[40]

If, for Levinas, "ethics provides the model worthy of transcendence,"
it is because he is a little nervous about theology providing the "model,"
particularly when it is a "worn-out theology... with its transcendence that
can be stepped over like a fence."[41] In other words, if there is any "reduction" to be spoken of, it is theology's complacent reduction of "the Most
High God," the God who commands our attention toward the "widow,
the orphan, the stranger and the beggar." This is the transcendence of God
that can never be scaled, the height of the Other that rises above us —
demanding our attention, commanding our response, requiring our love.
As though we could ever finally "jump the fence" and say to ourselves: "no
more is required of me." When all the time we are faced with that most
demanding of the Gospel sayings: "The poor you will always have with
you" (Matt. 26:11). The neighbor will always be there. I cannot escape
the Other; I will always be hostage to the height of the Other who asks
after me. "There will never cease to be poor in the land; I command you,
therefore: Always be open-handed with your neighbor, and with anyone
in your country who is in need and poor" (Deut. 15:11).

Levinas proposes no secular humanism; rather, he protests against the domesticating of the divine. The "low fence" of theology is the fence that reduces God to a "theme" for myself, as though God were simply "there" to be grasped and known by us, present to us (an easy jump!), when all the time "divinity keeps its distances" (*TI*, 297). As though theology were all about my identification with God, when it is often about God's identification with the other. Like the sensibilities of liberation theology, Levinas wants to keep the human neighbor between myself and God, such that we cannot too readily approach the invisible God without first encountering the height of our neighbor. "Is divinity possible without relation to a human Other?" asks Levinas.[42] Or is St. John says, How can we say we love God, whom we have not seen, unless we love a brother or a sister whom we have seen? (see 1 John 4:20–21). Or as Gutiérrez says:

> We stand before something which challenges our categories, the mystery of God who will not be *reduced* to our mode of thinking, and who judges us on the basis of our concrete, historical actions toward the poor.... Now we face a God who blocks the path of a false love which forgets sisters and brothers while claiming to direct itself spiritually toward God, more to domesticate God than to feel itself questioned by God's word.[43]

"BEING FACED"

> I tremble at what exceeds my seeing and my knowing... although it concerns the inner-most parts of me, right down to my soul, down to the bone, as we say.... It is the gift of infinite love, the dissymmetry that exists between the divine regard that sees me, and myself, who doesn't see what is looking at me...   —Jacques Derrida[44]

> An ethical meaning of the relation to the other, answering, in the form of responsibility before the face, to the *invisible that requires me;* answering to a demand that puts me in question and comes to me from *I know not where,* nor when, nor why.
> —Emmanuel Levinas[45]

It is difficult to talk about the experience of "being faced." It is more common and familiar to talk about the experience of "facing being."

Indeed, we probably can all resonate with this phrase, because we continually find ourselves "facing things." We face life's uncertainty, and we wonder about the future. We face life's difficulty, and we wonder whether we will ever find a measure of peace. We face life's profound ambiguity, and we wonder whether it will ever become clear to us. Facing being primarily means that our own being is a matter of concern for us. "We consider our being, question it, are troubled and afflicted by it, laden with it.... We do not engender our being; it is given to us, laid upon us; we are burdened with it and have to bear it. We do not exist, simply; we have to be."[46]

We face our lives — and at the same time we face our limitations (and that which outstrips us). We wonder what life is about and what it all means. We find ourselves facing questions that are of concern to us — about the shape of our lives, the shape of the world around us, questions about our future, our hopes for happiness, questions about pain and suffering. Facing being, we face the finitude of our existence and the vastness of our questions, and we feel caught up in life's great mystery or, more darkly, in its stark futility. Either way, we are lost in questions about life, its meaning, its purpose, its reason, its mystery, its elusiveness.

Mostly, we hold this experience and these questions in secret. Who can ever say to another what I feel when I find myself "facing being"? Philosophers, theologians, and other writers are probably the ones who most "break with secrecy" to talk about this experience. They think deeply about this question and give us all a certain vocabulary to talk about the experience of "facing being." They break with secrecy, such that "facing being" is filled with a multitude of responses. It "means" this. It is "about this." These are the "reasons." This is "why." This is "how it happens" or "fails to happen." The secret need no longer be secretive, and we are overwhelmed with these gallant and noble voices — all "facing being" together.

"Being faced," however, is different. The intuition in this phrase shifts attention from *my gaze*, which tries to bring everything under its surveillance, to *the gaze of the other*, which sees me without my knowing who is looking at me. The question of "facing being" *turns around* to become the question of "being faced" — "with the gaze, look, request, love, command, or call of the other."[47] It is no longer I who faces being, but the other who faces me. I am looked upon. I am asked after. Here, I lose a certain hold over myself, and find that I am no longer the one who interrogates and questions; rather, I am the one who is faced by the other's interrogation and questioning. This is not unlike the "resolution" to the Book of Job, when all those questioners suddenly find themselves placed in question ("Where were you when...?"). God questions more than God answers. The Jewish poet Edmond Jabès, for example, links God intrinsically to "The Book of Questions." Levinas goes so far as to say that God is an "abusive word" (*OBBE*, 156). Rather than our facing God, God faces us and we are left feeling "abused" and subjected. In the midst of all our questions and anxiety, God dares yet to face us and hold us in question, as though we were the ones accused, questioned, held responsible — as though we were meant to answer, not God.

Throughout his second major work, *Otherwise Than Being or Beyond Essence*, Levinas uses some very extreme words to describe the exposure we undergo in "being faced." He speaks of our being persecuted and held hostage by the face of the other. Rather than the notion of a free ego that chooses its commitments, Levinas speaks of the prior condition of being hostage to the other, a condition that is not rooted in our freedom or our choice, but in our being chosen or bound or tied to the other. Perhaps this is why Luke's Gospel has Jesus "sweating blood" when it comes to the moment of that most difficult of prayers: "Let your will be done, not mine" (22:43).

Prior to any choice or intentionality on our part, we are already exposed to the other. It is almost as if the other holds me against my will, against my ravenous desire to be the center of the universe. Prior to any decision on my part, I am born into a world where the other is always asking after me. I am bound and tied to you — to every you — and that is so from my first breath till my last. I am invested with responsibility even when I do not want to be. "The condition of being hostage is not chosen; if there had been a choice, the subject would have kept his 'as-for-me' (*OBBE*, 136). I am always and already obligated to you — chosen — even before I choose. Levinas cites a well-known passage from Talmud: "All in Israel are responsible for one another" (Tractate *Shevuot*, 39a).[48] We can read "Israel" as shorthand for "humanity," which means that being-for-the-other is written into the very fabric of life, is the way life is fundamentally structured. Levinas is also fond of quoting a passage from Dostoyevsky's *Brothers Karamazov*, "Each of us is guilty before everyone and for everyone, and I more than the others" (*OBBE*, 146). To which we could add Derrida's words: "This guilt is originary, like original sin. Before any fault is determined, I am guilty inasmuch as I am responsible. . . . Guilt is inherent in responsibility because responsibility is always unequal to itself: one is never responsible enough."[49] Or as Pope John Paul II says, "we are *all* really responsible *for all*" (*Sollicitudo Rei Socialis*, "On Social Concern," no. 38).

"Being faced" means finding ourselves faced by a continual requirement of obligation and responsibility to and for the other. Even a casual reflection on our lives will reveal how bound we are to others, how constantly we are beset by the demands of obligation and the requirements of love — to family and friends, to those we work with, to neighbors and strangers, to those in our society whom we do not know yet whose claim on our lives we feel nevertheless. "Being faced" is another way (maybe the exemplary way) of speaking of transcendence. As John Caputo notes: "We cannot transcend it, because it is transcendence itself. We are the ones transcended, overcome, lifted up or put down, overtaken, thrown. Obligation is the sphere of what I did not constitute. . . . Obligations come over us from the other whose transcendence shocks our freedom and autonomy."[50]

While "facing being" turns us inward upon our selves, to our own questioning and anxiety ("where our own being is a matter of concern for us"), "being faced" places us before the other who "opposes" me with the "absolute frankness of his gaze." The other addresses me, speaks to me, asks after me. The face of the other is "the epiphany of what can thus present itself directly, and therefore also exteriorly, to an I."[51] Being faced means I am no longer able to stay within the realms of my own "being"; rather, I am exposed to another who calls out from beyond my existence. "It is as though I were destined to the other before being destined to myself," Levinas says.[52] The presence of "me to myself" is broken, and I am no longer able to persevere in my being, in the project of myself. "*I am no longer able to have power. . . .* true exteriority is in this gaze which forbids me my conquest."[53] In a crystalline phrase of diamondlike insight, Levinas writes, "The Other must be closer to God than I."[54]

We may wonder about the excessive rhetoric that Levinas's language forces upon us. To be so bound to the other is indeed to be held hostage. Yet who of us has not known countless times in our lives when, faced with love's requirements, we have taken the very form "of worrying about the

other, a spending without counting, a generosity, goodness, love, obligation to others. A generosity without recompense, a love unconcerned with
reciprocity, duty performed without the 'salary' of a good-conscience-
for-duty-performed...."[55] How else would we describe the condition of
responsibility if not in this way? How else would we describe the requirements of love if not in this way? What else could obligation mean if it
did not mean this *kenosis* and hollowing out of ourselves?

> Is that not what the self emptying itself of itself would mean?...It
> is being divesting itself, emptying itself of its being, turning itself
> inside out, and if it can be put this way, the fact of "otherwise than
> being"....It is through the condition of being hostage that there
> can be in the world pity, compassion, pardon and proximity—even
> the little there is, even the simple "After you"...(*OBBE*, 111, 117)

Sometimes, as Kafka once wrote, we need texts that wound us and
in the process transform us: "A book must be the axe for the frozen sea
inside us."[56] Levinas knows what he is up against in trying to break the
hold of our own self-absorption and self-obsession. Unlike the ethical
theories of "social contract" or "rational agency" that attempt to *adjudicate*
self-interest (whereby the self is always primary, and the other a secondary
consideration requiring amelioration), Levinas is concerned with delimit-
ing and even *renouncing* self-interest.[57] Indeed, he leaves the reader feeling
both inundated by and resistant to the radical otherness he announces. It
is quite amazing, really, how much it takes to convince me of the "real
presence" of the Other, how much I am always blocking this announcement, resisting this impingement on my life. As Adriaan Peperzak says,
"*The Other* halts the movement through which the I tries to unfold." I do
not belong to myself, not because I am a mysterious essence, but because
"my essence consists in a being *toward* and *for the Other.*" There is quite a
real sense in which the Other "makes me suffer by urging me to endlessly
detach myself from the desire to return to myself as a ravenous center of
the universe."[58]

In her book *Saints and Postmodernism*, Edith Wyschogrod reminds
us that this language of extremity and excess (of self-denial and self-
giving, self-sacrifice and self-donation) has always been the language of
the saints.[59] Saintly life has always been connected to the compassion,

mercy, and love of the great religious traditions, for example, "the *ku-runa* or compassion of Buddhism, the *rachamim* or mercy of Judaism, or the *agape* of Christianity" (186). Saints are not people of moderation, reasonableness or nuanced argument. Rather, "the saintly desire for the Other is excessive and wild" (255). According to Wyschogrod, "a saintly life is defined as one in which compassion for the Other, irrespective of cost to the saint, is the primary trait" (xxiii). The world's religious traditions have always "addressed the problems of the wretched of the earth in the person of saints, those who put themselves totally at the disposal of the Other" (xiv). Saints are "fleshly signifiers of compassion, generosity, self-sacrifice" (59).

And lest we wonder whether the life of the saint is still a real and living presence for us today, lest we too readily dismiss the extremity and excess of Levinas's philosophy, Caputo does well to remind us:

> From time to time, here and there, it happens that men and women respond, answer a call, spend themselves, using themselves up entirely for the Other. They spend years, maybe a lifetime, serving others, giving themselves up for the good of others. . . . Fools spend their lives working to feed and house the poor, or teaching in crime-ridden schools, or protecting defenseless wildlife; they lead a celibate life serving the peasants in Central America, only to be dragged out of bed one night and shot to death by right-wing gangsters; they spend the better part of their adult life in prison, refusing to cut a deal with a racist government, trying to make a point.[60]

Saints are exemplary people whose exemplary stories we tell over and over again because their unbelievable lives are testimonies to the divine. Their lives are full of "insatiable compassion" which is a desire that is also a "diaconate." They place themselves in service, in the "welcome of the absolutely other."[61] Their lives are testimony to the transcendence of "being faced by the other." The only chance the Other has of interrupting our world is through the saint who bears witness to this revelation and this calling. As Levinas says, the witness of an answerability that says "Here I am" is the very "glory of the Infinite," because it witnesses to that which is before us, prior to us, that which is first and foremost and facing us, always engendering our response. "The glory of the Infinite is glorified in this responsibility" (*OBBE*, 144). It is not to us, but to the Other, to your Name, that glory is given (see Ps. 115:1). Levinas writes:

> When in the presence of the Other, I say "Here I am!," this "Here I am" is the place through which the Infinite enters into language, but without giving itself to be seen... I will say that the subject who says "here I am!" *testifies* to the Infinite. It is through this testimony... that the revelation of the Infinite occurs. It is through this testimony that the very glory of the Infinite glorifies *itself*.[62]

"Here I am" is a "prophetic signification" that recalls the Hebrew phrase of the scriptures, *heneni*. Abraham says *heneni* when called to sacrifice his son Isaac (Gen. 22:1); Moses says *heneni* when standing before the burning bush (Exod. 3:4); Isaiah says *heneni* when God asks who he shall send (Isa. 6:8). *Heneni* — "here I am" — is the very sign of "the-one-for-the-other" (*OBBE*, 151). Here I am, for You. This for-the-other is often perceived as "a seed of folly," an obsession, a "sickness" ("I am sick with love," Song 2:5), yet for Levinas, *heneni* is "a marvelous accusative: here I am under your gaze, obliged to you, your servant. In the name of God."[63]

"Here I am... for you... in the Name of God" expresses the deeply felt religious sensibility that when we clothe the naked or respond to the one in need, when we welcome the stranger or answer for the defenseless, we are "testifying" to God's presence. It is as if we sense that in these gestures of human response and love toward the other, we feel "the *passing itself* of the Infinite" (*OBBE*, 150). As though a touch of infinite goodness, a hint of immeasurable love, a trace of divinity *itself* passed this way. Indeed, this very passing of God, which can neither be contained nor caught nor stilled (nor least, "thematized" as a presence belonging to me) — "this is how God comes to mind."

"Here I am under your gaze." When speaking of the experience we undergo in being faced by the other, "Levinas employs a vocabulary so deeply religious as to awaken even the sleepiest reader that something unusual is going on."[64] Indeed, as Levinas himself says, "one is tempted to call the plot religious" (*OBBE*, 147). One such "religious plot" can be found in the story about Abraham welcoming the three strangers (Gen. 18:1–15). When we look at what the rabbis have to say about this story, it is striking how their commentary lingers at some length in the "space" between verse 1 and verse 2.[65] Verse 1 says: "The Lord appeared to him at the Oak of Mamre while he was sitting by the entrance of the tent during the hottest part of the day." Verse 2 says: "He looked up and there he saw three men standing near him. As soon as he saw them he ran from the entrance of the tent to meet them, and bowed to the ground." A large question looms in "the gap" between verse 1 and verse 2 that engages the rabbis' interpretive attention. They offer at least two possible readings (among others!), to which I will add Levinas's own voice (who is himself familiar and practiced in Talmudic commentary).

The first reading follows along these lines. Verse 1 suggests a revelation of God, and verse 2 that this revelation is "interrupted" by the appearance of three wandering strangers. According to this reading, the rabbis say: "The deed of hospitality is greater than the welcoming of the Divine Presence."[66] In other words, Abraham does not linger to enjoy communion between himself and God (v. 1), but runs in haste to attend to the needs of three desert travelers who require food, shelter, and rest (v. 2). Abraham becomes an exemplary model of true service and hospitality toward the stranger that has inspired generations of Jewish tradition: "The stranger did not lodge in the street; My doors I opened to the roadside" (Job 31:32). In the space between verse 1 and verse 2, the rabbis suggest that Abraham rightly interrupts his own peace and communion with God to attend to the real, concrete needs of tired and weary strangers. In a similar fashion, Levinas accords some sympathy with this reading when he writes: "To give, to-be-for-another, despite oneself, but in interrupting the for-oneself, is to take the bread out of one's mouth, to nourish the hunger of another with one's own fasting" (*OBBE*, 56).

(It is always interesting the way commentary leads to commentary. Here I offer a brief aside. When Levinas speaks of taking the bread out of one's own mouth, I wonder whether he is alluding to the inmates of the camps who gave their very own meager portion of bread, from their very mouths, to help keep another alive. Perhaps, in a similar way, Mark's Gospel speaks of the widow who did not give from her surplus, but from the "little she had, gives everything she possessed, *all she had to live on*" [13:44].)

The second reading (interpretation) wonders about the confusion evident in the opening verses (and much of chapter 18) between the speech of God and the speech of the strangers addressed to Abraham. According to this reading, the rabbis suggest that the strangers *are the way* God appears to Abraham. In this sense, the "gap" between verse 1 and verse 2 holds these two verses together, rather than separating and distinguishing them. As Levinas suggests in one of his own Talmudic readings, "The respect for the stranger and the sanctification of the name of the Eternal are strangely equivalent. And all the rest is a dead letter."[67] According to this reading, there is a certain confluence between the voice of "the Most High" and the arrival of three strangers requiring Abraham's attention. The "gap" between verse 1 and verse 2 suggests the very passing of God, of which Levinas says, "Is not this imposition on me, this devolving-upon-me of the stranger, the way by which there 'arrives on the scene,' or comes to mind, a God who loves the stranger who puts me in question by his demand, and to which my 'here I am' bears witness?"[68]

These are only two possible readings of the opening verses of Genesis 18. The gap between the first and second verse creates an immense opening that engages the rabbis' interpretive attention. In the story about Abraham and the strangers, they are wondering about the experience we undergo in being faced by the other, standing "under your gaze." Perhaps Levinas captures a sense of both these readings of God's revelation to Abraham when he writes: "The Justice rendered to the Other, to my neighbor, gives me an unsurpassable proximity to God. . . . One follows the Most High God, above all by drawing near to one's neighbor, and showing concern for 'the widow, the orphan, the stranger and the beggar,' an approach that must not be made with 'empty hands.' "[69]

Let me conclude with a story. I recall one afternoon when I was walking along the streets of Jerusalem. Like other major cities, Jerusalem has many beggars on its streets. It was easy to pass them by, just as I passed by so many other strangers. However, on this particular afternoon, I was suddenly gripped by the face of a woman who was begging, or rather, I felt her gaze. Her face pressed up against me, and against the myriad of other faces in a bustling street. She stood out, singularly, and I felt the "absolute frankness" of her gaze. Though she sat on a cobble-paved street in a pool of squalor — ragged, dirty, nursing an infant, her hand outstretched, pleading, begging, with completely "defenseless eyes" — she nevertheless looked at me with such commanding authority, such "height," such strength of appeal. She was the destitute one who nevertheless rises above me as the one "for whom I can do all and to whom I owe all."[70]

Though I knew that a handout to an outstretched hand was but a small charity, I nevertheless could not pass her by. I made my way through the crowded street and gave her some money, placing it in her empty hand, and she smiled and said in a language I did not understand, "Thank you." This incident is undoubtedly small, less than a mite, yet I felt as though in that place, on the streets of Jerusalem, "the Most High" was facing me.

EIGHT

"Go and Study" —
"Go and Do Likewise"

TO VENTURE

In one of his poetic reflections, Martin Heidegger tells us that each and
every life comes into existence as a *venturing*.[1] With every birth, life *ven-
tures forth*. In this *venturing* — which is perhaps like an adventure — life is
set forth "without special protection." Life does not emerge fully formed,
but enters the world as an openness that lacks protection and in this sense
stands exposed. If life were always shielded and protected, then nothing
would be truly ventured. Life would lack any sense of consequence. There
would be nothing that really *matters* because nothing would be "at stake"
or "at issue" in life.

However, Heidegger notes that we are not totally abandoned or unprotected, as though we were simply cast to the wind. There would be no
true *venturing* if we were simply flung into an abyss. If this were the case,
then who would really care what happens in life? Once again, life would
be robbed of its vitality as something that counts and that matters.

We are, Heidegger suggests, ventured forth such that our lives are put
in motion and brought to bear on events that could go this way or that. He
evokes the image of the scales, "an apparatus which moves by tipping one
way or the other," and notes that in the Middle Ages they used the word *die
Wage* for "balance." Our lives are always *held* in the balance, and in this sense
supported, yet they also *hang* in the balance, and in this sense put at risk.

In his beautifully meditative novel *The Unbearable Lightness of Being*,
Milan Kundera begins with a reflection on the "heaviness" and "lightness"
of life:

The heaviest of burdens crushes us, we sink beneath it, it pins us to the ground. But in the love poetry of every age . . . the heaviest of burdens is [also] an image of life's most intense fulfillment. The heavier the burden, the closer our lives come to earth, the more real and truthful they become.

Conversely, the absolute absence of a burden causes man to be lighter than air, to soar into the heights, take leave of the earth and his earthly being, and become only half real, his movements as free as they are insignificant.

What then shall we choose? Weight or lightness?[2]

We feel ourselves pulled in both directions. Often we feel weighed down by the burdens and troubles of life, and we long to "break free," to "cut loose," to "go with the flow." Yet we also know that it is our deep loves and commitments that bring weight and significance to our lives. Against "the sweet lightness of being," Kundera suggests that "only what is heavy has value." Without the difficulty and struggle of love, "human existence loses its dimensions and becomes unbearably light."[3]

Kundera's meditation suggests that we typically prefer lightness over weight. However, he asks us to consider whether the lightness of being — free, autonomous, unconstrained — is perhaps more unbearable than the weight of being — heavy with consequence, commitment, and concern.

Consider, for example, the following view of life, in which the author goes at lengths to espouse a supposedly "radical Christian worldview":

There is no Ultimate: everything is proximate. There is no Absolute: everything is relative. . . . Nothing is hidden, and this is all there is. . . . To say a wholehearted Yes to one's own, and the world's, lightness and transience is bliss. . . . To live in this way is to live on the basis of complete acceptance of one's own, and everything else's, contingency and transience. One finds eternal happiness in being fully merged into "the Fountain," the continual pouring-out and passing-away of everything. . . . Learn to live like that all the time, and you will be learning solar living, a way of living that forgets the past and the future and which simply burns, now.[4]

This passage not only strikes me as an *unbearably light* existence, it also strikes me as a *nontheological* existence. There is little in this passage that *weighs*. There is nothing that hangs in the balance. There is no gravity. Nothing here matters — neither the past nor the future. There is no remembrance and no hope — just forgetfulness. Existence simply "burns now" and couldn't really care less; it is simply wrapped up in its own "eternal happiness" that takes a perverse pleasure in the continuous "pouring-out and passing-away of everything."

"What then shall we choose? Weight or lightness?" Practical theology is in agreement with *weight* — "the closer our lives come to earth, the more real and truthful they become."

WHAT IS THE WORK OF MY LIFE?

Death has been on my mind lately. A good friend, Br. Ed Kiefer, S.M., died on January 7, 2004, after a long battle with cancer. My wife's father and my children's grandfather, Bernard O'Brien, died on May 2, 2004. May their names be held in God's memory.

Among many other thoughts and feelings, I have found myself drawn to the following question: *What is the work of my life?* This is more than an introductory question, such as "What is your name, and what do you do?" Rather, this is a question that goes to the heart of things — to the essential — "for where your treasure is, there your heart will be also" (Matt. 6:21).

"What is the work of my life?" It is too late to ask this question on my deathbed. It will be too late then to look back and ask, "Of what value my life?" "What has it amounted to or accounted for?" "What has it treasured?"

"What is the work of my life?" is a question we need to ask *today* — not retrospectively, looking back. Rather, this question is *in front of us now*.

"I call heaven and earth to witness against you today that I set before you life and death" (Deut. 30:19). The choice is before us now, and all of creation stands witness. The choice is not between theory and practice, but between "life and death."

"Choose life so that you and your descendants may live" (Deut. 30:19). Choose life while you can, while you're still living. Don't wait until you're on your deathbed. It will be too late then, because death will have already chosen you. "Where the corpse is," Jesus says, "there the vultures will gather" (Luke 17:37).

Eventually, I will have to handover my life. I will have no choice. At that moment I may finally see, perhaps as I've never seen before, what my whole life has been "about" — what the whole work of my life has been concerned with and devoted to.[5]

But it will be too late then. Better to choose the work of my life today. Better to hand myself over now, rather than wait for the final surrender. If we give of our lives — if we hand ourselves over now — then the choice for life will overcome the "sting of death." "Love is stronger than death" (Song 8:6), and the witnesses will say, "even though he dies, he has chosen life."

Where do I turn to discover the *work of my life?* This is not simply a question about the *meaning* of my life. The meaning (or theory) of life is one of those questions that lend themselves to endless speculation — fun, perhaps, to entertain — but about as profitable as a game of Scrabble.

To ask about the *work* (or practice) of my life *ties* the question of meaning to the question of purpose — or intention, or value, or orientation, or direction. It ties the question of life's meaning to the question of what I *contribute* with my life, what I *produce* with my life, what I *create* with my life, what I *make with my life*. *Work* has meaning, as Catholic social teaching continually reminds us, such that my life's *meaning* can never be divorced from my life's *work*. "My Father goes on working, and so do I," Jesus says (John 5:17).

A THEOLOGICAL LIFE

In his book *Philosophy as a Way of Life*, Pierre Hadot notes that one of the earliest definitions of philosophy comes from Plato, who called philosophy "a training for death."[6] This may strike us as a very strange definition, yet Hadot suggests that "to learn how to die" actually serves to focus one's attention on the "art of living."[7] We know, for example, that the birth of any new insight, behavior, or attitude is usually accompanied by the death of a preceding set of attitudes or behaviors that need to be changed and transformed. "This is what takes place in every spiritual exercise," writes Hadot, "it is necessary to change one's point of view, attitude, set of convictions, therefore to struggle with oneself."[8] We all know the saying of Jesus that says we must lose our life in order to save it: "For those who want to save their life will lose it, and those who lose their life for my sake will save it. For what does it profit them if they gain the whole world, but lose or forfeit themselves" (Luke 9:24–25). The "training for death" or the "losing of one's life" is for the sake of a new or renewed life. It is the process of conversion or *metanoia*, or what Plato calls "the turning of souls."[9] "Rather than aiming at the acquisition of a purely abstract knowledge," writes Hadot, "these exercises aim at realizing a transformation of one's vision of the world and a metamorphosis of one's personality."[10] Perhaps this is what lies behind that mysterious saying of St. Paul when he says, "I have been crucified with Christ, and it is no longer I who live but Christ who lives in me" (Gal. 2:19–20).

Hadot's work seeks to reclaim the ancient practice of philosophy as a spiritual exercise rather than simply as a theoretical discourse. He notes that philosophical "theory was never considered an end in itself, it is clearly and decidedly put in the service of practice."[11] The purpose of philosophy was to "form people and to transform souls."[12] In his introduction to Hadot's book, Arnold Davidson writes:

> The philosopher needed to be trained not only to know how to speak and debate, but also how to live. The exercise of philosophy was therefore not only intellectual, but could also be spiritual. Hence, the teaching and training of philosophy were intended not simply to train the intelligence of the disciple, but to transform all aspects of his being — intellect, imagination, sensibility, and will. Its goal was nothing less than the art of living, and so spiritual exercises were exercises in learning to live the philosophical life. Spiritual exercises were *exercises* because they were practical, required effort and training, and were lived; they were *spiritual* because they involved the entire spirit, one's whole way of being.[13]

In early Christianity, especially in the monastic movements, Christianity was also considered as a *philosophia*, a way of life that sought to live according to the paths of divine Wisdom.[14] Indeed, Ellen Charry has recently shown that early Christian doctrines and teachings were less concerned with developing conceptual theories and more concerned with the promotion of virtue and a life of "Christian excellence."[15] Knowing the truth implied "loving it, wanting it, and being transformed by it." Theory was not opposed to practice. Rather, theology was an exercise of life "nurtured through prayer, reflection, and study of God's word."[16]

To venture a theological life is *to live theologically*. It is not so much to ask about the ways that theology can be made practical; rather, it is to ask how the practices of my life can be made theological.

According to Paul Ricoeur, to venture or to wage a theological life requires a conviction to live within, or to enter, or to confess, or to have already entered, "a vast circuit involving a founding word, mediating texts, and traditions of interpretation."[17] It is a conviction based on a risk or a wager, rather than on proofs or certitudes. "It rests on a sort of wager: are there still enough people who will hear this word?"[18] The "small voice of Biblical writings" is often lost in the clamor of our world. "But the fate of the Biblical word is that of all poetic voices. Will they be heard at the level of public discourse?" "My hope," writes Ricoeur, "is that there will always be poets and ears to listen to them."[19]

The theological life is "the moment of adhering to a word reputed to have come from farther and from higher than myself, and this occurs in a kerygmatic reading within a profession of faith." At the religious level, there is a "dependence or a submission to an earlier word."[20] Conviction is rooted in a memory that stretches far beyond my own life, a memory that includes a "founding word, the mediation of writing, and the history of interpretation."[21] "I know this word," writes Ricoeur, "because it is written, this writing because it is received and read; and this reading is accepted by a community, which, as a result, accepts to be deciphered by its founding texts; and it is this community that reads them."[22]

Ricoeur is suggesting that at some point we have to risk the story of our faith tradition in the sense that we have to test it with our own lives. The story precedes us, is older than us, and while it offers us God's assurances, we have to venture this story in our own lives, *with* our own lives. "One has to be sure that the risk is taken," writes Derrida, "and to be sure that the risk is taken, one has to negotiate with the assurances."[23]

"GO AND STUDY" — "GO AND DO LIKEWISE"

In modern thought, practice is often contrasted with theory. Practical theology is an attempt to heal this dichotomy, so that thought and deed can *work together* rather than against each other. David Tracy refers to the dichotomy between theory and practice as a "fatal split."[24] When we divide theory and practice, we injure life, and it is the task of practical theology to heal this fatal wound.

Often, we are impatient with "theories." We can easily dismiss them as heady speculations. We want to get on with life. Unlike theory, or in contrast to theory, we typically associate the word "practical" with things that are *useful, workable, feasible, doable, realistic, sensible, functional, pragmatic, applied, hands-on, effective, relevant.* These "practical" words carry a positive content for our modern ears. Generally speaking, we don't like to suffer useless things. Rather, Western culture needs to feel productive. It likes progress and achievement. It likes things that are workable and effective. It likes concrete facts and ideas that are tested. It likes efficiency and control over events. It also likes profits and good returns, and it likes shopping malls that are filled with mostly *useless* things. Theology would lose its very soul if it were reduced to this understanding of the word "practical."

In a strange twist, however, there is also a sense in which we privilege theory over practice. Theory is the bright light that illumines all we do. Theory represents our "thinking selves," so highly prized in Western philosophy. It comes first and foremost. Practice plays second fiddle to theory because practice typically comes *after* theory, in second place, and no matter how hard it tries to win the race between them, practice always comes in second-best. Practice is what remains after theory has accomplished all its winning work — all that now needs to be done is for practice to demonstrate or test how well the theory works. Too often practice functions as the hand maiden of theory, the worker bee for the queen bee. In terms of theology, we have often considered "systematic" theology as the queen bee, and "pastoral" theology as the worker bee.

We can move backwards and forwards between theory and practice — now on the side of one, now on the side of the other — because we see them as opposites, caught in a tug-of-war, with each one pulling against the weight of the other.

Practical theology has no interest in refereeing this rather futile struggle. Rather, practical theology sees theory and practice as partners that belong together. They are made for each other. They require each other. Action requires reflection. Reflection requires action. They are not one or the other; they go hand-in-hand. The Talmud relates a famous story about the beloved Rabbi Hillel:

It happened that a certain heathen came before Shammai and said to him, "Convert me on the condition that you teach me the entire Torah while I am standing on one foot." Shammai drove him away with the builder's measuring stick that was in his hand. He then came before Hillel who converted him. Hillel said to him, "That which is hateful to you, do not do to your neighbor. This is the entire Torah; the rest is commentary—now go and study." (Shabbat 31a)[25]

Hillel teaches the entire Torah in a single verse. He makes it sound quite simple: "That which is hateful to you, do not do to your neighbor." There is no great mystery here; this is a very practical command that is within everyone's grasp. Just put this verse into practice. It's that simple. Or is it? Hillel reminds us that maybe it isn't as simple as it seems, for there is much commentary on this verse that requires our attention. *To practice the entire Torah requires much study.* We should not be lulled into thinking that the practice of the Torah is easy. Practice also requires reflection. Practice also requires learning. Practice also requires us to "go and study."

There is a story in the Gospels that is very similar to the story of Hillel. But first let me offer a brief aside. Scholars have noted that two schools of rabbinic thought were circulating during Jesus' time — the "house of Shammai" and the "house of Hillel."[26] Hillel was revered and beloved because his teachings reflected God's graciousness and a warm love for humanity, whereas Shammai's teachings found little favor because of their cold severity and strictness. Unlike Shammai who drove people away with his measuring stick, Hillel preached the mercy and compassion of God. "He will not break a bruised reed or quench a smoldering wick" (Matt. 12:20; Isa. 42:3). Jesus' teachings reflect the more compassionate and tolerant teachings of Hillel rather than the harsher teachings of Shammai. (Paul, by the way, was taught by Hillel's grandson, Gamaliel the Elder, as mentioned in Acts 22:3.) But back to the story:

A lawyer stood up to test Jesus. "Teacher," he said, "what must I do to inherit eternal life?" He said to him, "What is written in the law? What do you read there?" He answered, "You shall love the Lord your God with all your heart, and with all your soul, and with all your strength, and with all your mind; and your neighbor as yourself." And he said to him, "You have given the right answer; do this, and you will live." (Luke 10:25–28)

Whereas in the story of Hillel it is a "heathen" who comes to test the rabbis, in Luke's story it is a scholar of the law (the Torah) who comes to test the teacher, Jesus. Jesus takes the scholar's question and, in typical rabbinic fashion, bounces it straight back: "What do you read in Torah? What has your study taught you?" The scholar is obviously well versed in Torah and has studied it well, for he creatively brings together two seemingly disparate verses — the first from the book of Deuteronomy (6:5), and the second from the book of Leviticus (19:18). By combining these two verses, he manages to encapsulate the very essence of the Torah, to which Jesus replies, "You have given the right answer; do this, and you will live."

Such is Luke's version, which differs from Matthew's account, where it is Jesus himself who comes up with the brilliant reply (much like Hillel): "On these two commandments hang the whole Law, and the Prophets also" (22:40). Mark's version is different yet again, for he sets the scene in a more cordial environment of rabbinic discussion, without much hint of an acrimonious or testing exchange. The interlocutor in Mark's Gospel seems to appreciate Jesus' response and says, "Well spoken, teacher," to which Jesus replies, "You are not far from the kingdom of heaven" (12:34).

Luke's account, however, is interesting because, like the story of Hillel, it ends with a twist. The scholar in Luke's story offers the correct response, but when Jesus says, "do this and you will live," he feels a need to "justify himself" and so he challenges Jesus further: "And who is my neighbor?" (10:29). Jesus responds by offering a *commentary* on the "great commandment." He tells the story of the Good Samaritan. We need to consider, Jesus suggests, not only *who* my neighbor is, but also whether *I* can be a neighbor to another. We need to ask ourselves, Can I show mercy? Can I approach my neighbor with mercy and compassion, and thereby be a neighbor to the one who calls out to me and pleads for help? We need to go and study, to look more closely at the practices of our lives, to consider those we "pass by" too readily, or those we condemn too quickly, or those we judge too hastily.

To love our neighbor — to not do what is hateful — is a difficult teaching. If we think it is within easy reach of our comprehension, if we think that we are already fulfilling this commandment, then we are probably kidding ourselves (or trying to justify ourselves). Why else do we say, over and over again, "For I have sinned, in my thoughts and in my words, in what I have done and in what I have failed to do"? Why else do we pray, over and over again, "Lord have mercy"? It is difficult to live the *essence* of the Torah, yet we know it to be a beautiful teaching, as sweet as honey.

To practice the entire Torah will require much study. It will require much reflection on God's word and on the way we are living, and much practice in trying to live according to the ways of God, according to the essence of the Torah. We need to study the ways of God — "slow to anger and abounding in steadfast love" (Ps. 86:15) — with all our heart and soul and strength and mind, so that we can love our neighbor, so that we do not harden our hearts, so that we do not stray too far from the kingdom of heaven.

"Go and study." Go and study the ways of God and learn what God is teaching you, and "go and do likewise" (Luke 10:37). Don't just sit there. *Go! Study! Go! Do what you're learning!* Go and study. Go and do. This *rhythm* is a natural pattern for theology, a natural pattern for the people of God. It is the pattern of discipleship — of listening and responding, hearing and doing, reading ("This is the word of the Lord") and answering *(responsa)*, worshiping and going (*missa* — "to be sent forth"). This rhythm has sustained generations of faithful and prayerful people across the centuries, people who have sought to align their lives according to the ways and purposes of God, "on earth as it is in heaven" — as it is spoken in the scriptures, as it is taught in the Torah, as it is revealed by God's word. Go and study — go and do likewise.

FOR EXAMPLE

As a teacher, it is not uncommon for students to ask me, "Can you give an example of what you mean?" At that moment, I usually find myself searching for illustrations or instances, drawn from experience and from life, to help exemplify or activate the meaning I am seeking to convey. Trying to provide examples for students is often difficult as I struggle to find appropriate analogies or connections, yet I also find that this effort is often the moment when real understanding begins to take form.

Reflecting on this classroom experience has led me to wonder — maybe we can view practical theology in a similar way, as the effort to provide an example or an illustration of God's love and goodness in the world. This strikes me as quite a stunning proposal. It means choosing to pattern or model my life as an example of divine life. It means seeking to live in ways that bear witness to the life of God. It means that I am trying to live on earth as it is in heaven — as an example of God. This is a very daunting proposal — that the very work of my life might be seen as an example of God.

Viewed in this way, practical theology would always be *exemplary* or representative of God's mercy and justice. The answer to the question, "What is practical theology?" would always be "for example . . . " What are the works of mercy? Look at Mother Teresa's life for example. What are the works of justice? Look at Martin Luther King's life for example. What is the love of learning and the desire for God? Look at Thomas Aquinas's life for example. What is the spirit of the beatitudes and nonviolence? Look at Gandhi's life for example.

All of these lives are patterned, in one way or another, on the life and teachings of Jesus. Indeed, Tom Ryan notes that according to Aquinas, Christ's whole life can be viewed in this very way — as an exemplar of God. "Christ's life exemplifies a whole way of living — an *exemplum vitae*."[27] Many of Jesus' teachings and parables offer examples of the kingdom of God — "the kingdom of God is like . . . " Not only his teachings, but also his actions, as when Jesus responded to the misgivings of John the Baptist's disciples: "Go and tell John what you have seen and heard: the blind receive their sight, the lame walk, the lepers are cleansed, the deaf hear, the dead are raised, the poor have good news brought to them" (Luke 7:22). And then, during the Last Supper, Jesus provided a culminating example of his life's work. Assuming the role of a servant, he poured water into a basin and began washing the disciples feet, saying, "I have set you an example, that you should also do as I have done to you" (John 13:15).

Exemplary truths are often considered as high ideals, yet that does not mean they are therefore impractical. Rather, it means that they continually put us to the test. "Examine your selves to see if you are living in the faith. Test yourselves" (2 Cor. 13:5). As Levinas suggests, there is a very real sense in which "every truth must be attested," such that truth is always tied to "the veracity of the people who testify to it."[28] The Gospel saying, "You will know them by their fruits" (Matt. 7:16), suggests that truth is intimately linked with those who *testify* or *bear witness* to the truth they are living. The *practice* of truth is not something "added" to truth; rather, the practice of truth *inheres* in truth, such that without a living testimony or witness, truth would ring hollow or, as St. Paul says, it would simply be a "noisy gong or a clanging cymbal" (1 Cor. 13:1).

A CASE IN POINT

Two of the most prevalent words circulating around the globe at the moment are "war" and "terror." What troubles me is the way these words are associated — not, for example, as the "terror of war" — rather, as the "war on terror." It is difficult to imagine any war that does not involve terror, yet it is even more difficult to imagine that war could be considered as an answer to terror.

One of humanity's most complex and enduring tasks is to break cycles of violence — to choose life rather than death. I realize that many consider war as a way to end violence. However, it is difficult not to be struck by the amount of violence, conflict, and discord that the "war on terror" has unleashed in our world. Its frightening logic seems to have spiraled out of control, and the world seems helplessly caught in its grasp.

This depressing situation has led me to reflect further on the philosophy of nonviolence (especially in the works of Martin Luther King and Mohandas Gandhi). It was several years ago that I first began to ponder this approach, and I remember writing down my thoughts in a piece I titled "Silent Night" (see below). While this story does not reflect the enormous struggles that faced Dr. King and Gandhi, it nevertheless represents a time in my life when I struggled with a difficult situation and an equally difficult truth (and one that I continue to learn). Given the current state of the world, I feel compelled to keep venturing a theological life. "To not do what is hateful" requires much study and much practice. It really is a life's work — a venturing and a wager that lacks any final guarantees, except that "faith, hope, and love abide, these three; and the greatest of these is love" (1 Cor. 13:13).

Silent Night

Every week I see media reports of people caught in conflicts around the world. And every week I labor under the conflict of a neighborhood dispute. The huge burden of people caught in strife and war across the globe seems hardly comparable with the paltry burden of a neighborly relation gone sour. Yet it is this latter experience that causes many of my sleepless nights. It amazes me how much a seemingly trivial event like a fractious neighbor can eat away at my soul and my family's life like a deadly poison. Yet I find myself wondering whether this experience of conflict — in microcosm — grows from the same cancerous cells of division, intolerance, and hatred that affect us all in our human relations. Perhaps the distant conflicts of the world are not so far away after all. Perhaps their disturbance and distress are present in a nascent way in my own neighborhood, and in myself.

How have I handled this neighborhood conflict? My first response was not to handle it at all, not to hold it or feel it, but to ignore it. I would tell myself and my young children: "The best thing is to ignore it — ignore them." But the anxiety, the worry, and the restless nights didn't leave me — "ignorance" brought me no bliss, no peace. And I desperately yearned for peace, to be able to sleep well, to feel a healthy well-being (*shalom*) circulating in my relational world, with myself, my family, and my neighbors.

During this time I was studying the works of the Jewish philosopher Emmanuel Levinas. He kept telling me that we are responsible for each other, that wherever I turn, I see the face of another who looks at me and concerns me. I realized that I cannot ignore the face of my neighbor, even though whenever our eyes did meet (in the local supermarket, for example) we would turn our faces away from each other. How can I bring myself to take responsibility for the neighbor who offends me?

It is with a question like this that Levinas turns his attention in his Talmudic reading, "As Old as the World?":

How to preserve oneself from evil? By each taking upon himself the responsibility of the others. Men are not only and in their ultimate essence "for self" but "for others," and this "for others" must be probed deeply.[29]

If being-for-the-other, rather than violence, is embedded in life as its most ancient character, then this "for others" cannot simply mean that we "love those who love us" (Matt. 5:46). That would be too simple, too easy, too shallow a reading of that which is "as old as the world."

Rather, Levinas asks us to probe more deeply and to consider the ways in which *"I can be responsible for that which I did not do and take upon myself a distress which is not mine."* Responsibility for another extends even as far as bearing "responsibility for the sins you did not commit."[30] "For the other" becomes "for the fault of the other," taking on the sin of the other, "which wants absolutely and unto death to substitute itself for the other — for his sin and his distress."[31] When we ask: Is this love that gives itself, even in taking on the sin and fault of the other, "as old as the world?" — Levinas replies, "For the human world to be possible . . . at each moment there must be someone who can be responsible for the others."[32]

This thought kept me awake long into the night. I felt myself under a huge obligation. It was up to me to approach my neighbor, to meet face-to-face, to take responsibility not only for my own sin, but also for the sin and fault of another. I felt both repelled and attracted by this prospect. My resistance was strong: "Why me? Why should I be the one to make a move? Why don't they come and tell me what is bothering them so much? Why don't they express their grievance with me, rather than let it fester away?" Yet I also felt a desire to break this tireless, useless distance between us. I wanted to break through the hatred and anger. I wanted an end to it all and I realized it was up to me — no one else but me. "Yes, I am responsible for my neighbor. It is up to me to call both myself and them to a measure of responsibility and humanity within our ruptured relationship." Yet I still wasn't quite convinced, or maybe I simply lacked courage. It is not an easy thing to come face-to-face with an "enemy" — with someone who is against you.

And then, one night, I was listening to the music of Leonard Cohen. In a stunning song titled, "If It Be Your Will," Cohen reflects on the agony of Jesus in the garden of Gethsemane:

> If it be your will
> that I speak no more,
> and my voice be still
> as it was before;
> I will speak no more,
> I shall abide until
> I am spoken for,
> if it be your will.

If it be your will
that a voice be true,
from this broken hill
I will sing to you.
From this broken hill
all your praises they shall ring,
if it be your will
to let me sing.

If it be your will,
if there is a choice,
let the rivers fill,
let the hills rejoice.
Let your mercy spill
on all these burning hearts in hell,
if it be your will
to make us well.

And draw us near
and bind us tight,
all your children here
in their rags of light;
in our rags of light,
all dressed to kill;
and end this night,
if it be your will.[33]

Underlying this song is a very haunting thought — it is better to suffer violence than to perpetrate it. It is better to bear the fault of another's sin than to be the cause of further sin. Only in this way can we "end this night...all dressed to kill." Could it really be true that suffering for the fault of another is redemptive? I confess I have never fully understood this. And then, I encountered these words from Mohandas Gandhi:

It is difficult to observe truth, to suffer in order to put an end to suffering. And yet, the more I think about it, the more I see that there is no other way for us to fight our ills and those of others. I even feel that the world has no other really effective remedy to offer.... Satyagrahis [those who voices are true] bear no ill will, do not lay down their life in anger . . . but will always try to overcome evil by good, anger by love, untruth by truth, violence by nonviolence. There is no other way of purging the world of evil.[34]

I was feeling more resolved to approach my neighbor. Yet there was one last thought that came my way before I could finally make my move. Enter Nelson Mandela and his book *Long Walk to Freedom*. "How could it be," I thought, "that after a quarter of a century in prison, Mandela could still bring himself to meet around the table with his oppressors, in his efforts to create a new government for South Africa?" Near the end of his book, Mandela answered my question:

> It was during those long and lonely years in prison that my hunger for the freedom of my own people became a hunger for the freedom of all people, white and black. I knew as well as I knew anything that the oppressor must be liberated just as surely as the oppressed.
>
> When I walked out of prison, that was my mission, to liberate the oppressed and the oppressor both. Some say that has now been achieved. But I know that that is not the case. . . . We have not taken the final step on our journey, but the first step on a longer and even more difficult road. . . .
>
> I have walked that long road to freedom. I have tried not to falter; I have made missteps along the way. But I have discovered the secret that after climbing a great hill, one only finds that there are many more hills to climb. I have taken a moment here to rest, to steal a view of the glorious vista that surrounds me, to look back on the distance I have come. But I can only rest for a moment, for with freedom come responsibilities, and I dare not linger, for my long walk has not yet ended.[35]

Mandela's words reminded me of Paulo Freire, who wrote in his book *Pedagogy of the Oppressed*, "This is the great humanistic and historical task of the oppressed: to liberate themselves and their oppressors as well. Only the oppressed can initiate this task."[36] Similarly, Levinas says that "only the persecuted must answer for everyone, even for the persecutor."[37] "Only the persecuted" is similar to Freire's "only the oppressed" — only they have the ability to free the other, oppressed and oppressor both.

We are responsible for each other, even for those who offend us. It was up to me to approach my neighbor, to initiate a move out of oppression, to seek freedom for us both. This was my responsibility.

The moment finally arrived. I received an invitation in my mailbox to a Christmas street party. It was time to enact the words of Levinas, Gandhi, Mandela, Freire to "go and do likewise." With a great deal of nervous fear and trepidation, I prepared myself to encounter my neighbor — to face the other who I did not understand, who was causing me such pain and anxiety, who kept me awake night after night. Yet I felt a glimmer of hope that everything would go well. After all, it was Christmas, a time of "peace and goodwill" — the perfect time, I thought, to make a reconciliatory approach.

I arrived at the party, and gradually the room filled with people, shaking hands, smiling, greeting one another in festive cheer. There, in the midst of the crowded room, I saw my neighbor and his wife. I felt my heart beating, my palms sweating. I chatted with some people, sipped a glass of wine, and noticed again how they always looked away from me. After an hour or so, I took a deep breath and went to face my neighbor. I looked him in the eyes and said words to the effect: "There is a problem between us. I don't want this conflict to continue. I want to restore a relationship between us. I apologize for any offense I may have caused you. In the spirit of Christmas, can we find some goodwill between us?" But these words fell like seeds on dry, hard, barren ground. They had no transforming effect, no possibility of life. They were refused, and no miracle of peace occurred between us. I was devastated. I went to a dark corner and wept. It was going to go on and on and on. It was going to be a long road.

Now I do not know what to do. I do not know where I am, or where to turn. All I know is that on this small, suburban, cul-de-sac street, I felt the pain of a broken and torn world, and a deep longing to experience at least one holy night, one silent night, one night without turmoil and despair — one night of peace on earth.

SPEAKING OUR LIVES

The story did not eventually end there. A time did come when I was able to talk with my neighbor, and I felt a glimmer of hope that maybe my efforts had not gone astray after all. The tensions gradually eased, and I sensed a measure of peace and accord between us.

I continue to struggle with the difficult truth this situation brought to me, yet I continue to sense in this difficulty a deep truth of life—"as old as the world," as Levinas says.

I do not consider myself a violent or hateful person. However, I know that I have within me a propensity toward goodness and toward evil. The scales are always set. It frightens me to think that I can actually act in evil ways, that I can be the cause of evil in the world. Particularly in my thoughts and in my words, I have noticed how much anger and hatred can spew out of me—even with those closest to me.

"I have become keenly aware," writes Erazim Koh á k, "that I live my life in words, . . . I speak out my life as I live it."[38] We should keep in mind that words are never mere words. God created the world by uttering words. "The word that goes forth from my mouth does not return to me empty, without succeeding in what it was sent *to do*" (Isa. 55:11). Like the divine action of God's word, Paul Ricoeur reminds us that "human action is a speaking action."[39] Words are never neutral. They carry the power to build up or to tear down. When I love, I am speaking the word "love." When I hate, I am speaking the word "hate." We are all the time "speaking our lives" into the world. We are all the time saying who we are, announcing what we believe, and living what we do in the words we choose to speak.

Many of the great spiritual traditions of humanity urge us to take care with our words. In the Buddhist tradition, for example, we are urged to follow the path of "noble speech." We are cautioned to watch over our words, to notice how many times during the day we fail against virtuous speech. "Words can travel across thousands of miles. They are intended to build up understanding and love. Each word should be a jewel. A beautiful tapestry."[40]

"Death and life are in the power of the tongue" (Prov. 18:21). There is a Jewish commandment forbidding *lashon hara*—an "evil tongue" that goes about speaking and listening to gossip or malicious comments about other people.[41] "You shall not go about as a tale bearer among your people" (Lev. 19:16).

In the Gospels there is a seriousness and weight attributed to the words we speak. "It is by your words that you will be acquitted, and by your words that you will be condemned" (Matt. 12:37). The words we speak are not harmless. Nor are they spoken into a void. They matter and are full of consequence. Careless words can be devastating. The words we speak can do good or harm; they bear responsibility; they carry the weight of good or evil in the world.

Our words are often the measure of our holiness and purity, over against the ever-present garbage that can so easily spurt out of us. "It is the things that come out of a person that make a person unclean" (Mark 7:5). If we watch over our hearts, we will strive to speak only out of goodness, to let our words be bearers of goodness, to purify our speech and make our words holy. "A person's words flow out of what fills their heart" (Matt. 12:34).

St. Paul continually urged the communities he visited — many of which were mired in argument and conflict — to live a theological life, to be "imitators of God" (Eph. 5:1). How do we imitate God, we might well ask? Here is St. Paul's advice.

> But now you must get rid of all such things — anger, wrath, malice, slander, and abusive language from your mouth. Do not lie to one another, seeing that you have stripped off the old self with its practices and have clothed yourselves with the new self, which is being renewed in knowledge according to the image of its creator. . . .
>
> As God's chosen ones, holy and beloved, clothe yourselves with compassion, kindness, humility, meekness, and patience. Bear with one another and, if anyone has a complaint against another, forgive each other; just as the Lord has forgiven you, so you must also forgive. Above all, clothe yourselves with love, which binds everything together in perfect harmony. . . . And be thankful. Let the word of Christ dwell in you richly. . . . (Col. 3:8–16)

Go and study. Go and do likewise.

PART THREE

YOUR KINGDOM COME

NINE

"The Field Is the World"

Practical Theology and the Plurality of Cultures

THE APPLE

A living parable:

Slice an apple through its equator, and you will find five small chambers arrayed in a perfectly symmetrical starburst — a pentagram. Each of the chambers holds a seed (occasionally two) of such deep lustrous brown they might have been oiled and polished by a woodworker. . . .

Every seed in that apple . . . contains the genetic instructions for a completely new and different apple tree, one that, if planted, would bear only the most glancing resemblance to its parents. If not for grafting — the ancient technique for cloning trees — every apple in the world would be its own distinct variety, and it would be impossible to keep a good one going beyond the life span of that particular tree.

The botanical term for this variability is "heterozygosity," and while there are many species that share it (our own included), in the apple the tendency is extreme. More than any other single trait, it is the apple's genetic variability — its ineluctable wildness — that accounts for its ability to make itself at home in places as different from one another as New England, New Zealand, Kazakhstan and California. Wherever the apple tree goes, its offspring propose so many different variations on what it means to be an apple — at least five per apple, several thousand per tree — that a couple of these novelties are almost bound to have whatever qualities it takes to prosper in the tree's adopted home.

— Michael Pollan, *The Botany of Desire*[1]

This living parable is a celebration of life's inherent plurality, diversity, and variety — its "ineluctable wildness."

Can we imagine that God, like an artist in rapture, could be so wildly superfluous as to allow several thousand distinct varieties of apples to emerge from a single tree — each one never to be repeated?

"God said, 'Let the earth produce...'" (Gen. 1:11). "God said, 'Be fruitful, multiply...'" (1:22). "God saw that it was good" (Gen. 1:25). Better that life be full and rich and many and assorted, rather than uniform, identical, limited, one and the same.

Apples and humans, we are told, are "heterozygous." We are distinct, and we are plural. We are unique, and we are diverse. We do not emerge as mere replicas that are one and the same — a homogeneous mass. Rather, we burst forth as diverse and different — a heterogeneous flourishing.

We are filled with the glory of God, who colors all creation with a radiant heterogeneity — "the thousands of different languages spoken by humanity, the proliferation of cultures, the sheer variety of the imaginative expressions of the human spirit, in most of which, if we listen carefully, we will hear the voice of wisdom telling us something we need to know."[2]

This astonishing multiplicity does not mean that we are disparate and isolated from each other or from our fellow living creatures who share the earth. Rather, it means that we are inseparable and interconnected, bound and woven by the creative energy of God who has fashioned us to thrive like apple trees.

CULTURE

The wild apple, however, is perhaps a little too wild — reveling in an almost maddening and creative exuberance. Perhaps this is why humans, from early on, learned the ancient art of grafting as a way to tame the apple.

In a similar way, humans have also engaged in the art of "cultivating" their own human experience — attending to its otherwise wild and fertile "given-ness" in such ways as to nurture patterns of human significance and meaning. Indeed, Terry Eagleton notes that the etymology of the word "culture" can be traced to the activities of agriculture or the nurturing and tending of natural growth. "We derive our word for the finest of human activities from labor and agriculture, crops and cultivation."[3]

Culture, in other words, is a way of "tilling life" and bringing forth a world that is rich in human significance. It is one of humanity's finest activities. Along with the cultivation of the earth for crops and food, humans have also sought to cultivate the human spirit, to nurture those elements of sustenance required for human living — the nourishment of meaning and value, intimacy and sociality, art and creativity. Like rows of planted vines, human cultures are equally wondrous in their cultivation of a fruitful and enriched human existence.

"Culture," Eagleton tells us, is "one of the two or three most complex words in the English language."[4] Definitions abound, and it is easy to become more confused than enlightened when seeking to get a handle on this word. Part of the problem is that we are swimming in culture; it is like an ocean surrounding us, as water surrounds a fish. Or it is like the air we breathe. Or it is like a lens we see through, without us consciously noticing that we are wearing spectacles. Or it is like something entirely normal or "natural" to us, even though to a person of a different culture it may seem quite strange and foreign.

Culture can be like a canvas of possibilities for expressing human creativity, or it can be like a shadowy curtain of darker repressions and denials. It can be an authentic avenue of human insight, or it can be like a set of blinkers that block or cloud us from seeing other viewpoints.[5]

Culture, for all its shadow and light, is essential and intimate to humanity. And like any intimacy, no one "from outside" can ever fully share it, and no one "from inside" can ever fully describe it. Such is human culture.

This depth and complexity of culture reminds us of at least one important thing, namely, that I can never presume to fully know another, that I must assume a posture of reverence or humility before the intimacy and sacredness of another person's (or people's) cultural life.

I cannot respect the dignity of another human being, or enter into a dialogue with another human being, or seek to understand another human being, *without at the same time* respecting the dignity of their culture, entering into a dialogue with their culture, seeking to better understand their culture.

Maybe this seems all too obvious. After all, many of us are accustomed to living in an increasingly globalized world where we can access the World Wide Web with a click of the mouse, where our neighbors are ethnically diverse, where we can quite easily eat out at a Japanese or Indian or Thai restaurant. Perhaps we have taken the ancient art of grafting to a whole new level in human cultural interchange. Having myself lived in very vibrant, multicultural cities such as Sydney and Miami, I see real evidence of this creative possibility. However, I also wonder how much of this is just a surface play, an easy and liberal tolerance that Western societies like to take pride in as a sign of their supposedly mature and inclusive democracies.

I feel I would be naïve not to acknowledge that there remain real friction, real power plays, real domination of one cultural form over another. Indigenous peoples, and peoples whose histories are born of colonial oppression, for example, are particularly prone to the resistance and disregard of dominant cultures. Aboriginal Australians still suffer the effects of the "stolen generation" (where Aboriginal children were taken from their parents to be raised in white schools and white families).[6] African Americans still suffer the effects of slavery. Haitians, who live just a few hundred miles offshore from the United States, are nevertheless one of the poorest people in the world. Worse still, any hope of peacemaking in the conflict zones of the world now seems dismally overshadowed by the newly emergent rhetoric of the war on terror — a rhetoric that provides an all-too-easy justification for avoiding the patient trust and endurance required of peacemaking. According to Jonathan Sacks, we need a new theology of difference; we need to learn how to celebrate the "dignity of difference" — "why no one civilization has the right to impose itself on others by force: why God asks us to respect the freedom and dignity of those not like us."[7]

Unlike apple trees, it seems, human beings are not very good at dealing with the "hetero" — the other, the different, the various, the distinct, the "deep lustrous brown seeds." Perhaps we thought, as the Genesis story suggests, that by ingesting this wild fruit we could actually conquer it, that we ourselves would become "like gods" (Gen. 3:5), and be readily able to adjudicate between good and evil. Our task, perhaps, is less to sit in judgment upon others; rather, our task is to care for each other and for the world in which we live. A parable from the Midrash says:

When the Holy One created the first man, He took him and led him around all the trees of the Garden of Eden and said to him: "Behold my works, how beautiful, how splendid they are. All that I have created, I created for you. Take care, therefore, that you do not destroy the world, for if you do, there will be no one left to repair what you have destroyed." (Midrash, *Ecclesiastes Rabbah*)[8]

CONTEXTUAL THEOLOGY

A defining characteristic of practical theology is that it considers social and cultural context as built in to theology, and not merely as an extraneous factor that we can take or leave, or choose to regard or disregard. In his book *Models of Contextual Theology*, Stephen Bevans notes that "contextualization is not something on the fringes of the theological enterprise." Rather, "It is at the very center of what it means to do theology in today's world. Contextualization is a theological imperative."[9] His book offers numerous examples of the richness of theological reflection that is possible when a people's social and cultural context is engaged rather than ignored. Moreover, he reminds us that theological reflection throughout history has always taken place within particular social and historical contexts. "Even a cursory glance at the history of theology," he writes, "reveals that there has never been a genuine theology that was articulated in an ivory tower with no reference to or dependence on the events, the thought forms, or the culture of its particular time and place."[10]

According to Abraham Heschel, contextual thinking is best served when we become involved and engaged with the context and situation of life, rather than when we assume a posture of neutrality or disinterested detachment. "The attitude of the conceptual thinker is one of detachment: the subject facing an independent object. The attitude of the situational thinker is one of concern: the subject realizing that he is involved in a situation that is in need of understanding."[11]

Put simply, contextual theology means that theology cannot take place in a human vacuum — void of human reference. On the contrary, if the Christian theological principle of the incarnation means anything, it means that divinity and humanity are forever implicated and bound together. Those who think they know God, in isolation from any human consideration, are, as St. John bluntly says, "liars" — "for those who do not love a brother or a sister whom they have seen, cannot love God whom they have not seen" (1 John 4:20).

I often think of Gustavo Gutiérrez, for example. Born in Peru, he grew up in a poor village, and suffered physically as a child with an illness that left him with a permanent limp. Later in his life, he undertook studies for ordination into the Catholic priesthood. He completed his training in Europe, studying the great traditions of Western philosophy and theology. However, when he returned to the barrios of Peru, he found it increasingly difficult to relate his training in classical European theology to the cultural and socioeconomic context of his own people.

He began to read (or reread) the Gospels and the Christian tradition with the eyes of the poor, from the "underside of history," as he says — a side of history that was not well represented in the great halls of European learning. With a stunningly renewed attention to the context of the people of Latin America, who lived their lives in conditions far removed from the universities of Europe, Gutiérrez was able to creatively release the gospel message such that it became indeed good news for the poor. The preferred God of Europe became the God who preferred the poor and the "little ones." It took a Peruvian peasant, born south of the border, to remind those who were schooled in the great traditions of Western Christianity that the gospel is no gospel unless it is also a gospel of justice and liberation.

Practical theology's relationship to culture and context can appear daunting in its complexity. There is a great plurality of human cultural expression, along with a range of social, political, economic, and other contexts to consider. This complexity, however, need not overwhelm us. Rather, it can remind us of the natural richness of human life. It can help us notice the various interconnected domains that come into play when we consider the situations of human life. It can also teach us to reflect on situations and to notice their depth, rather than to jump to simplistic conclusions. An international aid worker writes:

> Complexity doesn't affect me negatively. I'm not cheered by it, I'm not glad it's complicated, but I'm not immobilized by it. Part of me

feels like it's more realistic. I get more depressed by superficiality: people saying, "it's very simple — this is all we need to do." Then I feel there's avoidance coming into play.[12]

The French philosopher Jacques Derrida is well known for his ability to ground his work in the fertile phenomenality of human life. He offers the following reflection on his approach to contextuality:

This is my starting-point: no meaning can be determined out of context, but no context permits saturation.[13]

The first and obvious thing to notice is Derrida's starting point — "no meaning can be determined out of context." This is his starting point because Derrida realizes that he has no other place from which to begin, except the very place in which he finds himself. He must begin from where he is — within his own context. Rather than ignore the very conditions of his life — his situatedness within social and cultural traditions — he affirms these as the starting point from which he and everyone must begin.

Far from detracting from the search for human meaning, context is usually the very thing we turn to when we want a fuller or richer under-standing of the subject before us. We often use the phrase "out of context," for example, to suggest that the meaning of something has been twisted or misconstrued because its context has been ignored. We realize that meanings take their shape and form within context, not out of context. Moreover, we are rarely satisfied with "bare facts." Rather, we like to hear the story behind things, as when we speak, for example, of a person's "life story," which is more than a sketch or an account, but rather a narrative rich in context and meaning. Situating people and events within meaning-ful narratives and contextual frameworks is a "natural" way that humans apprehend the world around them. So it seems quite natural that Derrida would choose to begin with context rather than "out of context."

We should notice, however, that while Derrida says he begins with con-text, he does not say that this is also where he ends, that his starting point takes him no further. Indeed, the second part of his statement suggests that context cannot be the be-all and end-all, the beginning and the end, because *"no context permits saturation."* In other words, we cannot think of context as a huge sponge that soaks up all meaning and value, that absorbs everything into itself, such that nothing else remains. Rather, context also reminds us that *there is always something more that resists being absorbed and assimilated.* There is always a "remainder" that refuses to be soaked up or wiped away.

Derrida is highlighting a certain sting or rub to contextual thinking that is rarely noticed. It is not uncommon, for example, to see the word "contextual" associated with the word "relative." Most of us have encountered the line of reasoning that suggests, "Everything is contextual, therefore everything is relative." However, Derrida is suggesting quite the contrary. He is suggesting that contextual awareness reminds us that there is always something "more than" or "other" that escapes every contextual framework. In other words, contextuality does not lock us into a world of purely immanent or relativized meaning; it also opens us to a world of transcendence. "No context permits saturation," which is to say that no context can soak up all meaning. No context absorbs every truth or determines all that can be said or done. To be aware of context is to be alert to the possibility of this "more than," of that which exceeds and surprises our contextual frameworks, such that there is always more that we can learn, more that we can understand, more that we can do and love in the world.

THEOLOGY AND CULTURE

Prior to the advent of the human sciences such as anthropology and sociology, culture was presumed to be static and normative and based on eternal verities and universal laws. Its opposite was barbarism and primitivism. Culture was equated with Christian European civilization.

This often-unconscious presumption that Western cultural achievements were somehow universal and normative found itself challenged by the newly emerging human sciences, and also by the encounter and engagement with non-Western cultures and religions. In the wake of a colonist mentality that sought to impose European standards across the globe, anthropologists and theologians began questioning the supposed normativity and superiority of Western culture.

The Second Vatican Council, especially in its document *Gaudium et spes* (the Pastoral Constitution dealing with the church in the modern world), initiated a profound shift in this mentality by highlighting the essential relationship between a human person and culture. "It is a fact bearing on the very person of man that he can come to an authentic and full humanity only through culture, that is, through the cultivation of natural goods and values. Wherever human life is involved, therefore, nature and culture are intimately connected" (no. 53). The document goes on to speak of a "plurality of cultures" that are expressions of human creativity and therefore deserve to be treated with respect and dignity.

This attention to the field of human culture was a defining character-istic of Pope John Paul II's papacy. In his travels to various countries, for example, John Paul II's custom was always to honor the local and indige-nous cultures of the lands he visited. "Every culture," he said "is an effort to ponder the mystery of the world and in particular of the human person: it is a way of giving expression to the transcendent dimension of human life."[14] Culture is the fundamental and essential dimension of human existence. "Culture is of humanity, by humanity, and for humanity."[15]

Pope John Paul II was following a deep theme of the Second Vati-can Council, which sought to encourage a "truly human dialogue" with all people of goodwill, so "that through sincere and patient dialogue" we "might learn of the riches which a bountiful God has distributed among the nations of the earth." We are encouraged to establish "re-lationships of respect and love" with cultural and religious traditions, to "uncover with gladness and respect those seeds of the Word which lie hidden among them."[16]

It was from within this newly emerging milieu of respect for human culture that practical theology took shape. Its emphasis on the essential link between faith and culture led to a great enrichment of theology. As David Tracy notes, since Vatican II we have witnessed a myriad of theological forms emerging from "the churches in Latin America, Asia, and Africa; the movements for social and individual emancipation in the centers of Eastern and Central Europe; in feminist theologies throughout the world; in the African-American and Native American theologies of North America; in the rethinking of the indigenous traditions of South and Central America."[17]

This enrichment, however, also brings new challenges and complexities. It is not an easy task to bring theological and cultural reflection together. Those of us who have ever lived in a different culture — encountering a different language, symbols, customs, beliefs — will surely appreciate the fine intricacies of the human cultural web. Indeed, the renowned cultural anthropologist Clifford Geertz compares culture to "webs of significance" that humanity has spun. His oft-cited definition of culture is that it

> denotes an historically transmitted pattern of meanings embodied in symbols, a system of inherited conceptions expressed in symbolic forms by means of which people communicate, perpetuate, and develop their knowledge about and attitudes toward life.[18]

To help us get a better feel for Geertz's definition, I would like to introduce you to Yossi Klein Halevi, an Israeli journalist who embarked on a "pilgrimage" in Israel "to encounter, as an Israeli Jew, my Christian and Muslim neighbors."[19] He recorded his journey in a book titled *At the Entrance to the Garden of Eden*. The following three stories of his encounters exemplify, in very human and poignant ways, some of the essential features of Geertz' rather dense definition of culture.

The Mosque

In the first story, Halevi is with a Jewish friend, Eliyahu, and they are visiting a Sufi mosque led by Sheykh Saud, at the invitation of their Muslim friend, Ibrahim.

> We sat down in a corner. The old men and teenagers pretended we weren't there, while the young boys frankly stared. Ibrahim had obviously neglected to mention to Sheykh Saud that the visitors he was bringing were Jews. We had come to a place where we didn't belong. . . .
> Fortunately, it was time for evening prayers, deflecting the awkwardness of our presence. The men arranged themselves in a straight line, the Islamic assembly of equality before God. To my surprise, Eliyahu simply stepped in. He waved me over, and before I quite realized what was happening, I too joined the Muslim prayer line.
> Ibrahim led the prayers. He shifted me forward and adjusted my shoulders so that I was fully aligned with the line. *"Allahu akbar,"* he called out, God is great, his voice deep and commanding. *"Allaaa-hu,"* he repeated, like a long exhalation, then quickly expelled *"akbar,"* as if any human description of His grandeur was superfluous. Israelis dreaded that call to prayer as incitement to murder: the terrorist's

cry before pressing the detonator on a crowded bus. But Ibrahim restored to those words their benign intensity.

I entered the flow of Muslim surrender, so caught in the rapid hypnotic movement that I forgot my self-consciousness, even forgot to feel elated for having broken the barrier of Islamic prayer. *Allahu akbar:* bow and stand. *Allahu akbar:* kneel and prostrate and kneel. *Allahu akbar:* prostrate and kneel. *Allahu akbar:* stand. And again, over and over, disorienting and reorienting, aligning the self with the prayer line and offering the body to God. *Allahu akbar:* prostrate and kneel. I wanted to remain prostrate, embraced by surrender, but the will of the line pulled me up to my knees. My body lost solidity, as if its bones had been extracted; turning to water, a particle in a wave of prayer.

Halevi then goes on to describe the Sufi prayer dance known as the *zikr:*

The dance began. Once again Eliyahu simply entered and waved me in. The tight circle opened and absorbed me. The two young men with drums stood outside the circle and beat the rhythm, only gradually accelerating. *La illaha ill'Allah*, there is no God but God. *La illaha ill'Allah!* Faster. *Allah-hu!* [Allah is He] Exhale. Twist left, inhale, twist right, exhale. . . .

The circle moved again. *Allah-hu, Allah-hu!* Spinning. Rapid exhalation: *Hu-Hu-Hu-Hu.* God's name merging into breath. . . .

Ibrahim held up a forefinger. *"Wa-had,"* one. Then: *"Eh-had,"* one, in Hebrew. It was a generous and daring nod to Eliyahu and me. The dancers were so focused that they followed Ibrahim's linguistic shift without hestitation, back and forth between Arabic and Hebrew. . . .

The *zikr* lasted perhaps an hour. I felt charged, cleansed, as if I'd been submerged underwater and had learned to breathe in a new way. To my surprise, I felt purged of my unease in this place, at home among the lovers of God. They obviously felt the same way toward me. For the first time, we made eye contact and exchanged smiles. We were at once too exhausted, too energized, and too exposed to hide behind wariness. Even though we didn't know each other's names, we had together inhaled the name of God. . . .

We drank intensely sugared tea, ate baklava, and talked of the sweetness of God. . . .

I asked Saud what he'd experienced during the *zikr*. "That our hearts kept getting closer and closer to God," he said, with the Sufi vagueness I'd so often encountered from Ibrahim. Yet that was as precise a definition of the experience as I needed.

Ibrahim, not to be poetically outdone, added, "Our souls went to heaven like clouds."

"When I first entered," I said, "I felt like a stranger. But now I feel we are brothers."

"When you pray together," said the sheykh's father, "you form one heart."

I felt sad.... Here was an Islam with which we could make peace, yet it was almost absurdly peripheral. Still, maybe the fact that even a handful of Muslims and Jews had danced together was enough for God to work with; perhaps He would magnify our prayers, widen the circle of ecstasy. (102–5)

The story begins by noting the strangeness of the encounter — "we had come to a place where we didn't belong" — suggesting the profound dissonance that can exist between human cultures ("us" and "them"). Yet it ends on the hopeful note that it is possible for humans to discover mutual belonging (to "widen the circle").

It highlights the power of symbolic and ritual forms — the straight line of the Islamic assembly that symbolizes equality before God, the ritual actions of kneeling and prostrating that symbolize surrender before God.

It articulates the centrality of language — the call to prayer and the mantralike chanting of God's name. It also signals the power of language, both in Ibrahim's inclusion of Hebrew along with Arabic to create an atmosphere of hospitality toward the guests, and in the troubling reference to the way many Israelis hear *"Allahu akbar"* — not as a call to prayer, but as the battle cry of a terrorist.

It speaks of one of the most basic and yet intimate expressions of cultural life — sharing food and drink, "sugared tea and baklava," and how humans always seem to discover a sense of communion ("the sweetness of God") when they eat and drink together.

Finally, it demonstrates that we can best understand a different culture, not by standing at a distance and observing or judging it — but by entering as best we can into its historic and symbolic world. "When I first entered, I felt like a stranger. But now I feel we are brothers."

The Church of the Holy Sepulcher

In the second story, Halevi finds himself in the Church of the Holy Sepulcher, after which he meets his friend, Sister Johanna, a Catholic nun.

I found myself inside the Church of the Holy Sepulcher, the Jerusalem shrine Christians revere as the site of Jesus' crucifixion, burial, and resurrection. In my few visits to the site, I'd had difficulty transcending my cultural barriers and appreciating its holiness. Like most Jews, I was put off by the accumulation of icons and statues, the gaudy new dome depicting the sun with thick gold rays, the competing denominations staking rival claims over every inch of sacred space.

And then, unexpectedly, the Holy Sepulcher penetrated me. Became me. The maze of alcoves entered my chest; the cupola fit the contours of my skull. Exhale: expelling darkness from the chest. Inhale: filling the head with light....

I'd grown up recoiling from the idea of even entering a church, which I'd feared as a place of menace; now a church — the ultimate church — had entered me.

Afterward, I met Johanna in the hallway. She looked at me carefully and said, "You're changing, friend. This place is changing you."

"Yes," I replied, "but not in the way you hoped for."

"How do you know what I hope for? What I hope for doesn't matter. Only what God wants...."

"I understand that for you it's inconceivable to reach God without Jesus," I said. "But other people have other ways."

"Maybe the Trinity teaches Christians that you can have distinctions and still be one in God. Maybe there are many roads." She smiled. "You see? I'm changing too." (130–31)

Again, this story highlights the sense of cultural and symbolic dissonance, and Halevi's struggle with "transcending cultural barriers." He notes that for many Jews, the idea of even entering a church is repellent. Yet here he was in this place of gaudiness and "menace" — locked in a battle between two different worlds of "historically transmitted meanings" — a holy site of Christian reverence, and a feared site of Jewish suspicion.

And again, we notice Halevi trying to open himself, to exhale his fears and to inhale the possibility of encountering God.

The story also refers to the central doctrines of Christianity — Jesus' death and resurrection and the Trinity, highlighting the "inherited conceptions of meaning" that Geertz speaks of. Yet it ends by suggesting that even these deep narratives need not be barriers to cultural and religious exchange — they can also open us to a mutual transformation and understanding of one another: "You're changing, friend.... I'm changing too."

Holy Week

The third story describes Halevi's apprehensive journey into the Christian celebration of Holy Week. It is a disturbing story because it shows that, along with authentically human meanings and values, cultures also carry with them disturbing distortions that can perpetuate themselves over many generations. "There is no document of civilization," writes Walter Benjamin, "which is not at the same time a document of barbarism."[20]

How does a Jew approach Holy Week?

Historically, it was a time of Jewish trauma. In my father's home town in Transylvania, Jews would lock themselves in their homes before Easter, hiding from their Christian neighbors, who blamed them personally for the crucifixion. Even for me, growing up in 1960s America...I would cross the street rather than pass my neighborhood's only church just to avoid the crucifix hanging outside, which seemed to me a celebration of Jewish death....

As Holy Week approached, I found myself suspiciously lethargic, unable to choose a Christian community with which to experience the progression from crucifixion to resurrection.... Finally I had to admit: I was afraid of Holy Week.

At lunch with a friend, a Conservative rabbi, I told him about my journey into Christianity and Islam. "How will you handle all those crosses?" he asked. I ignored the implicit rebuke and replied as reasonably as I could that the cross, while obviously not my symbol of devotion, inspired love for God among people whom I loved and respected. "You mean this?" he said, and he took two knives on the table and formed them into a cross. He defined my problem with brutal precision: Intimacy with the cross meant betraying all those Jews who'd been killed in its name.

The Jewish fear of the cross embodied the tragedy of Jewish-Christian relations. Where Christians saw God's love and self-sacrifice, we saw Christianity's crucifixion of the Jews. Until I overcame my lingering fear of the cross . . . my encounter with Christianity would remain blocked. There was no Christianity without crucifixion and resurrection. Yet Holy Week seemed an impenetrable border. Could a Jew really experience anything of Christianity's ultimate moment? . . .

Even among Christians whose denominations had repudiated deicide, its residue surely lingered. A charge that had been integral to Christianity almost since its inception could hardly be erased in a single generation. A Jew in a *kipah* showing up in church on Good Friday was pushing the limits of interfaith tolerance. To open myself to the spirit of Holy Week, I needed to be free of self-consciousness. Yet how could I relax in church if I'd be wondering whether worshippers were looking at me and seeing Judas Iscariot?

I confided my problem to my friend Rebecca, a New Age–style healer in Jerusalem. Rebecca had grown up in a home at once Orthodox and open to other faiths; Christian ministers were frequent guests. And she was an actively identifying Sephardi, descendent of Spanish Jewry, one of the most tolerant religious cultures the Diaspora had produced. If there were any Jew who could help me, I thought, it was Rebecca. But when I mentioned Holy Week, she whispered as if transformed into a Marrano hiding from the Inquisition: "Holy Week was when they burned the Spanish Jews." (137–39)

Halevi's journey is quite extraordinary. It is not easy to open one's heart to other cultures and traditions, especially when these exist in a fulcrum of tension and suspicion, and in a land that too often erupts into violence and hatred. Indeed, at the conclusion of his journey, Halevi's narrative descends into heart-wrenching sadness as a new round of violence prevents him from maintaining contact with his Muslim and Christian friends. After a suicide bombing that leads to a new tightening of borders between Israelis and Palestinians, Halevi calls his friend, Ibrahim:

> The voice that greeted me was thin and remote; he sounded like a man on his death-bed. . . .
> "Welcome, my brother," he said in English, avoiding Hebrew, perhaps out of fear. "I miss you, my brother. Are you safe? I pray to my God every night to stop the fire and help us to make forgiveness. . . . "
> "This is the time of the fanatics," he continued. "I am crying all the night, but the angels last week they promised me, 'Don't worry, the peace is coming.' The angels tell me that the future is for us, the peacemakers."
> *"Inshallah,"* I said.
> "Thank you, my brother, See you again."
> But I couldn't imagine when that might be. (313)

Halevi longs for Eden, the original garden, the garden of peace. He has experienced a foretaste of this garden, but now a profound sense of sadness fills his soul: "I stood at the entrance and glimpsed the garden, but that was all" (311).

"THE FIELD IS THE WORLD"

The Gospels frequently describe the kingdom of God in terms of small and humble beginnings — mustard seeds, yeast and leaven, the widow's mite, sprouting shoots, gatherings of two or three, praying in secret, treasures stored in the heart.

The struggles of ordinary and yet hope-filled people, like Halevi and Ibrahim and Joanna, are never too far removed from the yearning for peace, for *shalom* and well-being, for the coming of God's kingdom, "on earth as it is in heaven." *Inshallah* — "with God's help."

When Jesus spoke about the kingdom of God, he often compared it to the sowing of seeds. "The field is the world," he said (Matt. 13:38), and he warned against uprooting the weeds before the seeds take root, "for in gathering the weeds you would uproot the wheat along with them" (Matt. 13:29).

If we want to sow the seeds of God's kingdom, then we must sow them in the world. And we must nurture them, even (and especially) when we sense that the garden is about to be overtaken by weeds.

Toward the end of his journey, Halevi speaks of "the beautiful teachings of faith" he learned from his Christian and Muslim friends. "More than ever," he says, "the goal of a spiritual life in the Holy Land is to live with an open heart at the center of unbearable tension" (314). He realizes that he will never fully weed out all of his fears and suspicions and darkening doubts. "The best I can say is that I am struggling, and that maintaining a painful awareness of the gap between what I've been taught and my inability to embody those teachings defines my spiritual life" (314). He recognizes that even though there are weeds to contend with, it is the patient nurturing of fragile shoots that requires most of his care and attention, lest they be choked by the ever-recurring violence of a heedless world.

It is often difficult to see and attend to the seeds of goodness that are being sown in the world, especially when these seeds seem so small and fragile.

The kingdom of God is as if someone would scatter seed on the ground, and would sleep and rise night and day, and the seed would sprout and grow. . . . (Mark 4:26–27)

It is like a mustard seed, which, when sown upon the ground, is the smallest of all the seeds on earth. . . . (Mark 4:31)

Our attention to these small and tender shoots can often be overwhelmed by the weeds that seem to be constantly choking us. Of course, we would be foolish to ignore the weeds. We need a critical awareness that can alert us to the workings of injustice and ignorance. Yet we also need an appreciative or compassionate awareness that can awaken us to the presence of God, to the workings of grace and goodness. "Do not harden your hearts" (Ps. 95:8) — which is perhaps to say, don't let your hearts become worn down by heaviness and despair, or closed up in doubt and suspicion; rather "lift up your hearts" and see the goodness of God.

There is much we can learn from Yossi Halevi's story. To be aware of one's own culture, and to seek a deeper awareness and understanding of other cultural expressions, is crucial to practical theology. "If culture is where human beings become more human," writes Michael Paul Gallagher, "and if different cultures represent different ways of facing the question of the meaning of human existence, then the whole future of humanity is intimately linked with whatever happens in the field of culture."[21]

Halevi opened his heart to those who were strangers to him, even though they lived within the same land. He purposefully and patiently sought to learn from his Christian and Muslim brothers and sisters. He exposed himself to the religious and cultural tensions that have shaped the historical and political landscape of Israel and the Palestinian territory. He wrestled with his own cultural assumptions and with the cultural assumptions of others.

"The one enduring transformation that I carry with me," he writes, "is that I learned to venerate — to love — Christianity and Islam. . . . The cross and the minaret became for me cherished symbols of God's presence, reminders that He speaks to us in multiple languages — that He speaks to us at all" (314).

The efforts of Halevi and his friends, it seems, transformed themselves into a labor of love — "The harvest is plentiful, but the laborers are few" (Matt. 9:37).

TEN

Justice and Mercy
at the Gates of the City

I doubt I've come across a more apt and yet starkly evident description of the world than the one offered by Pope Paul VI in his encyclical *Populorum Progressio: On the Development of Peoples*, where he writes: "The world is sick" (no. 66). Jesus made a similar pronouncement when he was accused of dining with tax collectors and sinners — I have come for "those who are sick," he said (Matt. 9:12). There is perhaps no better rationale than these words for a practical theology that takes seriously the lack of well-being in the world. Indeed, practical theology is typically associated with the quest for justice and liberation, with the plight of the poor and the oppressed, with the need to address the social, political, and economic realities that shape the lives of millions of human beings who are too often left to suffer the sickness of the world. But what does it mean when Jesus says that he has come for those who are sick, and then he adds, "Go and learn what this means, 'I desire mercy, not sacrifice'" (v. 13). There is a strange connection here between the sickness of the world and the desire for mercy. "Go and learn what this means" — this is the task set before us in this chapter.

THE GOLDEN GATE

The walled city of Jerusalem has several large gates that allow access to the city. Yet there is one gate along its eastern wall that remains closed. It is called the "Golden Gate" and is one of the oldest and most beautiful gates of the city (referred to in Acts 3:2 as the "Beautiful Gate"). When I

175

lived in Jerusalem, I became fascinated by this gate. I can recall sitting on the Mount of Olives, overlooking Jerusalem, and gazing at this ancient city with its mysterious gate that has been sealed for hundreds of years.

I learned that the gate is shrouded in legend and holiness. Unlike the other gates of the city, this one has two large, arched doorways supported by wide columns. According to Jewish tradition, one of the doorways is known as the "Gate of Mercy" and the other as the "Gate of Repentance." Centuries ago, the Jewish people would pray in front of this gate, which faces the Temple area. They would first pray at the Gate of Repentance, and then turn to pray at the Gate of Mercy. According to Christian tradition, Jesus made his last entry into Jerusalem through the Mercy Gate (Matt. 21:1–11). In the Middle Ages, Arabic literature referred to this gate as the gate of Eternal Life.

While the other gates to the city remain open and allow for the comings and goings of people, Jewish tradition holds that this gate will remain closed until the coming of the Messiah, who will enter Jerusalem from the east (Ezek. 44:1–2). It stands as a symbol that the earthly city has not yet achieved the justice and the peace of the heavenly city.

Sitting on the Mount of Olives, I often felt pained at the sight of this beautiful and ancient city that is also troubled and torn by conflict. I remembered how Jesus also once wept over the city (Luke 19:41). The beautiful Golden Gate stared back at me, with its sealed archways, a reminder that the troubled ways of humanity have not yet achieved the lasting peace of God. And I remembered the vision of St. John: "I saw the holy city, the new Jerusalem" (Rev. 21:2). "Its gates will never be shut by day — and there will be no night there" (v. 25). Perhaps St. John was dreaming of a time when the doors of the Golden Gate will finally open, and "God will dwell with them as their God; they will be his peoples, and God himself will be with them; he will wipe every tear from their eyes. Death will be no more; mourning and crying and pain will be no more..." (vv. 3–4).

THE GATES OF THE CITY

The biblical writings contain many references to the gates of the city. The hospitality of the ancient city was extended to the stranger by meeting them at the gate (Gen. 19:1–2). Public markets were typically held at the gate (2 Kings 7:1), as its surrounding spaces were kept wide to allow for the movement and traffic of people, unlike the narrow and winding streets inside the city. The city gate was also the place of justice where the elders sat as a court. "Hate evil and love good, and establish justice at the city gate" (Amos 5:15; see also Job 31:21; Deut. 21:19; 25:17; Prov. 21:23).

Our word for politics is derived from the Greek word for "city" — *polis*. The metaphor of the "city gate" still functions as a striking image for us today. Just as the ancients once gathered at their city gates to conduct public affairs, politics retains this concern for participating in and promoting our shared life together. The task of establishing justice and offering hospitality at the gates of our cities (and our nations) remains as vital today as it did in biblical times. "For I know how many are your transgressions," the prophet Amos cries, "and how great are your sins — you who afflict the righteous and push aside the needy at the gate" (Amos 5:12).

In his encyclical *Octogesima Adveniens: A Call to Action*, Pope Paul VI tells us that we are responsible for "the good of the city" (no. 46), for the common good and for the welfare of the city:

> To build up the city, the place where humanity and their expanded communities exist, to create new modes of neighborliness and relationships, to perceive an original application of social justice and to undertake responsibility for this collective future, which is foreseen as difficult, is a task which Christians must share.... Let Christians, conscious of this new responsibility, not lose heart in view of the vast and faceless society; let them recall Jonah who traversed Niniveh, the great city, to proclaim therein the good news of God's mercy.... In the Bible, the city is often the place of sin and pride — the pride of man who feels secure enough to be able to build his life without God and even to affirm that he is powerful against God. But there is also the example of Jerusalem, the Holy City, the place where God is encountered, the promise of the city which comes from on high. (no. 12)

According to Michael Cowan and Bernard Lee, "God desires a social world characterized by justice and mercy," and the Christian community is "under biblical obligation to order our internal and our public life on behalf of the reign of God in history."[1] They evoke a passage from Jeremiah

who speaks of the "well being" or *shalom* of the city: "Seek the well being
of the city . . . for in its well being you will find your well being" (Jer. 29:7).
Shalom is a word that is rich in biblical meaning. "*Shalom* is the peace that
emerges when human beings are in right relationship with themselves,
their neighbors, the earth and all its creatures, and God."² "For we are
members of one another" (Eph. 4:25), St. Paul says, and the well-being
of one affects the well-being of all — "if one member suffers, all suffer
together with it" (1 Cor. 12:26).

Humans are primarily social beings, which means we are bound together. Yet while we seek fraternity and friendship, there is a troubling
sense in which we live in "gated communities," such that much of our collective existence is marked by what happens at our gates. We do not dwell
together in complete openness; rather, we dwell together via a network
of doorways that continually open and close. Hardly a day goes by where
we do not pass through doors of one kind or another — the doors of our
homes, the doors of our offices, the doors of supermarkets, the doors of
employment, the doors of airports, the doors of schools and universities,
the doors of hospitals and clinics, the doors of churches and temples, the
doors of business and government and law — doors that continually open
and close in an effort to monitor those who have access and those who are
denied. Each of these doorways represents the *shalom*, or well-being, of
the city; they represent the entrance of God's "Peace on Earth," as articulated by Pope John XXIII: access to a dignified life and a worthy standard
of living, access to cultural values and the dignity of personhood, access
to health care and education, to employment and decent working conditions, to freedom of association and freedom of movement, to praise
and worship of God, to participation in the city's life and to the common
good (*Pacem in Terris: Peace on Earth*, 8–38).

"BEFORE THE LAW"

It is in the gates of our cities that the task of social justice and the achievement of social good are either served or blocked. There are many persons
who stand at the gate, many who seek admittance, and many who spend
even their entire lives seeking entrance to the gateways that characterize
the *polis*.

In a very telling story titled "Before the Law," Franz Kafka suggests that at every gate there stands a doorkeeper, and that before this gate there is one who seeks permission to enter.

Before the Law stands a doorkeeper. To this doorkeeper there comes a man from the country and prays for admittance to the Law. But the doorkeeper says he cannot grant admittance at the moment. The man thinks it over and then asks if he will be allowed in later. "It is possible," the doorkeeper says, "but not at the moment." Since the gate stands open, as usual, and the doorkeeper steps to one side, the man stoops to peer through the gateway into the interior. Observing that, the doorkeeper laughs and says: "If you are so drawn to it, just try to go in despite my veto. But take note: I am powerful. And I am only the least of the doorkeepers. From hall to hall there is one doorkeeper after another, each more powerful than the last. . . ." These are difficulties the man from the country has not expected; the Law, he thinks, should surely be accessible at all times and to everyone. . . . The doorkeeper gives him a stool and lets him sit down at one side of the door. There he sits for days and for years. He makes many attempts to be admitted, and wearies the doorkeeper by his importunity. The doorkeeper frequently has little interviews with him, asking him questions about his home and many other things, but the questions are put indifferently, as great lords put them, and always finish with the statement that he cannot be let in yet. . . . During these many years the man fixes his attention almost continuously on the doorkeeper. He forgets the other doorkeepers, and this first one seems to him the sole obstacle preventing access to the Law. He curses his bad luck, in his early years boldly and loudly; later, as he grows old, he only grumbles to himself. He becomes childish, and since in his yearlong contemplation of the doorkeeper he has come to know even the fleas in his fur collar, he begs the fleas as well to help him and to change the doorkeeper's mind. At length his eyesight begins to fail, and he does not know whether the world is really darker or whether his eyes are only deceiving him. Yet in his darkness he is now aware of a radiance that streams inextinguishably from the gateway of the Law. Now he has not very long to live. Before he dies, all his experiences in these long years gather themselves in his head to one point, a question he has not yet asked the doorkeeper. He waves him nearer, since he can no longer raise his stiffening body. The doorkeeper has to bend low before him, for the difference in height between them has altered much to the man's disadvantage. "What do you want now?" asks the doorkeeper; "you are insatiable." "Everyone strives to reach the Law," says the man, "so how does it happen that for all these many years no one but myself has begged for admittance?" The doorkeeper recognizes that the man has reached his end, and, to let his failing senses catch the words, roars in his ear: "No one else could ever be admitted here, since this gate was made only for you. I am now going to shut it."[3]

The Law, which serves justice, is meant for everyone. It is meant to radiate its light for the good of all — a justice that is a *social justice* that serves the common good. Yet Kafka suggests that the Law must deal with each singular person — case by case — and in this sense the gate of the Law is not simply for everyone, but for each and every particular person — "for you alone." The Law is of no use to "everyone" unless it can be of particular use to *someone*. The Law's universal reach often fails to reach each and every person who seeks access to justice. In this sense, whenever there is one who has been denied access to the Law, then the Law has failed to serve justice's universal claims.

When Martin Luther King delivered his "I Have a Dream" speech, he stood before the Lincoln Memorial in Washington, D.C., one of the country's key symbolic gateways of justice and the *polis*. He cited the Law — "that all men, yes, black men as well as white men, would be guaranteed the unalienable rights of life, liberty, and the pursuit of happiness."[4] The Law is meant to serve justice and the well-being of all, and yet "the life of the Negro is still sadly crippled by the manacles of segregation and the chains of discrimination . . . the Negro still lives on a lonely island of poverty . . . the Negro is still languished in the corners of American society and finds himself in exile in his own land" (217).

Dr. King is claiming the Law's universality — it is for the well-being of all people — yet he makes his appeal for *this particular people* — the "Negro" who stands before the Law, seeking justice. For more than "one hundred years" African Americans have been denied access to justice by the gatekeepers of the Law. Many have spent their whole lives seeking admittance, and many have died outside its gates. Dr. King speaks on their behalf, coming to their defense before the Law. And while the Law radiates its promise (King calls it a "promissory note"), he has come to the gateway of the nation's capital "to cash a check," and he says that the check has come back with "insufficient funds" (217). The check is void; the gate is shut, and there is "no admittance" to the nation's Law that promises life, liberty, and well-being for all. And yet King has a dream that "one day every valley shall be exalted, every hill and mountain shall be made low, the rough places shall be made plain, and the crooked places shall be made straight and the glory of the Lord will be revealed and all flesh shall see it together" (219). He dreams of that day when the nation will be transformed into a "beautiful symphony" of brotherhood and sisterhood. He dreams of that bright day when the Golden Gate will open its doors "into the palace of justice" (218).

For the biblical prophets, the gates of heaven can never be closed to the gates of the city. God tells Jeremiah to "stand at the gate of the Lord's house, and proclaim there this word.... You that enter these gates to worship the Lord... Amend your ways and your doings, and let me dwell with you in this place.... If you do not oppress the alien, the orphan, and the widow... then I will dwell with you in this place..." (Jer. 7:2–7). Commenting on this passage, Gustavo Gutiérrez notes that Jeremiah "makes it perfectly clear that until there is a commitment to the rights of the poor, God will not dwell with them in the temple; God is absent because the people do not practice justice, especially towards the weakest among them."[5]

It is to the guardians of the Law that Jesus says, "You shut up the kingdom of heaven in men's faces, neither going in yourselves nor allowing others to go in who want to" (Matt. 23:13, JB). Many of Jesus' parables and many of his actions were concerned with defending those whose access to justice was denied, those who were left standing outside the gates of the Law, those who were cast off from the promises of God's kingdom — the excluded, the accused, the debarred, the victims, the least, the poor, the disadvantaged. It is for these that the Law exists — "the Sabbath was made for humankind" (Mark 2:27) — and yet it is often these whom the Law leaves waiting and languishing at its gates. Instead of being the "preferred ones" before the Law — the ones whose claims are most urgent, the ones who suffer injustice and a lack of well-being —

they are too often treated as "the least" before the Law. In the kingdom of heaven, however, it is these "least" and "last" who are of special concern to God, who receive the "preferential love of God." As Jesus says on another occasion to the gatekeepers of the Law, "the tax collectors and the prostitutes are going into the kingdom of God ahead of you" (Matt. 21:31).

God's "preferential option for the poor" challenges our notion of the Law's presumed impartiality and equality, often symbolized as a blind-folded woman ("Lady Justice") who sees no distinctions between people, and who holds a set of scales that balances everything with perfect equi-librium. By contrast, the biblical kingdom favors the poor and criticizes the rich, which is a great joy to Jesus' mother, Mary. "My soul magnifies the Lord," she sings, "for he has scattered the proud in the thoughts of their hearts. He has brought down the powerful from their thrones, and lifted up the lowly; he has filled the hungry with good things and sent the rich away empty" (Luke 1:51–54).

Citing John Paul II, the U.S. bishops note that the option for the poor is "a call to have a special openness with the small and the weak, those that suffer and weep, those that are humiliated and left on the margin of society, so as to help them win their dignity as human persons and children of God" (*Economic Justice for All*, no. 87). They go on to say that the option for the poor is not a pitting of one group over another; rather, "it states that the deprivation and powerlessness of the poor wounds the whole community. The extent of their suffering is the measure of how far we are from being a true community of persons" (no. 88).

The poor are always in our midst. They are not only the "economically poor," but all those "who cannot cope" and who find themselves suddenly burdened or stricken for one reason or another — the unemployed worker, the single parent, the illegal immigrant, those overwhelmed by debt, or evicted by the landlord, or arrested on the streets. It is these who are members of the *polis* — who stand at our city gates, seeking justice — and yet who are often most ignored. According to Gutiérrez, "the poor are non-persons, the *in-significant*, those who do not count in society and all too often in Christian churches as well." He goes on to say: "We do not know the names of the poor; they are anonymous and remain so. They are insignificant in society *but not before God*."[6]

There are many who do not count "before the Law," but they do count "before God." If there are any among us who find ourselves serving as gatekeepers of the Law, then our task is to help those who come before us to gain access to justice — to life and liberty and well-being, to the *shalom* of the city. If we are teachers, if we are pastors, if we are health-care workers, if we are lawyers, if we are in positions of authority, if we are business leaders, if we are shopkeepers, if we are police officers, if we are public servants, if we are parents or neighbors or citizens — if we are members of one another — then we need to ensure that everyone who comes our way is enabled access to dignity and justice in all the gates of our city.

JUSTICE AND MERCY

It is difficult to be a "gatekeeper," especially when this requires us to mediate between the demands of justice and the petition for mercy. There is much that is unjust in our society, yet I have often wondered whether it is the lack of mercy that causes injustice to prevail. Or rather, that without mercy, justice is perilously close to becoming unjust. This had led me to believe that mercy is not the opposite of justice — or the complement of justice — but its very condition.

Others have taught me that it is not so much a lack of mercy that causes injustice; rather, it is a lack of attention to social sin. Injustice requires collective actions to address social and structural factors that perpetuate suffering in society. While we need "acts of charity" to serve the immediate needs of those who suffer the effects of social injustice, we also need "acts of justice" to transform the root causes of injustice that are systemic ills embedded in economic and political arrangements. While it is good to perform acts of charity for the poor, providing direct services such as food, clothing, and shelter, it is also good to seek to change the structures that create poverty and hardship.

An earlier Christian tradition speaks of a different distinction, not between justice and charity, but between "corporal works of mercy" and "spiritual works of mercy" (*Catechism*, no. 2447). The seven corporal works of mercy are based on the passage from Isaiah that speaks of "the fasting that pleases God" (Isa. 58:6–10) and Jesus' parable of the Last Judgment (Matt. 25:34–40). The corporal works of mercy are very similar to what we call today "acts of charity"—to feed the hungry, to give drink to the thirsty, to clothe the naked, to shelter the homeless, to visit the sick, to visit those in prison, to bury the dead. The spiritual works of mercy are to admonish the sinner, to instruct the ignorant, to counsel the doubtful, to comfort the sorrowful, to bear wrongs patiently, to forgive all injuries and to pray for the living and the dead.

The overarching motif is that our works are best described as works of mercy. So, what of justice? Wherever we find people who lack basic human rights that are rooted in their very dignity as human persons, then justice is *owing*. Justice is a debt that we owe to those who have been denied the well-being of human flourishing. Justice serves the *common good* and not simply the good of a few. St. John Chrysostom writes: "Not to enable the poor to share in our goods is to steal from them and deprive them of life. The goods we possess are not ours, but theirs" (*Catechism*, no. 2446). The beggar on the street is not asking for a handout; the beggar is asking why we have stolen so much.[7] When we attend to those who are in need, we are not giving them what is ours; rather, we are giving them what is theirs—"we are paying a debt of justice" (*Catechism*, no. 2446).

Justice is what we *owe* and places us in debt, though it is not uncommon to hear people saying that the beggar on the street has already received their just deserts, that they are on the street because of a fault that they bear, and that should we decide to give them anything, then we consider it an act of charity—giving them something that belongs to us—rather than a debt of justice, giving them something that belongs to them.

We do not typically feel *in debt* to the beggar or to those who sit at our gates. And yet in his encyclical *Sollicitudo Rei Socialis: On Social Concern*, Pope John Paul II notes that "at stake is the *dignity of the human person*, whose *defense* and *promotion* have been entrusted to us by the Creator, and to whom the men and women at every moment in history are strictly and responsibly *in debt*" (no. 47). In one of Jesus' most haunting parables, we find ourselves face-to-face with this debt. "There was a rich man who was dressed in purple and fine linen and who feasted sumptuously every day. And at his gate lay a poor man named Lazarus, covered with sores, who longed to satisfy his hunger with what fell from the rich man's table..." (Luke 16:19–21). The poor man dies and is carried away by angels to be with Abraham. The rich man dies and is sent to Hades where he is tormented by scorching flames. The rich man begs Abraham for mercy.

But Abraham replies, "Child, remember that during your lifetime you received your good things, and Lazarus in like manner evil things; but now he is comforted here, and you are in agony" (v. 25). Justice is served. The debt is paid. Here we are face-to-face with the debt of justice pure and simple, exacting and unrelenting: Once you were rich and comfortable, now you are in agony. Once you neglected the cries of the suffering, now your own cries are neglected. Moreover, the severity of justice is such that "a great chasm has been fixed" so that none can cross from the fires of justice into the balm of mercy. It is a terrifying scene, repeated in the Letter of St. James:

> Come now, you rich people, weep and wail for the miseries that are coming to you. Your riches have rotted, and your clothes are moth-eaten. Your gold and silver have rusted, and their rust will be evidence against you, and it will eat your flesh like fire. Listen! The wages of the laborers who mowed your fields, which you kept back by fraud, cry out, and the cries of the harvesters have reached the ears of the Lord of hosts. You have lived on earth in luxury and pleasure; you have fattened your hearts in a day of slaughter. (5:1–5)

The prophet Amos warns us not to be too quick to long for the day of justice. "Alas for you who desire the day of the Lord! Why do you want the day of the Lord? It is darkness, not light; as if someone fled from a lion, and was met by a bear; or went into the house ... and was bitten by a snake. Is not the day of the Lord darkness, not light, and gloom with no brightness in it?" (5:18–20).

We should be wary of evoking the word "justice" too readily, especially when we consider Jesus' words, "Let anyone among you who is without sin be the first to throw a stone ... " (John 8:7). "It might seem strange to say this," writes Gutiérrez, "but justice can become an idol."[8] We can all too easily think that we are acting justly, that our laws are just, that our society is just, that the guilty are rightfully judged, the poor are taken care of, and the accused are justly locked away. We can turn justice into an idol, bowing to the civilized rule of law, trumpeting our own righteousness, parading our supposed freedom and democracy for all to see and to admire. "God, I thank you that I am not like the other people" (Luke 18:11). If we have this attitude, Jesus says, we will not find favor in God's sight, but if we pray, "God, be merciful to me, a sinner," God will look with favor upon us.

In his encyclical letter *Dives in Misericordia: Rich in Mercy*, John Paul II notes that "human action can deviate from justice itself, even when it is being undertaken in the name of justice" (no. 12). We can easily deceive ourselves into thinking that we are acting justly and, for this reason, John Paul II suggests that without mercy, justice cannot be established. Justice alone is not enough. It can even lead to the negation and destruction of itself if it is not tempered by mercy. The pope refers to the ancient saying, *summum ius, summa iniuria* (no. 12), which can be translated as "the more justice, the more injury" or "the more law, the less justice."[9] Justice requires mercy to ensure that our practices of judgment and justice are not harsh or severe, so that we can act *humanely* with tolerance and restraint, "bearing with one another in love" (Eph. 4:2). The pope writes:

> Society can become ever more human only if we introduce into the many-sided setting of interpersonal and social relationships, not merely justice, but also that "merciful love" which constitutes the messianic message of the Gospel.... A world from which forgiveness was eliminated would be nothing but a world of cold and unfeeling justice, in the name of which each person would claim his or her own rights vis-à-vis others; the various kinds of selfishness latent in man would transform life and human society into an arena of permanent strife between one group and another. (no. 14)

Many of Jesus' parables are scandalous and irritating because they offend our human sense of justice as fairness, equality, and rights. "For the kingdom of heaven is like a landowner who went out early in the morning to hire laborers for his vineyard. After agreeing with the laborers for the usual daily wage, he sent them into the vineyard" (Matt. 20:1–2). That seems fair and just. But the story continues. Toward the end of the day, the landowner sees some workers who have not been hired, and so he says, "You also go into the vineyard." The workers are then called to receive their wages. Those who came first and spent a whole day working in the field receive the same wages as those who came last and spent only an hour working in the field. The workers who came first are scandalized at the injustice of it all, saying, "These last worked only one hour, and you have made them equal to us who have borne the burden of the day and the scorching heat" (v. 12). The landowner replies that he has paid them what they agreed to, and that surely he can be generous to the other workers if it pleases him. Our notions of equality and justice can often be offended by acts of generosity. The parable of the prodigal son and the disgruntled brother (Luke 15:11–32) makes a similar point — God is gracious and "rich in mercy" (Eph. 2:4).

Perhaps the most telling parable concerning the relationship between justice and mercy is the parable of the unmerciful servant (Matt. 18:23–35). In this parable, the kingdom of heaven is like a king who is collecting debts from his servants. One of the servants owes him ten thousand talents (note, this is an enormous debt; one talent is worth about fifteen years of labor). The servant cannot pay and so the king orders that the servant, his wife, his children and all his possessions be sold. The servant falls to his knees and begs for mercy, and out of pity for him, the king releases him and forgives all his debt. The servant then meets someone who owes him a small amount and demands that just repayment be made. His fellow servants are scandalized that he is demanding justice after having himself received mercy. They report his actions to the king who decides that the servant will now be subjected to the demands of justice, handing him over to be tortured until he pays his entire debt. Jesus concludes the parable with these haunting words, "So my heavenly Father will also do to every one of you, if you do not forgive your brother or sister from your heart" (v. 35).

THE GATES OF MERCY AND REPENTANCE

In the early 1980s Poland was torn by conflict and violence. The Polish composer, Henryk Górecki, responded to the tragic events with his symphony for voice titled *Miserere*. Its unaccompanied form consists of a text of only five words — "Domine Deus noster, Miserere nobis" — "Lord our God, have mercy on us." Over an extraordinarily beautiful and sustained span of some twenty-five minutes, the voices rise and fall with their plaintive and lamenting appeal — "Domine Deus noster." These three words fill the main body of the work, repeated over and over again in waves of choral voice — "Domine Deus noster" — "Lord our God," "Lord our God," "Lord our God." The final words, "Miserere nobis" (Have mercy on us), are saved until the concluding three minutes. It is as if Górecki senses the long, suffering cries of the human heart, pleading to God in the midst of so much heedless violence and human hatred, only to finally surrender in the last moments to the mercy of God. "Something of a sigh of mercy, of compassion, is hidden in the deepest depths of reality," writes Edward Schillebeeckx, "and in it believers hear the name of God."[10]

God's mercy is "from generation to generation" (Luke 1:50) and "showing mercy is, despite everything, the deepest purpose that God intends to fulfill in history."[11] According to the Canadian theologian Heather Chappell, mercy is at the heart of reality, at the heart of God, and at the heart of the gospel message proclaimed by Jesus. Mercy is a rich and deeply layered word:

Mercy towards suffering: an affective response that seeks to actively relieve someone's distress; a charity influenced by a softening or a change of mind and heart; an inclining of the heart toward another; compassion toward another's pain.

Mercy towards sin: forgiveness and clemency; the gift of release, yielding, staying the hand against someone; a letting go, a setting free.

Mercy as a surprise blessing: unexpected leniency; the gift of tolerance, forbearance, restraint, moderation, mildness; a disposition against all strictness and severity; a kindly refraining from the infliction of punishment or pain; a blessing regarded as an act of divine favor or compassion.[12]

Mercy is not simply something that we "feel" or "offer" to another. Rather, "mercy *requires something of us:* that we relent, that we change our mind and heart, that we give up a previous understanding of another, that we release them from the bondage of our preconception, and finally that we stoop down and bear with them in their suffering."[13] Mercy therefore contains within itself the movement of repentance, conversion, or *metanoia.* "Be merciful, just as your Father is merciful" (Luke 6:36).

If we know that we are sinful and wretched, and yet God has dealt kindly with us, then we should deal kindly with others. If we have experienced God's "amazing grace," then we should be no less amazing in our actions toward one another. If we have felt the generosity of God's love, then we should extend this generosity in everything we say and do. If we truly believe in the "glad tidings" of the gospel, then our lives should also be good news for others. Schillebeeckx writes:

God's merciful dealing — demonstrated clearly in Jesus' own compassion for people — must be exemplary for anyone who wishes
to enter the kingdom of God. . . . For since God's lordship is the
universal, compassionate disposition of God towards humanity, the
metanoia demanded by the kingdom takes concrete form in empathy
with and dedicated commitment to one's fellow human beings.[14]

Mercy and *metanoia* are intimately linked. It is because we know the
"gate of mercy" that we are able to pray at "the gate of repentance."
Without the offer of mercy, repentance would be futile. To confess our sin,
to change our ways, to repent of our wrongdoing, to turn to our neighbor
with compassion, are possible only if we know that mercy, rather than
condemnation, awaits us at the gate of repentance. We are all trespassers
before God and before each other, and without mercy there would be no
hope for any of us. It is only within the context of mercy that deep and
practical *metanoia* is possible. As Chappell notes, "In all conversions from
suffering to hope, from sin to release, and from despair to faith, mercy is
the effective element which offers a future and enables change."[15] Only
mercy can transform "hearts of stone" into "hearts of flesh" (Ezek. 36:26).

"THE LITTLE ACT OF GOODNESS"

"Politics left to itself," writes Emmanuel Levinas, "bears a tyranny within
itself; it deforms the I and the other who have given rise to it, for it judges
them according to universal rules, and thus *in absentia*."[16] As Kafka's
parable suggests, the workings and determinations of justice are often
conducted in the great halls of the law, in the manner of a "politics left
to itself" and its own devices, as though politics had no other concern
than its own concern, whereas all the time it should be concerned with
the well-being of the *polis* and the common good. And all too often, rules
and legislation and judgments are made in the absence of the one who
stands outside — "in absentia" — as though the law didn't really care about
those left standing outside its gates, whereas all the time it is meant to be
concerned for the welfare of all, even and especially for the least of all.

Left to itself, the wheels of politics and the laws of justice can turn
with unrelenting power. "Every attempt to organize humanity fails," writes
Levinas.[17] Many a system has been tried, and many a system has failed. Even

the much-lauded system of "democracy" has not yet achieved what it seeks, as Martin Luther King's speech in Washington, D.C., powerfully attests.

"Is there a need to stress the possible ambiguity of every social ideology?" asks Pope Paul VI. He continues:

> Sometimes it leads political or social activity to be simply the application of an abstract, purely theoretical idea. . . . There is also the danger of giving adherence to an ideology which does not rest on a true and organic doctrine, to take refuge in it as a final and sufficient explanation of everything, and thus to build a new idol, accepting, at times without being aware of doing so, its totalitarian and coercive character. And people imagine they find in it a justification for their activity, even violent activity, and an adequate response to a desire to serve. The desire remains but it allows itself to be consumed by an ideology which, even if it suggests certain paths to man's liberation, ends up by making him a slave. (*Octogesima Adveniens: A Call to Action*, nos. 27–28)

Paul VI worries that "politics left to itself" holds the inherent danger, even under the banner of a desire to serve, of turning the law and politics into an idol. Even democracy can be turned into an idol as, for example, the way it is currently invoked by those who seek a justification for the war on terror. Violence can spread even in the name of democracy and freedom, especially if these are taken as "a final and sufficient explanation of everything." Paul VI offers the following caution: "Politics are a demanding manner — but not the only one — of living the Christian commitment to service to others. . . . The domain of politics is wide and comprehensive, but it is not exclusive. An attitude of encroachment which would tend to set up politics as an absolute value would bring serious danger" (*A Call to Action*, nos. 46).

This is a concern that Levinas also shares, for he has personally witnessed and suffered the dangers of social and political systems that can all too easily assume the tyranny of coercive and totalitarian practices. Collective structures always harbor a tendency to forget or exclude or oppress the very relation that "gives rise" to political activity, namely, the "I and the other" of human fraternity and ethical responsibility. Levinas's insistence on the face-to-face relation is not an apolitical stance; rather, it is the very prompting of a transformed conception of politics and society, one that keeps before us the fundamental responsibility of the ethical relation, the face of the human other that is irreducible to any form of totalizing politics.[18]

"Left to itself," politics "deforms the I and the other." In other words, the ethical relation must continually inspire the social and political order. Paul VI writes:

> Human rights are still too often disregarded, if not scoffed at, or else they receive only formal recognition. In many cases legislation does not keep up with real situations. Legislation is necessary, but it is not sufficient for setting up true relationships of justice and equality.... If beyond legal rules, there is no deeper feeling of respect for and service to others, then even equality before the law can serve as an alibi for fragrant discrimination, continued exploitation, and actual contempt. (*A Call to Action,* no. 23)

One of the cardinal points of Catholic social teaching is that the human person "is the foundation, cause, and end of all social institutions" (*Mater et Magistra: Christianity and Social Progress,* 219). The "beginning, the subject, and the goal of all social institutions is and must be the human person" (*A Call to Action,* no. 14).

In other words, while we must necessarily attend to the social fabric of our institutional structures, political administrations, and judicial systems, we must recognize that all these social institutions are not so much the *foundation* or basis of ethical relations, but the *consequences* or "guardianships" of the more originary ethical relation that comes to us, not from our well-constructed social theories or ethical codes, but from the fundamental relationship of the "I and the other." If our social and political frameworks are not directed toward or inspired by this fundamental ethical relation, then our "collective measures lose their human meaning because they have forgotten or masked real faces and real speech. This forgetfulness is the beginning of tyranny."[19]

The true aim of all social and political activity "should be to help individual members of the social body, but never to destroy or absorb them" (*A Call to Action,* no. 46). Levinas notes, however, that there is a "ceaseless deep remorse of justice,"[20] for while the dignity of each and every person is unique and incomparable, there are nevertheless times when it is necessary for the law to calculate and make comparisons, to weigh and to measure. Justice that seeks to be true and good is always saddened by its inability to be truly just for each and every person who comes before the law, because it knows that it must necessarily weigh individual cases according to universal principles, and yet it also knows that no universal principle is ever adequate to deal with each and every human particularity that comes before it in all its special instance and circumstance. "Legislation is always unfinished, always resumed." While the law aims to approximate the justice due to every person, it is nevertheless "distanced by the necessary calculations imposed by a multiple sociality, calculations constantly starting over again."[21] In other words, the law — when it is functioning well or as best it can — is nevertheless painfully and "remorsefully" aware of its own pitfalls and shortcomings.

"Justice is necessary," Levinas says, "that is, comparison, coexistence, assembling, order, thematization... the intelligibility of a system, and thence also a copresence on an equal footing as before a court of justice."[22] However, this "reasonable justice" that is based on fairness and equality and universal principles is nevertheless "bound by legal strictures and cannot equal the goodness that solicits and inspires it."[23] Underlying all quests for justice stands "the whole gravity of love" — a love that does not measure or boast; rather, a love that "bears all things" (1 Cor. 13:7). In the name of this love, Levinas prefers to "reserve another word: *miséricorde*, mercy, when one assumes responsibility for the suffering of another."[24] He even goes so far as to suggest that

> the little act of goodness (*la petite bonté*) from one person to their neighbor is lost and deformed as soon as it seeks organization and universality and system, as soon as it opts for doctrine, a treatise of politics, a party, a state, and even a church. Yet it remains the sole refuge of the good in being. Unbeaten, it undergoes violence and evil, which, as little goodness, it can neither vanquish nor drive out.[25]

"Justice itself is born of charity."[26] If it is inspired by goodness, if it is founded on charity, if it is chastened and softened by mercy, then it may be possible for justice to best approximate what it seeks. Otherwise, it will always be deformed and wounded — unable to rise to the heights of justice that always wells up from the concern and responsibility of one for another. "God is the God of justice, but his principle attribute is mercy."[27] Love disarms justice. It unsettles justice. It watches over justice.

Acts of charity and mercy may seem small and insignificant in the face of the huge demands of social justice and the necessary concerns of politics in the world. However, it is these often small and fragile acts of love that ultimately watch over justice. Just as the parent watches over the child who is sick, or the lover watches for the beloved, sitting up through the night — "faint with love" (Song 5:8) — unable to sleep but rather full of concern and solicitude, so too "love must watch over justice."[28] As Chappell suggests, "mercy not only crowns or seasons justice, but ultimately even supplants it."[29] The seemingly fragile acts of tenderness and love — "acts of charity" — should not be considered as mere Band-Aids. Rather, they are the very sign of God's goodness in the world. A rabbinic parable speaks of the Messiah who is found at the city gates, attending to the afflicted and the suffering, "binding up their wounds," and says that while "others bind an *entire* area covering *several* wounds with one bandage, the Messiah dresses *each wound separately*" (*San.* 98a).

Acts of mercy and charity may often appear as mere supplements to the grander works of justice; they may even appear as "foolish" in the eyes of the world, and yet St. Paul says:

God chose what is foolish in the world to shame the wise; God chose what is weak in the world to shame the strong; God chose what is low and despised in the world, things that are not, to reduce to nothing things that are.... None of the rulers of this age have understood this. (1 Cor. 1:27–28; 2:8)

"Various models have been tried," Paul VI says, "but none of them gives complete satisfaction." Nevertheless, "the Christian has the duty to take part in this search and in the organization and life of political society" (*A Call to Action,* no. 24). The gates of the city that open onto the public spaces of the *polis* are a crucial arena for the voices of those who bear the gospel message — especially as that message advocates for the rights of the little ones who are jostled and crowded at the entrance — continually scrutinized by the "gatekeepers" of the law. Perhaps this is why Jesus refers to another gate that also marks an entrance to the city — the gate that is narrow and cannot even accommodate a camel, the gate that only allows for a person at a time to pass through, the gate that is a sign of the kingdom of God — "and only a few find it" (Matt. 7:14).

ELEVEN

To Dwell Poetically in the World

I have always sensed that the *practical* and the *poetical* are intimately related. I am thinking of poetry in its broadest sense — "an exploration of the human powers to make (*poiesis*) a world in which we may poetically dwell."[1] Humans construct the way they want to dwell in the world; human existence is essentially world-building activity in which we "make a world."

We do not typically question or notice these constructions *as constructions*. Rather, we consider the world in which we live and our particular social arrangements as the "real" world.[2] Shopping malls, freeways, credit cards, television, newspapers, democracy, and freedom — this is the "real" world. However, it is also a "fabrication" in the sense that it is the product of our human powers "to make a world."

"I've been walking in a largely peach-colored, air-conditioned shopping mall," writes the American poet Adrienne Rich. "I enter this mall rarely," she says. "But this time I am on a search."

Inside, in a space the size of a small village, are clothing-chain outlets, fast-food parlors, stores selling computers and camcorders, stuffed animals, papier-mâché cactuses, mugs inscribed with names and mottoes, athletic shoes, real and plastic houseplants, paper plates, cups, napkins. . . . The shops are stocked, to the inch, mostly with repetitions of identical merchandise, a plethora of tiny-choice variants on a single model; nothing here is eccentric, nothing bears the imprint of an individual maker. . . .

194

Here is a chain bookstore, stacked novels, computer manuals, in-timacy manuals, parenting manuals, investment-management man-uals, grief-management manuals, college-entrance manuals, medita-tion manuals . . . I ask the young clerk at the register where the poetry is. He walks me toward the back of the store: "Those two shelves down there."

(*What Is Found There: Notebooks on Poetry and Politics*)[3]

Adrienne Rich is on a search for poetry in the mall, yet all she manages to find are two small shelves buried at the back of the store. "Poetry is underneath," she says, and "awfully low 'down there'." No one seems very interested in poetry, preferring instead the supposed reality of the shopping mall (which is full of copies, fakes, and fabrications) to the reality of the poetic world, a world in which we may "poetically dwell."[4]

Rich bemoans the lack of poetry in the mall. She believes that poetry can stir the human imagination and help us redescribe and reconstruct our world. The work of a poem "reminds you (for you have known, some-how, all along, maybe lost track) where and when and how you are living and might live — it is a wick of desire."[5] Poetry can "break open locked chambers of possibility, restore numbed zones to feeling, recharge desire."[6] Poetry *makes* the world appear differently — as strange, as new, or even as freshly remembered, as though we had forgotten something essential. "Over so many millennia, so many cultures, humans have reached into preexisting nature and made art: to celebrate, to drive off evil, to nourish memory, to conjure the desired vision."[7] The poetic word breaks open, energizes, and restores. And it invites us to dwell in this newly opened, recharged, and restored world.

"TELL ME MY NAME"

How do we dwell poetically in the world? More often than not, the poetic word comes to us as a visitation. It cannot be forced, but requires a cer-tain patience or receptivity. This is how the Jewish poet Edmond Jabés describes it:

I have developed a habit; every morning, before going to my desk, say — in any case, before attending to any business — I sit for a

moment in the armchair in one corner of the room, which is my
refuge. My chair, as I have long adopted it.

This particular day at the usual hour, I tried, eyes half closed, to
empty my mind and give free rein to the various thoughts assailing
me, to be led by them without any precise aim, meaning neither to
obey nor to bristle.

I was still waiting for my reflections and meditations to take off
when I heard a knock at the door — I always take the precaution of
closing it so that I will not be needlessly bothered — and, almost at
the same moment, saw a young woman enter. I did not dare speak
at first, paralyzed by her airy manner and the silence she imposed.
A silence more exacting than that of the room.

She sat down in the matching arm chair opposite mine, watched
me for a brief moment, then asked me point-blank to be so kind as
to tell her her name — but with so blighted a smile, such painfully
insistent eyes that I trembled.

She must have realized that I was upset because she immediately
got up again, embarrassed, it seemed, went toward the door — which
she had left ajar on coming in — and, without paying me any more
heed, disappeared.

Of this woman, of whom I know only that she one morning
burst into my room only to vanish as suddenly, but whose strange
request harries my memory, of this woman nothing much will be
said in this book. Not of her infinitely sweet voice, nor even of the
incurable wound she had come to pit against mine.

But her face and voice are only more present in these pages. Her
face, to feed my imagination, her voice, irrefutable proof that she
is real.   ("The Dream")[8]

What is my name? This is the question that causes poets and artists
to tremble. The world stands shrouded and nameless, *mysticus* (full of
mystery), and yet it calls out, pleading almost, "Tell me my name." Poets
tremble because no matter how hard they struggle with words — or the
artist with paint or the sculptor with marble or the musician with wood
and string — no matter how hard they struggle, they know that nothing
of what they say or create can ever actually name the nameless. To express
the inexpressible, to name the unnamable, to reveal the hidden mystery —

this is the "incurable wound" of the poet. Yet it is also the poet's most crucial vocation. "Ever since the book," writes Jabés, "my life has been a wake of writing in the space between limits, under the resplendent sign of the unpronounceable Name."[9]

In his essay "Poetry and the Christian," Karl Rahner suggests that Christianity has a "special intrinsic relationship to the *word* and hence cannot be without a special relationship to the *poetic* word."[10] One of the great tasks of the poet is to respond to the "infinitely sweet voice" of the nameless, the immense, the incomprehensible, the abiding mystery we call God. "It is this nameless being that words try to name when they speak of things.... One can miss this when one hears words," says Rahner (359). Our common experience of language is that words express, designate, name, define, distinguish, compare, determine. However, we can forget that "the small, limited region of the determinative word lies within the vast, silent desert of the godhead" (359). Even as words seek to name and to define, the one who has a listening heart "experiences something totally different: the silent, mystic presence of the nameless" (358). We need the poetic word to help us understand that their whole meaning is to utter the unutterable, to enable the nameless mystery to touch one's heart. Rahner writes:

> Christianity needs such words; it needs practice in learning to hear such words. For all its words would be misunderstood, if they were not heard as words of the mystery, as the coming of the blessed, gripping, incomprehensibility of the holy. For they speak of God. And if God's incomprehensibility does not grip us in a word, if it does not draw us on into his superluminous darkness, if it does not call us out of the little house of our homely, close-hugged truths into the strangeness of the night that is our real home, we have misunderstood or failed to understand the words of Christianity. (359)

THE LANGUAGE OF POETRY

Martin Heidegger introduces his essay on "The Nature of Language" by saying that his reflections

are intended to bring us face to face with a possibility of undergoing an experience with language. To undergo an experience with
something — be it a thing, a person, or [the divine] — means that
this something befalls us, strikes us, comes over us, overwhelms and
transforms us. When we talk of "undergoing" an experience, we
mean specifically that the experience is not of our own making;
to undergo here means that we endure it, suffer it, receive it as it
strikes us and submit to it. It is this something itself that comes
about, comes to pass, happens.[11]

Heidegger then goes on to ask how we can possibly undergo an experience of language? Especially because we can never "extract" ourselves
from language. "Language is the house of being"[12] — we swim in language
as a fish swims in the ocean. This leads Heidegger to ask:

But when does language speak itself as language? Curiously enough,
when we cannot find the right word for something that concerns
us, carries us away, oppresses or encourages us. Then we leave
unspoken what we have in mind and, without rightly giving it
thought, undergo moments in which language itself has distantly
and fleetingly touched us with its essential being.[13]

Often, language "grants its being" precisely at those moments when
words fail us, when we realize that we are not in control of language,
that every word's "is" (it is this) also reminds us of a deeper, hidden "is
not" (we never quite capture it in words). Hence, the importance of listening to what language both reveals (grants/gives) and what it conceals
(what remains hidden and unspoken in language). To undergo an experience with language is to undergo those moments when we are "without
words," when words fail us, when the hidden depths of language reveals
the nameless and the unsayable.

This reminds us that language is not just a tool or an instrument that we
use or control. Against our everyday, ordinary, and conventional "use" of
language, it is *poetic language* especially that brings into the open the hidden source of language. Poetry alters our relation to language. In poetry,
the uncanny — the strange, the hidden, the unsayable — brings us up
short such that we "undergo an experience of language." Poetry is an
event in which language interrupts our attempts to reduce it conceptually

and instrumentally...*it takes itself out of our hands*. It is what happens when language suddenly deprives us of subjective control, as when the poet T. S. Eliot, says:

So here I am, in the middle way, having had twenty years —
Twenty years largely wasted....
Trying to learn to use words, and every attempt
Is a wholly new start, and a different kind of failure
Because one has only learned to get the better of words
For the thing one no longer has to say, or the way in which
One is no longer disposed to say it. And so each venture
Is a new beginning, a raid on the inarticulate....(*Four Quartets*)[14]

If you can imagine this, you are "on your way to language," you are on your way to poetry.

Paul Celan, Jewish poet and survivor of the Holocaust, writes of the poetic experience in the following words:

Reachable, near and not lost, there remained in the midst of the losses this one thing: language.

It remained, not lost, yes in spite of everything. But it had to pass through its own answerlessness, pass through frightful muting, pass through the thousand darknesses of deathbringing speech. It passed through and gave back no words for that which happened; yet it passed through this happening. Passed through and could come to light again, "enriched" by all this.

In this language I have sought, during those years and the years since then, to write poems: so as to speak, to orient myself, to find out where I was and where I was meant to go, to sketch out reality for myself.

It was, you see, event, movement, a being underway, it was an attempt to gain direction....

A poem, as a manifestation of language and thus essentially dialogue, can be a message in a bottle, sent out in the — not always greatly hopeful — belief that somewhere and sometime it could wash up on land, on heartland perhaps. Poems in this sense are underway: they are making toward something.

Toward what? Toward something open . . . toward an addressable
Thou, toward an addressable reality.

(*Selected Poems and Prose*)[15]

Poetry as a whole is always inclined toward a more or less distant, unknown addressee. This distance, this strangeness, is not an obstacle to be
overcome but rather something the poem makes room for — welcomes —
and, so to speak, invites. The poem is hospitality to the "addressable thou."
Like Augustine's *Confessions*, one of the finest testimonies of an "I saying you" (the pronoun "you" occurs in 381 of the 453 paragraphs of the
Confessions), Paul Celan's poetry is always directed toward "you."

> You prayer —, you blasphemy —, you
> prayer-sharp knives
> of my
> silence.
>
> You my words being crippled
> together with me, you
> my hale ones.
>
> And you:
> you, you, you
> my later of roses
> daily worn true and
> more true. . . .

(" . . . Plashes the Fountain")[16]

Poetic movement is not toward a point of completion, but a ceaseless,
searching, open-ended yearning and movement toward what is always
elsewhere and otherwise, toward what is coming, toward an unexpected
"arrival" or "event" or "announcement" that is not of my own making, not
in my hands, as when the angel Gabriel appears to Mary and all she can
do is say, "Be it done to me according to your word" (Luke 1:38). Poetic
movement is not a quest that I undertake through mastery and control.
Rather, as Heidegger suggests, it is responsiveness to mystery;[17] it is an
"event of releasement," letting go or letting it be done, as when Jesus prays
in the garden, "Not my will, but yours be done" (Luke 22:42).

In his book *Real Presences*, George Steiner notes that there is language and art because there is "the other," because there is "you." Hèléne Cixous, for example, says that it is always "the other" that brings her to writing:

> Another? The other! Ah, the other, here is the name of the mystery, the name of You, the desired one.... The other to love. The other who puts love to the test: How to love the other, the strange, the unknown, the "not-me-at-all?"[18]

No poetic work finally encompasses all of life's meanings or strangeness. Understanding is patiently won and, at all times, open to revision. We know too well "that our comprehension, even as it deepens into intimacy, most particularly where it deepens into intimacy, remains partial, fragmentary, subject to error and revaluation."[19] The poetic work witnesses to the "weight of otherness" that haunts all our efforts toward communion. They tell us of the "obstinacies of the impenetrable," of the strange transcendence that we come up against "in the labyrinth of intimacy" (138–40). At times, they even aim to make us feel this strangeness as even more strange, lest we too quickly domesticate the transcendent and make familiar what is always a greater mystery.

The poetic experience is one of expectancy, of hospitality, and of the decision taken to open the door to the one who knocks. "We lay a clean cloth on the table when we hear a guest at our threshold.... We light a lamp at the window" (149). In the biblical tradition, the guest often comes as the stranger. There is a certain *trust* and *risk* involved in welcoming the stranger. We have to trust that the stranger will not overwhelm us, yet we must also risk a true welcome. The stranger *comes to call on us* — and often calls upon us to change our life. In the presence of a poetic text (or a painting or a symphony), we seek to hear and welcome its message. The artistic work, says Steiner, comes as a visitation and a summons — "an Annunciation of a terrible beauty or gravity breaking into the small house of our cautionary being. If we have heard rightly the wing-beat and provocation of that visit, our house is no longer habitable in quite the same way as before" (143).

As with any great poem, novel, painting, or musical composition, they bring with them a radical call towards change, towards a new way of dwelling in the world. The awakening, the enrichment, the consternation, the unsettling of sensibility and understanding which follow our experience of art *prompt us to action.* In a wholly fundamental sense, the poem, the painting, the sonata "are not so much read, viewed or heard as they are *lived*" (143). Great works of art say to us: "Change your life." They address our lives and call upon us: "What do you feel, what do you think of the possibilities of life, of the alternative shapes of being which are implicit in your experience of me, in our encounter?" (142).

CREATIVE INTUITION

In *Higher Education and the Human Spirit*, Bernard Meland argues that rational ways of knowing have tended to neglect deeper, intuitive ways of knowing, what he calls an *appreciative consciousness* or a "felt wisdom."[20] Feeling the sense of life's "unsayableness" has given way to the rationalist's quest for what is distinctly clear and "sayable." Yet according to Meland, *we live more deeply than we think.* If we are to be faithful to lived experience, this "more deeply" should be reflected in our ways of knowing. The deep, rich, intuitive realm of the unsayable requires a perceptive, intuitive grasp of experience that is irreducible to rational analysis and logical thinking. Meland argues for a knowing that is appreciative and intuitive of this deeper sense. He appeals to an appreciative consciousness that is attuned to humanity's way of apprehending the world through a sense of value, a sense of beauty, of feeling, affection, intuition — through moral, religious, and aesthetic experience.

The Catholic philosopher Jacques Maritain places *creative intuition* at the heart of the poetic and artistic experience. He does not oppose reason to intuition; rather he argues that in poetic experience, reason is freed from being purely logical and conceptual, and touches its deeper source in what he calls "intuitive reason" (*intuitis rationis*).[21] Poetic experience depends on the recognition of a "spiritual unconscious" or "musical unconscious" (92). In the same way that music touches our hearts, Maritain suggests that poetic experience taps a "reserve of vitality" that is not constrained by "the workings of rational knowledge and the disciplines of logical thought" (110).

"The poetic sense alone gleams in the dark of unknowing" (75). Maritain is not disregarding the intellectual life, but he is suggesting that our use of reason often functions like a thin layer of oil that is floating on a deeper body of water. Paul Ricoeur, for example, suggests that it is the realm of the poetic and the symbolic that "gives rise to thought" (348). The production of concepts and ideas, which often appear to us as clear and distinct, are like thin abstractions of meaning that float on a vaster reserve of poetic and intuitive life. As Bernard Lee notes, poetic perception — rather than being vague or indistinct — is often more in touch with the depth of human experience than the generalized abstractions of rational consciousness.[22] "Here it is," says Maritain, "in this free life of the imagination, at the single root of the soul's powers, and in the unconscious life of the spirit, that poetry, I think, has its source" (111).

Maritain insists that the poetic is not a vague realm accessible only to a few mystical or esoteric souls. For example, he says that "it is enough to think of the ordinary and everyday functioning of intelligence, and of the way in which ideas arise in our minds, or how every genuine intellectual grasping, or every new discovery, is brought about" (93). There is poetic intuition *at work* in science and mathematics; there is poetic intuition *at work* in the primary insights of philosophical thought; there is poetic intuition *at work* in the lives of saints and prophets — think of St. Francis's "Brother Sun and Sister Moon" or St. John of the Cross's "Dark Night of the Soul." Poetry is a "secret labor" that is at work in all of humanity's intellectual and spiritual gifts.

"What matters most," says Maritain, "is that there exists a common root of all the powers of the soul, which is hidden in the spiritual unconscious, and that there is in this spiritual unconscious a root activity in which the intellect and the imagination, as well as the senses and the powers of desire, love, and emotion, are engaged in common" (110). He offers another example, saying: "It is enough to think about the way in which our free decisions, when they are really free, are made, especially those decisions which commit our entire life — to realize that there exists a deep unconscious world of intuitive activity, for the intellect and the will, from which the acts and fruits of human consciousness emerge" (93–94). Most of humanity's profound acts of saying "yes" — "yes" to another in marriage, "yes" to the call of religious life, "yes" to birthing and raising children, "yes" to a particular vocation or life's work — most of these avowals are not born of a purely logical or rational choosing; rather, they are born of the creative intuition and secret labor of the soul. They are, at their heart, *poetic acts*.

The creativity of the poet is his or her person as *person* — the creative self marked with the expressiveness proper to the movements of the spirit. Poetry's *I* is not found in self-centered ego, but in the substantial depth of living and loving attentively, creatively and responsively. Poetry's *I* resembles the *I* of the saint. The creative self is both revealing and sacrificing; it dies to itself in order to live for the work. As such, egoism is the natural enemy of poetic activity. The very engagement of the poet is *for the sake of the work* — for the sake of goodness and creativity — not for the sake of the self (142–43). What we receive from the poet is a *gift of intellect and imagination, of desire and hope, a new way of naming and living in the world* — a participation in poetic knowledge and poetic intuition through which the poet has perceived a certain unique mystery of the world, an incomparable knowing, a gift, a fleeting or deepening revelation of God's glory and goodness. "Not to us, O Lord, not to us, but to your name be the glory" (Ps. 115:1).

THE MYSTICAL AND THE PROPHETIC

Johannes Metz claims that "the radical nature of following Christ is mystical and political at one and the same time."[23] My own sense is that the *poetic* is similarly both *mystical* and *prophetic*, and that both these sensibilities are crucial to practical theology. Citing a passage that contrasts Aristotle with Marx and Hegel, British theologian Duncan Forrester captures something of these two distinctive approaches:

Aristotle philosophises out of "wonder," out of intellectual curiosity which is half awe, half the desire to adjust man's existence to the order of being, to the cosmos. Both Hegel and Marx, on the contrary, philosophise out of unhappiness and dissatisfaction, out of the "experience" that the world is not as it ought to be. Accordingly, while Aristotle primarily aims at understanding, at discovering structures and laws to which man's thought and actions have to adjust, Hegel and Marx aim at "revolutionising." . . . The problem for Aristotle does not consist in correcting the universe. . . . It consists in discovering its inherent order and rationality and adjusting oneself to it. In Hegel and Marx almost everything is wrong and consequently has to be transfigured, transformed, revolutionised.[24]

Following David Tracy,[25] we may call the first approach (the way of wonder) a mystical or "analogical imagination" that sees the natural and human world as a reflection or mirror of God's creative hand and God's gracious goodness. The other approach (the way of transformation) we may call a prophetic or "dialectical imagination" that sees the world as marred and distorted by sin and therefore distanced or estranged from God.

This strikes me as a "sic et non" distinction — "yes and no" — as famously found in the medieval writings of Abelard, who was the first to coin the word *theologia* as a relentlessly inquisitive and open-ended inquiry — "on the one hand, on the other hand."[26] On the one hand, the world is drawn and magnetized by God's creative goodness; on the other hand, it is cracked and broken by sin. As for myself, I have come to believe that life is ultimately gracious, yet I am also aware that this can be a somewhat naïve belief, unmindful of life's suffering and affliction. However, it can also be an incredibly amazing belief — beyond belief — that is deemed "faith" by many a great religious writer and saint.

The Analogical or Mystical Imagination

It is good sometimes to remind ourselves that everything lives in God. Often, we do not notice this, which is why we need poets. The poet finds signs of heaven here on earth, seeing all things "in God." The ocean is in God. The night is in God. The child, the flower, the grain of sand. "Look at the birds of the air," Jesus says. "Consider the lilies of the field..." (Matt. 6:26–28). Listen to the wind, whose sound and movement is like the Spirit of God (John 3:8). Everything lives and moves and has its being "in God" (Acts 17:28). Even your "enemy," even the poor and the despised — these too live in God. This is surely one of the great gifts of poets, who do not just see the moon, but "Sister moon," who do not just see another person in need, but "the face of Christ."

Such is the way of the analogical imagination (the *analogia entis*), which sees everything as God's creation, lovingly crafted in God's image. This instinct or aspiration toward beauty and goodness draws us to consider the world as a "correspondence of heaven" or an "analogy of heaven." Those who achieve this poetic vision are those who live on earth "as if" they were living in heaven, as if everything was alive in God — even those who have died, even the sinner. "Christians must go to the Mass of life as we go to the Mass of the altar," Rahner says.[27] The mystical or analogical imagination does not pull me out of this world to some other world; rather, it changes what it means to be in this world. The great process philosopher Alfred North Whitehead put it this way:

> What is done in the world is transformed into a reality in heaven, and the reality in heaven passes back into the world. By reason of this reciprocal relation, the love in the world passes into the love in heaven, and floods back again into the world. In this sense, God is the great companion — the fellow-sufferer who understands.[28]

The analogical imagination perceives that a moral and vital "law of life" pervades the universe, and it is the human vocation to align their lives with this creative goodness. It is a profound affirmation, a *yes* to life and to the holiness of life. In the mystical tradition this is known as the experience of *kataphasis* — affirmation, wonder, giving thanks, and speaking with rather than against life's goodness and beauty. It is a great *Amen* — to the world and to humanity — and to the God who affirms and sustains all existence.

In a way that is reminiscent of Julian of Norwich's testimony that "all will be well," Erazim Kohák believes that what survives the inexorable forces of time and history, death and suffering, is the absolute value of the Good. "Though we seldom acknowledge it amid the shipwrecks of life," writes Kohák, "love and hope continue to survive by clinging to an extreme confidence: *it will be all right*, whatever comes, unwanted, unacceptable, unavoidable, it will be all right, in ways that we may not be able to imagine or pray for, it will somehow be all right. We could not go on living if we ceased to believe that."[29] Kohák acknowledges that if we remain only within the order of time, if we give everything over to the judgment of history, if we stay only within the realms of an anguished finitude and the passing moments of transience, then such a conviction in *infinite goodness* is impossible to make. As he says:

> In the order of time alone it is often not all right. There is so desperately much death and pain, love lost, lives destroyed, hopes scattered before the wind and washed away by the flood-crest of history. Within the order of time, the very "happy end" is the ultimate mockery, being both happy — and an end. Humans can confront the

anguish of finite goodness only in the recognition that it is not only caught up in the flow of time but also, in its goodness.... What is good, insofar as it is good, cannot perish: it is forever inscribed in eternity.[30]

Though at times it seems that goodness has been crushed in our world, the task and vocation of humanity is not to turn away from the world, but to continue to embody, to enact, to watch over, and to cherish the holiness of life in all its truth and goodness and beauty. The poet, like the saint, is one who bears witness to life's inherent goodness and holiness — even, and perhaps especially, in times of darkness and despair. Kohák writes:

> It is those humans who are willing to suffer and to die — needlessly, as time judges need — so that the goodness, the truth and the beauty of the eternal, would not perish but would rise to eternal validity. It is Václav Benda, recently released after surviving a four-year prison term because he refused to collaborate with the political police, saying simply, "There is this commandment, 'Thou shalt not bear false witness.'" It is all those who choose to live in truth, [including] the millions of nameless, unnoted others who have suffered and died — and often far less dramatically, who have *lived* — so that the good, the true, the beautiful will not dissipate unnoted into the cosmos. They are the salt of the earth.... It is they who remind us of the full and specific sense of our humanity and our place in the cosmos, as the beings who, living at the intersection of time and eternity, can bring the eternal into time — and raise time to eternity.[31]

One of the great tasks of the poet is to bear witness to the *via superlativa* of God's overflowing love. God is not so much the "Wholly Other" that exists in some transcendent realm apart from our lives. Rather, transcendence is "excedence" or "surplus" or "more than" — there is always more that I can know, more that I can love, more that I can cherish. We are always in relation with that which exceeds our lives. *"Inquietum cor nostrum,"* as St. Augustine says — our hearts are always restless (*Confessions*, Book 1, 1). *"Nihil sufficit animae, nisi ejus capacitatem excedat,"* St. Bonaventure says — "Nothing suffices for the soul but that which exceeds its capacity."[32] This desire does not so much emerge from a lack —

a *via negativa* — but from a positive overflowing, a surplus, a *via super-lativa.*[33] When we read poetry, when we love, when we pray, we experience this "more than" or this great surplus that continually overflows our lives, and we seek to summon this overflowing love into the world.

The Dialectical or Prophetic Imagination

There is also — on the other hand — the dialectical or prophetic imagination, an imagination that is common to many religious traditions, an imagination that is concerned with "renouncing the world" — "for the present form of this world is passing away" (1 Cor. 7:31). In the mystical tradition, this is often known as *apophasis* — negation, undoing, stripping away, speaking against. Dorothee Soelle suggests that mysticism has always included forms of resistance that have taken various expressions: "Whether it be withdrawal, renunciation, disagreement, divergence, dissent, reform, rebellion, or revolution, in all these there is a *No!* to the world as it exists now."[34]

Maritain notes that poetic art is not subservient, but rather eminently free in its desire to speak the truth and to name things as they really are, no matter how shocking or uncomfortable or unconventional. Poetic art seeks to break down "social and utilitarian connotations, worn-out meanings, and habit."[35] In this sense, poetic experience is not simply a beautiful "inspiration" but also something "negative" and profoundly transformative — "the breaking down of strong habitual barriers." In poetry, we find an entrance "where everything is other than as usual."[36]

Similarly, Rahner reminds us that we cannot approach poetry as something that is simply edifying, "for the sake of sheltered people." Rather, when we come upon real poetry, we often encounter prophetic voices that disturb and unsettle conventional opinions and routines, that see through or unmask enshrined habits and customs, that name realities and truths that many are either blind to see or don't want to be seen. We need the poet "to say frankly what he or she finds in us, and to divine what the future brings, so that they may be the poets and witnesses of our own age, of *its* pain, of *its* happiness, of *its* tasks, its death and of eternal life."[37]

The mystical strain in the Jewish tradition (the Kabbalah) suggests that each person has the inherent capacity to affect the life of God. Every proper word and deed releases divine energy while every improper action serves to reinforce the disunity with divine life. Earthly deeds stimulate or arouse divine life in such a way as to cause energy from the upper world to descend to the lower world. Humanity's fallenness has caused an injury to God. God is broken and shattered (*shevirah*) — and only shards of divine light remain in the world. Prayer and good deeds are vehicles for "repairing" (*tikkun*) divine life and enabling divine abundance to flow back to the lower realm. For the kabbalists, we not only enable God, we help mend or heal God's brokenness in the world.[38]

On the night before he delivered his inaugural lecture in Paris (March 1256), the young Aquinas prayed: "Salva me, Domine, quoniam diminutae sunt veritates inter filios hominum" ("Save me, Lord; I am going down among the children of men where your truths are smashed to bits").[39] The Christian tradition also knows of God's brokenness and the *via dolorosa* or the "way of sorrows" — the *via crucis*. It knows of God's suffering in the passion of suffering people — the "little ones" and the "forgotten ones." The poet is often the one who seeks to name God in the world, as though God were lost and nameless — unidentified, unrecognized, unknown. "You are my witnesses," Isaiah says (44:8). In the "Book of Poverty and Death," Rainer Maria Rilke seeks to witness to the suffering of God in the suffering of humanity:

You are the poor one, you the destitute.
You are the stone that has no resting place.
You are the diseased one
whom we fear to touch.
Only the wind is yours.

You are poor like spring rain
that gently caresses the city;
like wishes muttered in a prison cell, without a world to hold them;
and like the invalid, turning in his bed to ease the pain.

Like flowers along the tracks, shuddering
as the train roars by, and like the hand
that covers our face when we cry — that poor.
Yours is the suffering of birds on freezing nights,
of dogs who go hungry for days.
Yours the long sad waiting of animals
who are locked up and forgotten.

You are the beggar who averts his face,
the homeless person who has given up asking;
you howl in the storm.[40]

Poets and artists are often the first to be banished by tyrannical regimes, or excommunicated by the guardians of truth, or censored by the socially comfortable. "You are the one we fear to touch.... You howl in the storm." The poet, as Walter Brueggemann notes, is often the one who "cries out" in a "public processing of pain." This poetic and prophetic act "releases new social imagination" such that "the cry of pain begins the formation of a counter-community around an alternate perception of reality." "Juices are set free which enable those who have not hoped for a long time to hope, those who have not imagined for a long time to imagine."[41] Dorothy Day is perhaps one example of a prophetic voice whose typewriter and Catholic Worker houses sought to witness to and alleviate the world's pain.

The poetical renaming and reimagining of the world is essential to the prophetic task. In the midst of a world too often frozen over with cold indifference, there is still this prayer that asks: "*What if?* — the possible. *What if — ? —* the first revolutionary question, the question the dying forces don't know how to ask."[42] Only living forces know how to feel the world with "question-prayers," to imagine what things might be like, to believe that something else might be the case than is the case, to envision different futures, to name new possibilities. Perhaps this is why poets and prophets never tire of saying, "I have a dream . . ." or "the kingdom of God is like . . ." — so that we might transform despair, indifference, anger, and isolation into the startling poetical, practical, prophetic, question-prayer: "What if . . . ?" What would we create then, what might the world look like, what might the revelation of *shalom* mean if it broke through and captured a people's heart and imagination? "A revolutionary poem," says Adrienne Rich, "is a wick of desire." She writes:

It may do its work in the language and images of dreams, lists, love letters, prison letters, meditations, cries of pain, documentary fragments, blues, late-night long-distance calls.... Any truly revolutionary art is an alchemy through which waste, greed, brutality, frozen indifference, and anger are transmuted into some drenching recognition of the *What if?* — the possible.... In depicting lives ordinarily downpressed, shredded, erased, this art reveals through fierce attention their innate and latent vitality and beauty.... Revolutionary art dwells, by its nature, on edges. This is its power: the tension between the *is* and what can be. Edges between ruin and celebration. Naming and mourning damage, keeping pain vocal so it cannot become normalized and acceptable. Yet, through that burning gauze in a poem which flickers over words and images, through the energy of desire, summoning a different reality.[43]

COMBINING THE LETTERS AND NAMING THE WORLD

"God said, 'Let there be light,' and there was light" (Gen. 1:3). God created the world with words. In Hebrew, God's word *dabar* is active, creative, continually bringing forth life and existence. According to the mystical tradition of Judaism, all of creation is dependent on God's word. The Hebrew "aleph-bait" (from which we derive our word "alphabet"), consists of the "letters of creation" by which God made heaven and earth. "Twenty-two elemental letters," the Kabbalah says, "God engraved them, carved them, weighed them, permuted them, and transposed them, forming with them everything formed and everything destined to be formed."[44]

The Kabbalah tells us that we too can learn "to combine the letters by which heaven and earth were made."[45] It advises us to do good deeds and to engage in study, to combine the letters and receive the abundant flow of God's word:

Take hold of ink, pen, and tablet. Realize that you are about to serve your God in joy. Begin to combine letters, a few or many, permuting and revolving them rapidly until your mind warms up. Delight in how they move and in what you generate by revolving them. When you feel within that your mind is very, very warm from combining the letters, and that through the combinations you understand new things... then you are ready to receive the abundant flow, and the abundance flows upon you, arousing you again and again.[46]

When we begin "to combine letters" we are seeking, as Paulo Freire suggests, to *name* the world. "To exist humanly, is to *name* the world....

Human beings are not beings in silence, but in word, in work, in action-reflection."[47] There are many ways to name the world, which is more than simply placing "tags" on things, as though existence were simply waiting for us to label it. Rather, the very way we "combine the letters" and name the world creates the type of world that thereby comes into being. Moreover, it creates what we are able to see or fail to see; it creates the way we respond and act; it creates the limit or the expanse of our horizon — our "view of the world." The next time you watch the news or read the headlines, or the next time you are in a conversation, or the next time you hear descriptions of the world or situations, ask yourself: "Is this the best way to combine the letters? Is this the best way to name what is happening? Or is there perhaps another way?"

By recognizing the power of the creative word, we are seeking to enliven our poetic ability for seeing and naming the world which can too often be smothered in lazy familiarity or buried in unquestioned assumptions. Our day-to-day life, with its familiar patterns and objects, can all too easily become a husk that prevents anything fresh from coming in. It is in contrast to this dullness that Freire writes, "The naming of the world is an act of creation and re-creation." It requires "an intense faith in humankind, faith in their power to make and remake, to create and re-create, faith in their vocation to be fully human."[48]

Poetic intuition makes its way back to the creative source, to the word of God — creating, speaking, endowing life. Such is the supreme analogue of poetry — poetry is engaged in the free creativity of God's spirit. "Poetic knowledge knows," Maritain says, "not in order to know, but in order to produce. It is toward creation that it tends."[49] The poetic word is sacramental, helping to effect what it signifies. In *Rilke's Book of Hours*, Rilke writes:

> The hour is striking so close above me,
> so clear and sharp,
> that all my senses ring with it.
> I feel it now: there's a power in me
> to grasp and give shape to my world.
>
> I know that nothing has ever been real
> without my beholding it.
> All becoming has needed me.

> My looking ripens things
> and they come toward me, to meet and be met.[50]

The world exists because it is beheld and loved into being. We are in the world to love and name the world, to create, to bring forth life. Poetic knowing involves a certain *alert receptivity* — a keen reflective attentiveness and response to concrete existence. As the mystic suffers divine things, so too the poet suffers the things of this world, suffers them so much that he or she is enabled to speak of them, to see them, to bring them to light. The poet, in the words of David Tracy,

> embarks upon a journey of intensification into the concreteness of each particular reality — *this* body, *this* people, *this* community, *this* tradition, *this* tree, *this* place, *this* moment, *this* neighbor — until the very concreteness in any particularity releases us to sense the concreteness of the whole as internally related through and through.[51]

In attending to the concrete existence of singular reality, poetic intuition "makes things diaphanous and alive, and populated with infinite horizons. As grasped by poetic knowledge, things abound with significance, and swarm with meanings."[52]

The Christian tradition wagers that there is an intimate relationship between the poetic word — living, animated, suffering, turbulent, joyous — and the word of God — born, crucified, and risen. Life is full of joyous, sorrowful, and glorious mysteries. The poetic word is never a gloss or escape from the life of Christian faith. Rather, it signals the very possibility of hearing "the Word become flesh."

"Ever since this Word has been heard in its human embodiment," writes Rahner, "there is a brightness and a secret promise in every word."[53] The poetical and the practical are intimately related because in every authentically human word the gracious incarnation of God's own word can take place. "If one is to grow ever more profoundly Christian, one must never cease to practice listening for this incarnational possibility in the human word."[54]

"This aspect of Christ," writes Luce Irigaray, "is still to be discovered":

> Always he is in society, in company, loved, helped. Living in a society of living people, from which he does not emerge as a solitary

man. Sharing needs and desires . . . eats, drinks, sleeps, goes off alone and comes back, speaks or is silent, listens and answers, walks or stops, lives secretly or in the open, goes into hiding or comes forth publicly, loves and suffers desperation and betrayal, has close friends, political enemies, judges, admirers. . . .

He sees the divine dimension. It determines everything he does or doesn't do and say. It is impossible to pin down. Impossible to lay a hand on, yet always present. Breathed into the core of his flesh. Inapparent, yet feeding all that appears. Shining through each of his acts. . . . Paralysis was never his rhythm. Even when dead, he rose again. Is body, ascends into heaven, comes back in the spirit. Lives, lives again, lives on through it all.[55]

TWELVE

Practical Theology Is "Like a Rolling Stone"

Practical theology — always moving and restless — cannot stop to gather and formalize itself into a neat and tidy system or specialization of theology. "Once upon a time you dressed so fine," Dylan says.[1] Yet while it is tempting to debate the formalities and proprieties of practical theology in academic journals and convention halls, practical theology nevertheless finds itself continually underdressed for the occasion, like an unruly itinerant, always on the move, on the way, *viatores*, as Aquinas said, "people on the road."[2] There is a very real sense in which practical theology is "without a home/like a complete unknown/like a rolling stone" (Dylan). It resembles its teacher who had "nowhere to lay his head" (Matt. 8:20), and who sent his disciples out into the world to move from town to town, "with no bag for your journey, or sandals, or a staff," proclaiming that the "kingdom of heaven has come near" (Matt. 10:10, 7).

So what does it mean to do practical theology? How does it feel? It feels like "being-on-the-road, being-underway, even being homeless, in brief: discipleship."[3] In this chapter, I would like to explore this movement of practical theology in the experience of people whose lives are similarly marked by movement — the immigrant and the refugee.

"A DAY IN THE LIFE OF AN ALIEN"

Lines. They begin outside the building. A throng of people all corralled into lines. They continue inside the building. Security

215

screening first, of course, and relinquishing my cigarette lighter — a possible weapon no doubt.

"Form one line!" "Only those with appointments!" "Have your papers and identification ready!" Confusion. Anxiety written over many faces. The authorities! "Line up here!" "Fill out these forms!" "Take your number and have a seat!" Desperate souls herded into a huge processing machine, like cans of beans on a factory line.

Memories of the unemployment office. And now it is the immigration office. The same feelings. Humiliation. A thing to be processed and dealt with. A case. An issue. A number. A reject in the system. A herded crowd. Not to be trusted. Always under suspicion. Under the law. Regulated. Controlled. Gatekeepers! Gatekeepers!

Here I was again. The drill. Assigned my number, following directions, holding onto my forms, anxious, unsure, waiting for that all-decisive "yes" or "no." To the left. To the right.

I have an alien number. It is A099147068. Who would have guessed that on this beautiful blue planet, I would be given a number that identifies me as an alien? I can't fathom this. It actually boggles my mind more than the most inscrutable mysteries of God.

We all had numbers and we all sat together, in tidy and orderly straight rows, glancing up occasionally when we heard the chime as the number for the next ticket-holder moved from B608 to B609. I was B638, so I knew I had a while to wait. Plenty of time to gaze at the faces around me — wonderful faces — with different features and complexions — old and young, some sitting silently alone, others with family or a partner. Plenty of time to imagine their stories and the journeys that brought them here. A room full of aliens.

I attempted to go to the restrooms, but was quickly pounced upon by a security guard, as though leaving my seat was a breach of orderly conduct. "Where is your ticket, Sir? You need your number to go to the restrooms." She spoke in a very loud voice (like a commandant...I wondered why she couldn't be a little more discrete), and I felt the eyes of the whole room gazing at me. I had a sudden flashback and felt like a school kid again, busted by the principal. "Never mind," I said, "I can wait," and I resumed my seat, figuring that a leak wasn't worth an interrogation. God, I felt like jumping up and spewing my guts against this whole system and the indignity of it all. I felt the rage of a wild and unruly Amos. But then I sat down and rejoined my fellow compatriots, felt myself being absorbed into the room, into the crowd, into the people — sat with them, with them, with them — an alien among aliens.

READING THE SIGNS OF THE TIMES

This is how practical theology typically begins. Of course, it could begin with innumerable other scenarios — positive or negative — but it typically begins with a situation, a concern, a question, an experience, an issue, an event — something, at least, that claims attention. So one of the first things we can say about practical theology is that it is a theology *generated* by concern — there is always something that sets it off and gets it going. This is in contrast, if you like, with a theology that can take its course no matter what is going on around it, as though it were quite indifferent to circumstances or particularities and would rather not be bothered by them, preferring instead to function in a more removed or detached manner. But that is not the way of practical theology, which finds itself caught in situations and insists on trying to work its way from within these situations rather than aside from them.

To do practical theology means, therefore, a commitment not to swerve from the presentations of life or the signs of the times. Reading the signs of the times, however, is often an excruciatingly difficult task. David Tracy calls it "naming the present" and suggests that our attempts to name our current situation are always fraught with a groping and tentative search rather than any clear-sighted awareness.[4] It may be possible for later generations to look back on our own times and, with the benefit of hindsight, paint a fuller picture of the signs and events that have shaped and colored our age. Those of us living now, however, have to deal with what Gutiérrez calls "the density of the present" — we are caught in the midst of complex realities and never released from trying to read the full import of events that continually press upon us.[5] I would never have guessed, back in the year 2000, that a tragic and fateful day was lurking just around the corner, a day that would plunge much of the world into the language of "war" and "terror." Indeed, when the year 2000 approached, I felt optimistic about the new millennium and couldn't wait to get the twentieth century behind us, so to speak, hoping that we may have learned some vital lessons from it. Little did I know then that the whole dynamics of the world would shift into the language of terrorism, security, war, and conflict. How naïve I was to think that the twenty-first century might actually portend a brighter future for humanity. So, here we are again, trying to "discern the signs of the times." What a perennial task...

> Generations have trod, have trod, have trod;
> And all is seared with trade; bleared, smeared with toil;
> And wears man's smudge and shares man's smell. . . .
>   (Gerard Manley Hopkins, "God's Grandeur")[6]

Are we simply trudging our way through history? Unfortunately, this is the sad lot of many in the world today. The Pontifical Council for the Pastoral Care of Migrants and Itinerant People writes:

> Today's migration makes up *the vastest movement of people of all times.* In these last decades, the phenomenon, now involving about two hundred million individuals, has turned into *a structural reality of contemporary society.* It is becoming an increasingly complex problem from the social, cultural, political, religious, economic and pastoral points of view. (*Erga migrantes caritas Christi* — *The Love of Christ toward Migrants,* Introduction)

Here we have a description of "the signs of the times" — "a structural reality of contemporary society" that involves "the vastest movement of people of all times." This phenomenon is something *unique* to our own age and, as such, should claim our attention as a reality that is particularly pressing for us today. Moreover, it is a "structural reality" — which means that it is *built into* the vast and complex webs of our global existence, involving political, economic, cultural, and religious concerns.

It is my own experience of being an immigrant — alien number A099147068 — that has led me to take an interest in the plight of the refugee, the asylum seeker, the exile and the itinerant. One of the ways we can connect with the large and complex issues of the signs of the times is to examine our own lives and see whether there are affinities in our experience that can bring us into solidarity with the concerns and struggles affecting people in our society and our world. This is not to say that everything must be reduced to "my experience." Rather, it is to say that a keener reflection on my own experience can often generate real social concern.

I cannot imagine any truly lived human life that is not affected — at some point and somewhere along the way — with the smear and the smudge of humanity's faltering journey on this planet. If there are any among us who have been affected or touched by the suffering or injustices of our world, then we have an opportunity and a responsibility to try to connect or enlarge our experience by joining with others who are similarly afflicted. I have no doubt that my own immigrant experience is but a poor reflection of the plight of itinerants and asylum seekers in our world. Nevertheless, it at least provides me with a way to become involved in their concern, to feel something of their human condition, to want to speak on their behalf and to join in their struggle.

BORDER CONTROL

Perhaps nothing comes as close to humanity's most original sin than its desire to construct borders — borders that determine who is "in" and who is "out," who belongs and who is outcast — borders that demarcate those who own and possess, and those who are deprived and dispossessed.

It seems doubtful that we will ever be able to live without borders, even though, as Robert Frost suggests, there is something within us "that doesn't love a wall, that wants it down."[7] Perhaps we feel within us the lure of God's own original blessing fighting against the pull of our own original sin. Perhaps we are torn by a world that is economically and politically divided between "mine" and "yours" — and a world in which there are no more borders, or, as St. Paul says, "no more distinctions between Jew and Greek, slave and free, male and female . . ." (Gal. 3:28).

If we have to deal with borders, then let's try at least to make them as open and porous and permeable as possible — especially for *people* — yes, even for the immigrant and the itinerant, but most especially for the poor and the exiled.

We live in an age where money and information travel virtually un-hindered and freely around the globe, paying scant regard to barriers and borders. Yet the movement of *people* is still crassly and crudely blocked and constrained. The Pontifical Council for the Pastoral Care of Migrants and Itinerants writes:

> The ever-increasing migration phenomenon today is an important component of that growing interdependence among nation states that goes to make up globalization, which has flung markets wide open but not frontiers, has demolished boundaries for the free circulation of information and capital, but not to the same extent for the free circulation of people. (*The Love of Christ toward Migrants*, no. 4)

We continue to draw national lines and to insist on the right of nation-states to control their borders, such that the very concept of open borders seems to create a wave of frenzy and panic among national populations. "Asians go home!" was a common graffiti I saw scrawled on walls and subways during a particularly dark period in Australia's recent history. In the wake of September 11, 2001, a new tightening of borders is now made even more justifiable, such that a whole new department has been created in the United States that seeks to protect and secure "the homeland." There seems even less hope now for the stranger, the immigrant, the itinerant, the refugee — for human beings who find themselves, for one reason or another, "on the move" across our wondrously round earth-land.

For all those who want to insist on the right of sovereign states to control their borders, Catholic social teaching willingly nods its head. It admits — almost begrudgingly — that this is indeed a right.[8] Yet the right to control borders can never stand as a right on its own. The right to control borders must face a variety of other equally important human rights before it can parade itself as if it were the single and most important right. Indeed, border control can easily become a vehicle for abuse and injustice. Left to its own devices, border control can even lead to some of the worst of human atrocities (to cite but one tragic example, over seven hundred immigrants died on the U.S./Mexico border between 1997 and 2000, as reported in the *Houston Chronicle*, June 13, 2000, and these deaths continue today).

It is typically assumed that the primary duty of a state is toward its own citizens, yet we seldom ask about a state's obligation toward those who are not its citizens. In acknowledging the right of a state to control its borders, Catholic social teaching says that this right should be exercised "in furtherance of the common good," suggesting that a nation does not exist simply as an isolated nation unto its own, but rather exists within a "family of nations" and thus also shares duties and responsibilities to the wider global community.[9] The state, therefore, has "collective moral obligations to citizens of other countries."[10]

This is perhaps most evident in the internationally recognized duty of states toward refugees and asylum seekers. As Michael Dummett notes, the Geneva Convention of 1951 affirms that "every human being has a right to refuge from persecution; to deny refuge to the persecuted is to deny them their due: it is a manifest injustice."[11] According to Catholic social teaching, not only does the state have a duty to those who flee to it for refuge from intolerable conditions, it also has a duty to provide a true welcome and reception toward those who seek refuge (*Refugees: A Challenge to Solidarity*, no. 13–14). Yet, as Dummett notes, "this duty is currently violated by almost all 'developed' states."[12] Pope John Paul II writes:

> In many regions of the world today people live in tragic situations of instability and uncertainty...in such contexts the poor and the destitute make plans to escape, to seek a new land that can offer them bread, dignity and peace. This is the migration of the desperate: men and women who have no alternative than to leave their own country to venture into the unknown. Every day thousands of people take even critical risks in their attempts to escape from a life with no future. *Unfortunately, the reality they find in host nations is frequently a source of further disappointment.* ("Message of the Holy Father for the World Migration Day 2000," no. 4; emphasis added)

In Australia, for example, asylum seekers are detained in prison-like conditions for periods as long as three to four years, including children, and have even been subjected to beatings and tear gas.[13] Recently, 167 Haitian asylum seekers arrived on the shores of Miami. I sought visitation along with a group of pastoral workers but was denied access, and was stunned by the high walls, barbed wire, and guards that surrounded the immigration facility. Rather than offer a true human welcome, especially for people who have undergone enormous trials and suffering, these "exiles of despair" (John Paul II) are detained in "processing centers" that are, in reality, prisons — kept under lock and key, behind barbed wire, and controlled by uniformed guards. This is no way for a state to exercise its "right to control borders."

This right is also challenged by the horrifying inequality of the world order that places a special burden of responsibility on the more developed and wealthy nations of our world. "Migration raises a truly ethical question: the search for a new international economic order for a more equitable distribution of the goods of the earth" (*The Love of Christ*, no. 8). As long as there exists an ever-widening gap between rich nations and poor nations, justice requires that, along with seeking to reduce this disparity, wealthy nations should not raise and strengthen their barriers against the poor. There is a "collective egoism" of wealthy countries that, despite having relative abundance, continue to close their borders to those who do not share equally in the world's gifts. Michael Dummett writes:

> Until the condition of impoverished countries has been improved, justice requires that the rich countries should not shut their doors against the poor.... It would remain a foul injustice for Western nations to continue to say to them "Keep out! Starve if you have to, but do not threaten our prosperity...." At present, European nations, while piously protesting their disapproval of racism and xenophobia, in practice behave like a Dives whose response to the sight of Lazarus at his gates is to strengthen the locks.[14]

OPEN BORDERS

The concept of open borders is often perceived as a scandalous idea, particularly among those who fear that it will create a "flood of immigrants." Others see it as a naïve or idealistic conception that simply wouldn't work in the real world. It seems to me, however, that "open borders" is the very ideal we should be striving toward, and that it is a rather moderate ideal, far less radical, for example, than the more messianic, utopian, or eschatological ideal of *no borders*. Humankind has not yet discovered a satisfactory way to live peaceably without borders. Yet the possibility of living without borders often functions as the very inspiration that leads many prophetic and compassionate souls to serve their fellow human beings on this planet as if there were no borders — "Doctors Without Borders" (*Médicins Sans*

Frontières), for example, along with many other international relief agencies and humanitarian organizations. It seems to me that the people of God — no less — should be a people without borders, people who recognize, along with St. Paul, that "you are no longer strangers and aliens, but you are citizens with the saints and also members of the household of God" (Eph. 2:19).

In his encyclical *Pacem in Terris: Peace on Earth*, Pope John XXIII comes "dangerously" close to advocating the principle of open borders:

> Every human being has the right to freedom of movement... and, when there are just reasons for it, the right to emigrate to other countries and take up residence there. The fact that one is a citizen of a particular state does not detract in any way from his membership in the human family as a whole, nor from his citizenship in the world community. (no. 25)

To advocate for open borders is to advocate for the lessening of restrictions and the breaking down of barriers that unduly block the movement of people. It is to advocate for a more humane treatment of those who seek refuge on other shores; it is to seek the dismantling of costly and oppressive bureaucratic procedures of immigration systems, what Hannah Arendt calls "the infinitely complex red-tape existence" that burdens the life of every immigrant.[15] As Michael Blume notes, "The dignity of a person does not expire as a visa or a passport does."[16] To advocate for open borders is to speak against restrictive and unjust immigration policies that have created a huge underclass of illegal and undocumented immigrants. Dummett writes:

> One of the greatest social evils from which the countries of the West now suffer — those of North America as well as European ones — is the presence of illegal immigrants. This is not an evil because those people are there, in those countries: it is an evil because they are illegally there. Being in the country illegally, they are denied the rights to social security, to health care, to work and so on, that everyone ought to have, and they are also at the mercy of exploiters.... The barriers erected with the intention of keeping them out... fail to fulfil their intended purpose [and result in] calamitous unintended

consequences. The solution is not to build them higher yet: it is to lower them or, better, to dismantle them all together.[17]

To advocate for open borders is to also directly challenge the ingrained and media-driven racism, nationalism, and xenophobia that drives much of the world's immigration policies. We are all too familiar, as Dummett notes, with the standard litany of complaints that are directed against foreigners — "they are dirty, they are noisy, they steal, they will not work but just want to live on welfare, they fill up the hospitals, they crowd out the schools, they will not adopt our ways, they run down the neighborhood, the Government does more for them than it does for us."[18] This is the type of propaganda that too readily spews forth from the popular press, perpetuating ethnocentric and anti-immigrant bias — to prevent the stranger and the foreigner, as John Caputo says, "from crossing over 'our' borders, from taking 'our' jobs, from enjoying 'our' benefits and going to 'our' schools, from disturbing 'our' language, culture, religion and public institutions."[19] The Pontifical Council for the Pastoral Care of Migrants and Itinerants writes:

> The precarious situation of so many foreigners, which should arouse everyone's solidarity, instead brings about fear in many, who feel that immigrants are a burden, regard them with suspicion and even consider them a danger and a threat. This often provokes manifestations of intolerance, xenophobia and racism. (*The Love of Christ*, no. 6)

What is required is "a conversion of mind and heart" that confronts "attitudes of cultural superiority, indifference, and racism; accepting migrants not as foreboding aliens, terrorists, or economic threats, but rather as persons with dignity and rights."[20] The idea or vision of open borders should not be a remote aspiration; it should be the very principle of human hospitality and solidarity, and it should, as John Paul II says, open our ears and our hearts: "The Church hears the suffering cry of all who are uprooted from their own land, of families forcefully separated, of those who, in the rapid changes of our day, are without any security, at the mercy of every kind of exploitation, and she supports them in their unhappiness" ("Message of the Holy Father for the World Migration Day 2000," no. 6).

We should remember, too, that many developed nations — countries such as Australia, Canada, and the United States — from their founding to the present time, are nations of immigrants who have welcomed new people to their shores. At times, memories can fade as people forget the positive fruits that have been borne of the immigrant experience — the new energy, hope, and cultural diversity that enriches a nation's life. Sometimes, and here I am speaking of the American context, we can forget the great ideals of a nation that have inspired a generous hospitality to those from other lands. Such ideals are enshrined, for example, on the pedestal of the Statue of Liberty, which stands at the gateway to one of America's greatest cities, and which reads:

> Not like the brazen giant of Greek fame,
> With conquering limbs astride from land to land;
> Here at our sea-washed, sunset gates shall stand
> A mighty woman with a torch, whose flame
> Is the imprisoned lightning, and her name
> Mother of Exiles. From her beacon-hand
> Glows world-wide welcome; her mild eyes command
> The air-bridged harbor that twin cities frame.
> "Keep ancient lands, your storied pomp!" cries she
> With silent lips. "Give me your tired, your poor,
> Your huddled masses yearning to breathe free,
> The wretched refuse of your teeming shore.
> Send these, the homeless, tempest-tost to me,
> I lift my lamp beside the golden door!"
>
> (Emma Lazarus)

SEARCHING THE SCRIPTURES AND TRADITIONS OF HOSPITALITY

Abraham is a very enigmatic figure, yet he looms large as the shared ancestor of three great religious traditions: Judaism, Christianity, and Islam. His origins can be traced to the nomadic world of Semitic tribes in the ancient Near East. According to Bruce Feiler, "The bible alludes to this lifestyle, calling Abraham a *Hebrew* and an *Aramean*. These and other variants, *Aramu* and *Arabu*, were common terms for 'seminomad,' until they were replaced by the catchall *Arab*."[21]

The first word Abraham received from God was the word to depart. "Go from your country and your kindred and your father's house to the land I will show you" (Gen. 12:1). So Abraham departed, "not knowing where he was going" (Heb. 11:8). He had no clear indication of where the journey would lead, nor if he would ever return. "The lesson of Abraham's early life," writes Feiler, "is that being human is not being safe, or comfortable. Being human is being uncertain, being on the way to an unknown place. Being on the way to God."[22]

The desert wanderers of the Semitic world had a keen sense of their reliance on each other in order to survive. This was expressed in the nomadic code of hospitality — the duty owed to a fellow traveler — to offer rest and refuge, food and water. Nomadic hospitality was often symbolized by the pile of ashes under the cooking pots, and by the size of the pots themselves — signs and symbols of welcome and generosity.[23] For the desert nomads, to be human is to offer hospitality and to welcome fellow sojourners.

There is perhaps no better exemplar of this nomadic hospitality than the story of Abraham and Sarah welcoming the three strangers. "The Lord appeared to Abraham by the oaks of Mamre, as he sat at the entrance of his tent in the heat of the day. He looked up and saw three men standing near him. When he saw them, he ran from the tent entrance to meet them, and bowed down to the ground" (Gen. 18:1–2). He rushes to Sarah's tent and asks her to bake bread. He rushes to choose a tender calf and have it prepared. And he waits on them to make sure they are well served. A rabbinic legend says that Abraham's tent had no less than four entrances in order to welcome a guest approaching from any direction. God's appearance to Abraham comes with the arrival of three strangers requiring Abraham's attention. In welcoming strangers and offering them food and rest, Abraham is welcoming God. As Emmanuel Levinas notes, "The respect for the stranger and the sanctification of the name of the Eternal are strangely equivalent."[24]

In the book of Deuteronomy, we find one of the earliest "creeds" of the Hebrew people — the *habiru* — this group of wandering people without any settled place in the world, who were often known in the ancient Near East as "strangers" and "outsiders":[25]

A wandering Aramean was my ancestor; he went down into Egypt and lived there as an alien, a few in number, and there he became a great nation.... When the Egyptians treated us harshly and afflicted us, by imposing hard labor on us, we cried to the Lord, the God of our ancestors; the Lord heard our voice and saw our affliction, our toil, and our oppression. The Lord brought us out of Egypt with a mighty hand and outstretched arm ... and with signs and wonders; and he brought us into this place ... a land flowing with milk and honey. (Deut. 26:5–9)

This story captures the central experience of the Hebrews — a displaced people who lived as aliens in Egypt, without status or identity, oppressed by a powerful empire, who "groaned and cried out" (Exod. 2:23). God saw their misery, heard their cries, and "came down to deliver them" (Exod. 3:7–8). These profound experiences became crucial in Israel's development of a social ethic of hospitality and justice toward the stranger. The stranger and the alien (in Hebrew, *ger*) — those lacking status and protection — are to be treated with justice and humanity, especially because of Israel's memory of its own past:

You shall not oppress a resident alien; you know the heart of an alien, for you were aliens in the land of Egypt. (Exod. 23:9; cf. 22:21)

For the Lord your God is God of gods and Lord of lords, the great God, mighty and awesome, who is not partial and takes no bribe, who executes justice for the orphan and the widow, and who loves the strangers, providing them food and clothing. You shall also love the stranger, for you were strangers in the land of Egypt. (Deut. 10:17–19; cf. 24:17)

When an alien resides with you in your land, you shall not oppress the alien. The alien who resides with you shall be to you as the citizen among you; you shall love the alien as yourself, for you were aliens in the land of Egypt: I am the Lord your God. (Lev. 19:33–34)

Thus says the Lord: Act with justice and righteousness ... and do no wrong or violence to the alien, the orphan, and the widow. (Jer. 22:3)

The Gospel writers situate the birth of Jesus in the context of this Hebraic concern for the displaced and oppressed (Isa. 61:1–2; Luke 4:16–19). Jesus was born into a family that could find no lodging in Bethlehem (Luke 2:7), and experienced exile in Egypt (Matt. 2:14). When I lived in

Houston, I was struck with the way these traditional Christmas stories had a powerful resonance for Hispanic people, many of whom had experienced displacement and rejection, and who saw in Christ's story a profound identification with their own experience. In their Advent tradition known as *Las Posadas,* they ritually participate in the experience of Christ who "became flesh and lived among us" and who was "in the world...yet the world did not know him" (John 1:14, 10). As Ana María Pineda explains, *Las Posadas* is a ritual that lasts for several nights as the people reenact the story of Mary and Joseph going from door to door seeking shelter.[26] They are weary from travel and Mary is heavy with child, yet there is "no room" for them. At each designated site, an ancient exchange is repeated:

En nombre del cielo,	In the name of God,
buenos moradores,	we ask those who dwell here
dad a unos viajeros	give to some travelers
posada esta noche.	lodging this evening.
Aquí no es mesón;	This is not an inn;
sigan adelante;	move on;
Yo no puedo abrir	I cannot open
no sea algun tunante.	lest you be a scoundrel.

This scene of being rejected and turned away is reenacted for eight days until finally, on the ninth day, the eve of Christmas, a humble innkeeper offers the travelers the only shelter he has left — a stable. The people celebrate the hospitality of the innkeeper and the *posada* (shelter) given to Mary and Joseph so that their holy child could be born.

Jesus is often portrayed in the Gospels as a needy stranger seeking shelter — "I was a stranger and you welcomed me" (Matt. 25:35). He had "nowhere to lay his head" (Matt. 8:20) and asked those he met for hospitality. To Zacchaeus he said, "I must stay at your house today" (Luke 19:5). As he sent out his disciples into the cities and towns, he said, "Whoever welcomes you welcomes me, and whoever welcomes me welcomes the one who sent me" (Matt. 10:40).

Jesus is also portrayed as a gracious host, welcoming the little children and the poor, the outcast and prostitutes, tax collectors and sinners. His table fellowship — "he welcomes sinners and eats with them" (Luke 15:2) — encapsulates the heart of his hospitality. He spent much of his public life on the move, going through towns and villages (Luke 13:22; Matt. 9:35), proclaiming the gracious hospitality of God's kingdom. His parable of the banquet, for example, portrays an open invitation for a place at the table to those who, for reason of class or ritual impurity, would normally never get an invitation: "When you give a banquet, invite the poor, the crippled, the lame, and the blind, and you will be blessed because they cannot repay you" (Luke 14:13).

In the Gospel of Luke's postresurrection story, Jesus appears as a stranger to the disciples on the road to Emmaus. They welcome him as a guest and only then recognize him in the breaking of the bread (Luke 24:35). Welcoming the stranger and the "breaking of bread" became central practices in the early Christian community (Acts 2:42–47), a foretaste of the joy and the welcome of sharing in the kingdom's "banquet table."

This tradition of hospitality continued in the practices and spirituality of early Christianity. During the first three centuries, along the southern coastline of the Mediterranean, groups of Christians took seriously Jesus' words to "leave everything and follow him" (Luke 5:11; 18:22). Echoing the flight of Jesus into Egypt, the desert fathers, as they came to be known, were the forerunners of Western monasticism. As Douglas Burton-Christie notes, life in the desert provided endless opportunities to learn and to practice love and hospitality. The monks "knew how difficult it was to engage in even the smallest acts of love, much less to allow the power of love to transform one. The *Sayings* are full of questions of how to overcome the legion of dark impulses within oneself that prevented one from loving."[27] In one of the *Sayings*, for example, we are told: "God sells righteousness at a very low price to those who wish to buy it: a little piece of bread, a cloak of no value, a cup of cold water."[28] The monks speak in direct and realistic language about the need to offer hospitality — a practice that surmounted all other spiritual practices, much like Abraham who rushed to attend to the concrete needs of three traveling strangers.

A brother came to a hermit: and as he was taking his leave, he said, "Forgive me, abba, for preventing you from keeping your rule." The hermit answered, "My rule is to welcome you with hospitality, and to send you on your way in peace."

A hermit who was very holy lived near to a community of monks. Some visitors to the community happened to go to see him and eat, though it was not the proper time. Later the monks of the community said to him, "Weren't you upset, abba?" He answered, "I am upset when I do my own will."

When visitors come we should welcome them and celebrate with them. It is when we are by ourselves that we ought to be sorrowful.[29]

Hospitality became an essential feature of the sixth-century *Rule of St. Benedict*, which inspired centuries of Western monasticism. In chapter 53 of the *Rule*, we read: "All humility should be shown in addressing a guest on arrival.... By a bow of the head or by a complete prostration of the body, Christ is to be adored because he is indeed welcomed in them.... The abbot shall pour water on the hands of the guests, and with the entire community shall wash their feet. After the washing they will recite this verse: *God, we have received your mercy in the midst of your temple.*"

"Contribute to the needs of the saints," writes St. Paul, "extend hospitality to strangers" (Rom. 12:13). This desire to extend hospitality has continued to inspire many small Christian communities, including, for example, Jean Vanier's L'Arche communities and the Catholic Worker Houses founded by Peter Maurin and Dorothy Day, to name but two examples. The goodness and beauty of hospitality remains a difficulty for us, and often requires us to form bonds with others whose communal commitments are marginal to prevailing understandings of power, status and possessions.[30] "Welcome is one of the signs that a community is alive," writes Jean Vanier.

To invite others, whether strangers or visitors, is a sign that we are not afraid, that we have a treasure of truth and of peace to share. If a community is closing its doors, that is a sign that hearts are closing as well.... A community which refuses welcome — whether through fear, weariness, insecurity, a desire to cling to comfort, or just because it is fed up — is dying spiritually.[31]

We are all "temporary residents" on this planet, or, as St. Paul says, we have here no lasting home; we are tent-dwellers (2 Cor. 5:1; cf. Lev. 25:23). We live under the shelter of God and in the shelter of each other. When we break unjust chains, when we share food, when we offer shelter to each other — then we "shall be like a watered garden, like a spring of water, whose waters never fail" (Isa. 58:11).

"AND YOU WELCOMED ME"

The best of the scriptures and the best of Christian tradition do not place any limit or condition on hospitality. As Jacques Derrida notes, if hospitality were always set by conditions and limits, it would not be true hospitality. However, neither can hospitality be left as a lofty and remote ideal.[32] The unconditional claims of hospitality need to be continually tried and tested within the difficult conditions of our neighborhoods, our societies, and our nations — all of which are crisscrossed with fences, restrictions, and borders. Only by practicing the difficult demands of hospitality can we ever approximate the lasting peace it promises to the human community. Derrida writes:

> To the extent that we are looking for criteria, for conditions, for passports, borders and so on, we are limiting hospitality.... But if we want to understand what hospitality means, we have to think of unconditional hospitality, that is, openness to whomever, to any new comer. And of course, if I want to know in advance who is the good one, who is the bad one — in advance! — if I want to have an available criterion to distinguish between the good immigrant and the bad immigrant, then I would have no relation to the other as such. So to welcome the other, you have to suspend the use of criteria. I would not recommend giving up all criteria, all knowledge and politics. I would simply say that if I want to improve hospitality, the politics of hospitality, I have to refer to pure hospitality... if only to control the distance between in-hospitality, less hospitality, and more hospitality.[33]

Derrida wonders whether it is possible to translate unconditional or "pure" hospitality into the regulated and conditioned structures of political and social institutions. He suggests that while such attempts must always be made, they must be made with a keen awareness of the *risk* involved in offering hospitality, which is always without condition, without criteria, without regulation. There will never be a time when we can say that our social and political institutions are completely open, welcoming, and hospitable. We are always dealing with passports, borders, and criteria. However, maybe this impossibility of hospitality is not so much a *failure* as it is a sign of the *very excess of hospitality* that continually goes beyond and exceeds our political arrangements, such that they are continually called to become *more hospitable, more open, more welcoming.*[34]

True hospitality is unguarded (and therefore exposed to risk), yet it is often caught in questions of power — the power to welcome, for example — such that we guard the threshold, screening those who can cross and those who can't. "Who goes there?" If we're not quite certain — "in advance," as Derrida says — then we typically close the doors, "just to be sure" — *to be on the safe side.* It is very rare, in other words, that we ever actually welcome a *stranger.* And yet, this is the true test of hospitality — "I was a *stranger* and you welcomed me" (Matt. 25:35). If we follow this parable further, it goes on to say that those who welcomed the stranger are those who didn't realize or didn't know: "When was it that we saw you a stranger and welcomed you?" they ask incredulously. According to the parable, the virtuous are those who didn't know beforehand — in advance — how or when or in whom the presence of the Christ would appear.

Hospitality always involves a certain inconvenience or interruption to my world. It is rarely within my control to prepare — in advance! — for the arrival of an unannounced or unexpected guest or stranger, or for a person who is suddenly in need of my attention. In other words, while we can seek to create hospitable conditions, we can never entirely "plan" to be hospitable. Hospitality can never be an entirely structured or institutionalized or "plan-able event."

Such is the quandary of practicing hospitality — we cannot fully "prepare" for it; rather, it always places us in the position of *having to receive,* rather than being able to control. Here we come upon a very strange structure of hospitality — it is not simply something that *I offer* — rather, hospitality means that *I receive.* Hospitality is always about *reception* and in this sense, cannot be mastered. Rather, to be hospitable means that I am in the position of the one who receives — such that it is the stranger who offers or presents themselves to me.

Hospitality, in this sense, is quite "defenseless" — it lets its guard down and stands unprotected. Perhaps this is why hospitality is so difficult, because we are so fearful. Ana María Pineda observes that the Greek word for stranger is *xenos*. Our English word, *xenophobia*, means "fear of the stranger." If we turn this word around, we get the New Testament word for hospitality: *philoxenia*, "love of the stranger."[35] Pure hospitality, like perfect love, casts out all fear (1 John 4:18). It is not easy to create this deep trust in one another, to convert *xenophobia* into *philoxenia*.

John Caputo notes that even the word "community" — perhaps one of our most warm and welcoming words — can become an arena of fortification: "to have a *communio* is to be fortified on all sides, to build a 'common' (*com*) 'defense' (*munis*), as when a wall is put up around the city to keep the stranger or the foreigner out."[36] This self-protective (en)closure of community, this defense of the homeland — making the homeland secure — is perilously close to becoming a xenophobia.

Community can create those who are "in" and those who are "out," leading to exclusionary and excommunicative practices. Even the phrase "unity in diversity" (*E pluribus unum*), while a noble sentiment, can nevertheless suggest that strangeness, difference, uniqueness, and diversity are welcomed and celebrated — but only if there is "unity" — as though there were a secret fear that the stranger might actually disrupt or threaten the gathering together of a community or a society or a nation. Welcome is extended, but only insofar as unity is preserved and not threatened. Perhaps this is why immigration policy is always such a controversial subject, because people fear the breakdown of society. We tend to prefer unified and harmonious worlds of peace and oneness, which is not always good news for the alien or for the one who doesn't fit.

It is difficult to talk of the immigrant experience without touching upon the issue of nationalism.[37] The emergence of nation-states was initially seen as a great hope for displaced peoples and for those without any protection of country and citizenship. Nation-states were envisaged as a way to gather humankind into safe, democratic, and law-abiding states that could guarantee citizen rights and citizen participation under the ideals of democracy. This is perhaps the "bright side" of the emergence of nation-states that sought constructive ways for humans to be together and to coexist together. The diversity of flags representing various nations at the Olympic Games is perhaps one image of the positive attempt to celebrate our diverse national identities in the context of a universal brotherhood and sisterhood.

There is, however, a dark side to the concept of nation-states, particularly in their tendency (never too far away) to border on nationalism and excessive patriotic pride. In this context, national flags can become idols of collective egoism, rather than expressions of deeper cultural values. Jean Vanier writes:

> We human beings have a great facility for living illusions, for protecting our self-image with power, for justifying it all by thinking we are the favoured ones of God.... How difficult it is for human beings to move from the recognition of the value of their own particular culture and way of life to the acceptance of the value of other cultures and ways of living. This movement implies a weakening in our own certitudes and identity, a shifting of consciousness and a lowering of protective walls. The discovery of our common humanity, beneath our differences, seems for many to be dangerous. It not only means that we have to lose some of our power, privilege, and self-image, but also that we have to look at the shadow side in ourselves, the brokenness, and even the evil in our own hearts and culture; it implies moving into a certain insecurity.[38]

Recently, I was taken aback when I saw Arnold Schwarzenegger's televised speech at the 2004 Republican National Convention. He spoke under the mantle of being an immigrant, yet he whipped the crowd into a fervor of nationalism, as they all chanted in one voice: "USA! USA! USA!" I began to wonder whether "of the people" might not be a dangerous principle. There is something frightening about rallying cries made under the banner of flag and country. Religion is often critiqued for its zealot like fervor that creates so much conflict in the world, yet Schwarzenegger's speech shows that nationalistic fervor is also eerily alive and well.

Jacques Derrida is particularly concerned with the role that nation-states play in holding immigrants hostage to their plight. We live, Derrida says, "at a moment in the history of humanity and of the Nation-States when the persecution of all these hostages — the foreigner, the immigrant (with or without papers), the exile, those without a country, the displaced person or population — seems, on every continent, open to a cruelty without precedent."[39] We see from border to border, close to us or far away, "what is happening today, not only in Israel but in Europe and in France, in Africa, America, and Asia ... everywhere refugees of every kind, immigrants with or without citizenship, exiled or forced from their homes, with or without papers."[40] There is no room in the inn, no refuge for the stranger, no sense of human fraternity — such that what we are witnessing today, Derrida suggests, are "crimes against hospitality."[41]

For Derrida, this is an urgent matter of our time — "millions of 'undocumented immigrants' [*sans papiers*], of 'homeless' [*sans domicile fixe*], call out for another international law, another border politics, another humanitarian politics, indeed a humanitarian commitment that *effectively* operates beyond the interests of Nation-States."[42] What, we may well ask, is the alternative to states, nations, and nationalisms? Derrida wonders whether a "new international" could possibly be conceived, one that is beyond nationality and national citizenship and toward something more open, more hospitable — "something which would go beyond the current stage of internationality, perhaps beyond citizenship, beyond belonging to a state, to a given nation-state.... Not a new way of associating citizens belonging to given nation-states, but a new concept of citizenship, of hospitality, a new concept of the state, of democracy...."[43]

Is this a crazy dream? Or could it possibly be the hope of a new reality, one that awaits a more mature humanity, one that we have not yet imagined — beyond flags and pledges and anthems and uniforms and commanders — beyond this sliced-up planet — a reconfiguration that still awaits us as we continue the ongoing experiment of learning to live together in friendship and welcome. Is this a dream, or the reality of an abiding vision, one that is close to the heart of God?

> Is it not to share your bread with the hungry,
>   and bring the homeless poor into your house;
> when you see the naked, to cover them,
>   and not to hide yourself from your own kin?
> Then your light shall break forth like the dawn,
>   And your healing shall spring up quickly...
>   (Isa. 58:7–8)

"Further On up the Road"

THEOLOGICAL METHOD — A WAY OF LIFE

Method and theory are closely related words. Method comes from the Greek word *methodos*, which means the way (*hodos*) of knowledge or the pursuit of knowledge. To attain knowledge, one must necessarily have a way or a path or a method. In other words, anyone who proposes a theory typically brings with them a path or a method of inquiry that helped them arrive at the theory. In this sense, method and theory are closely related. For this reason, people are often interested in the *path of thought* as much as they are in the resulting *theory*. Indeed, following a particular thinker's path of thought and the way he or she traveled from one place to another can often be as interesting, if not more interesting, than knowing that thinker's actual destination. A person's method or way of pursuing knowledge is crucial — not simply as a forerunner to great theories or ideas — but as the very "stuff" of theory, the very thing that makes theories interesting, because we are able to witness the unique and particular paths that have been traversed and traveled in the pursuit of knowledge and human inquiry. Often, the path is so crucial or fascinating that it can even generate bands of disciples who become so intrigued by a particular *method* or *path* that they too want to follow and become disciples (we even have words for such followers, for example, Lonerganians or Thomists, existentialists or Marxists, Franciscans or Buddhists, and so on).

Method, however, can be too closely associated with theory, which is always a great temptation, such that we think that a particular method or way of attaining something is the truth itself. Or we think that our method gives us a certain control that steers everything in accord with our well-worked theory. Or method becomes a set of rules or procedures that drives everything according to established norms and conventions. What is lost in these conceptions of method is the original sounding behind the word that suggests a path — a way, a search, or a pursuit — but not necessarily a controlled destination or an assured arrival. While it is tempting to see method as a controlling device that offers measures for successful outcomes, it's more original meaning points to a path — a way.

To ask the question of method is to ask: What is the way? Methodological questions are questions about the best way to go, the path to follow, the way ahead. To seek a method, therefore, is to ask: What will guide me? What will move me? What will lead me?

According to Pierre Hadot, the ancients approached the task of philosophy with questions such as these. Their goal was never simply knowledge, but the practice of a way of life. Rather than offer abstract principles, philosophical discourse "always intended to produce an effect, to create a *habitus* within the soul, or to provoke a transformation of the self."[1] It sought to "render active, efficacious, alive... to inspire judgments which generate useful acts, and choices in favor of the good" (176). The philosophical way was always in search of the best way to live. "From this perspective," Hadot says, "we can define philosophical discourse as a spiritual exercise — in other words, as a practice intended to carry out a radical change in our being" (176). Unlike the many how-to books that fill the shelves of our bookstores today, "Knowledge was not an ensemble of propositions or formulas which could be written, communicated or sold ready-made" (26).

Hadot seeks to undo our long-standing association of philosophy as a realm of abstract discourse and theoretical speculation. Rather "practical reason takes primacy over theoretical reason" (273). He seeks to remind us that the ancient task of philosophy was always considered as a *way of life:*

> We must discern the philosopher's underlying intention, which was not to develop a discourse which had its end in itself but to act upon souls.... Whether the goal was to convert, to console, to cure or to exhort the audience, the point was always and above all not to communicate to them some ready-made knowledge but to *form* them. The goal was to... *transform* — that is, to change people's way of living and of seeing the world. (274)

Hadot notes that the "choice for a way of life" was not located *at the end* of the process of philosophical activity, like a kind of "accessory or appendix"; rather, the choice for a way of life stood at the very beginning: can I practice *this way of life?* The choice meant following "a certain way of life and existential option which demands from the individual a total change of lifestyle, a conversion of one's entire being, and ultimately a certain desire to be and to live in a certain way" (3). "The real problem is therefore not the problem of knowing this or that, but of *being* in this or that way" (29).

Philosophy was never conceived by the ancients as a *mastery of life* — borne of speculative theorizing — but always as a *practice*, a *discipline*, a *way to follow*, a *questioning*, and a *searching*. While the ancient philosophical schools were guided by ideals and *forms of life* — the true, the good, and the beautiful, for example — these were never considered as remote ideals or detached theories; rather, they were tasks to be enacted in our world. The ancients knew that the great universals such as "the true, the good, and the beautiful" would remain great abstractions unless they were invested with a real weight or "heaviness" that anchors them in actual existence. They considered that humans were the "bearers" of these virtues in such ways that unless we learned to *practice* them, we would remain mired in falsity and illusion — in lies, in hatred, and in ugliness. Wisdom, however, "is radiant and unfading" and "hastens to make herself known to those who desire her."

> There is in her a spirit that is intelligent, holy,
> unique, manifold, subtle,
> mobile, clear, unpolluted,
> distinct, invulnerable, loving the good, keen,
> irresistible, beneficent, humane,
> steadfast, sure, free from anxiety,
> all-powerful, overseeing all,
> and penetrating through all spirits . . .
>   in every generation she passes into holy souls
> and makes them friends of God, and prophets. . . .
> For she is an initiate in the knowledge of God,
> and an associate in his works.
> If riches are a desirable possession in life,
> what is richer than wisdom, the active cause of all things?
>   (Wisd. 6:12–13; 7:22, 27; 8:4–5)

While reading Hadot's work, one can sense his untiring efforts to re-claim philosophy as a practice and a way of life. He is all the time striving to counter our ingrained assumptions that philosophy is nothing but the well-worked theories of great minds. Indeed, if we think that philosophy is little more than ivory-tower speculation, detached and removed from the world, we would do well to remember that Socrates was sentenced to death for his philosophical activity. His relentless searching and inquiry disturbed many people; he did not simply follow the patterns of the world but chose instead to question and to search for the *way* of wisdom:

> I have no concern at all for what people are concerned about: financial affairs, administration of property, appointments to gen-eralships, oratorical triumphs in public, magistracies, coalitions, political factions. *I did not take this path. . . .* but rather the one where I could do the most good to each one of you in particular, by per-suading you to be less concerned with what you *have* than with what you *are. . . .* [2]

In one of his Socratic dialogues, Plato notes that the philosophical way of life is often considered a "madness" by those who are comfortably ac-climatized to the world's normality. Those who follow the routine ways of the world are often scandalized by the philosopher who follows the inspiration of "divine madness" — "the vulgar deem him mad, and rebuke him; they do not see that he is inspired." [3] Every great "thought-project" that signals a pattern of life has a "madness" to it somewhere — some-thing very attractive and yet maddening at the same time. Jesus was often accused of "raving" and "being out of his mind" (John 19:20). Paul also spoke of the gospel as a "madness" or a "foolishness." He seems to say it right up front, rather than try to hide its madness and make it appear more reasonable. He tells the Corinthians he has come to preach "Christ crucified" — a "foolishness" and a "stumbling block" to all those who think themselves wise, or knowledgeable, or successful, or powerful (see 1 Cor. 1:18–31).

Maddening ideas are maddening because they cannot simply be "thought." Rather, they irritate and unsettle by constantly prodding and poking us toward new attitudes and transformed behaviors. Perhaps there is some truth in saying that there is often a "method in madness," as, for example, when Jacques Derrida says that "a madness must watch over thinking."[4] We need to keep looking for what is "mad" and "unstable" in systems of thought that have, over time, forgotten the madness and become stabilized and calmly coherent. The gospel message harbors "dangerous memories," as J.-B. Metz well reminds us.[5] We need only think, for example, of the mad lives of saints and prophets who were gripped by a wild and foolish passion for God. In his biography of four "God-obsessed" American Catholic lives, Paul Elie captures the maddening quality of Dorothy Day's Catholic Worker movement:

> The Catholic Workers were "holy fools," like Prince Myshkin in *The Idiot* or the Berrigan brothers in jail, in that they were determined to share the sufferings of others. They were anarchists, insofar as Christianity was anarchic. "Love God and do as you will." "For such, there is no law." "If anyone asks for your cloak, give him your coat too." They were demonstrators of "the providence of God, how God loves us." They were writers and journalists who had put their words to the test with their lives: "This work came about because we started writing of the love of God we should have for each other, in order to show our love for God. It's the only way we can know we love God."[6]

It would be a mistake to assume that practical theology is simply arguing for a "practical method" — something that will turn our systematic workings into practical workings. Rather, it is arguing for the somewhat maddening idea that we actually have to live the gospel message much more than we think. J.-B. Metz says: "In itself, the Christian idea of God is a practical idea. God cannot be thought of at all unless this idea irritates and encroaches on the immediate interests of the person who is trying to think it." He then offers this rather maddening statement about the "folly" of Christ: "Christ has always to be thought of in such a way that he is not simply thought of." Rather, "All Christology is nourished, for the sake of its own truth, by praxis and particularly the praxis of the imitation of Christ. It is, in other words, expressed in practical knowledge."[7] Two simple verses from Luke's Gospel are enough to exemplify Metz's point: "Do not judge, and you will not be judged; do not condemn, and you will not be condemned. Forgive, and you will be forgiven; give, and it will be given to you" (Luke 6:36–38).

To imitate Christ is to follow the way of Christ, and it is in following this way that we are led into truth and life (John 14:6). This, in a nutshell, is the method of theology, the "theological method." And this is what it means to speak of practical theology as a way of life. We can always travel, as Van Morrison suggests, "further on up the road."[8]

"If God were a theory," writes Abraham Heschel, "the study of theology would be a way to understand him."[9] What if God were not a theory, but a method? What if we were meant to be studying not the "theory" of God, but rather the "way" of God — God's method, God's ways, God's thoughts, God's hopes, God's desires, God's concerns — or, in traditional theological language — God's will? At its simplest — and yet most difficult — practical theology is a way of life that needs to be practiced. The method of practical theology is this — to become disciples, followers, listeners and doers of the Word, people of faith, people who walk the paths of God, people who seek to know and practice the purposes of God, who desire God and the *ways of God.* "Thy will be done, on earth as it is in heaven."

"ANONYMOUS CHRISTIANITY"

The phrase "anonymous Christians" was made famous by Karl Rahner, suggesting that those of other religious traditions who sought earnestly for God's truth and wisdom could well be considered "anonymous Christians."[10] I have often wondered whether this phrase could also apply to Christians themselves, and not simply to those of other faith traditions. Perhaps there are many practicing Christians who do so in "anonymous" ways, preferring to remain hidden in the world rather than clearly identified. We know that Jesus spent much of his time moving from village to village, moving among the people — the "crowds" of the Gospels: "When he saw the crowds, he had compassion for them, for they were harassed and helpless, like sheep without a shepherd" (Matt. 9:36). Yet it seems that Jesus was nevertheless uncomfortable with being identified in any clearly defined way (Matt. 16:20). He said we should "beware of practicing your piety before others in order to be seen." He cautioned against "sounding a trumpet before you" (Matt. 6:1–2). "Whenever you pray," he said, "go into your room and shut the door and pray to your Father who is in secret; and your Father who sees in secret will reward you" (Matt. 6:6). Perhaps we should practice our faith "anonymously," without our own name or our own professed identities writ large "for all to see."

In his work titled *To Begin Where I Am*, Czeslaw Milosz writes: "If only this could be said: 'I am a Christian, and my Christianity is such and such.' Surely there are people who are capable of making such a statement, but not everyone has that gift. . . . It is worthwhile to ponder the difficulty of labeling oneself a Christian."[11]

In many ways, the deepest and most profound way to belong to a religious tradition is to continually engage the question: What does it mean to belong to this people, this history, this tradition? What does it mean to follow this path, this way? "What does it mean to be Jewish?" asks Edmond Jabès: "I for one am tempted to reply it means being the person this question addresses, who quietly keeps asking it of himself."[12]

I find a great difficulty with the various identities and labels that we human beings are apt to place on ourselves and others. I'm not sure I want to be another one of those who too confidently says, "I am this. . . . " I think it is better to have the question put to me, such that I must continually and secretly work it out and give an answer with my own life: "Who are you?" "Are you a Christian?" "Are you Catholic?"

The philosopher and mystic Simone Weil, born into a Jewish family and yet profoundly attracted to the Catholic tradition, struggled most of her life with the question of receiving baptism and becoming a member of the Catholic Church. In many ways, she saw this struggle as the very expression of her vocation. She writes:

> When I think of the act by which I should enter the Church as something concrete which might happen quite soon, nothing gives me more pain than the idea of separating myself from the immense and unfortunate multitude of unbelievers. I have the essential need, and I think I can say vocation, to move among men of every class and complexion, mixing with them and sharing their life and outlook, so far that is to say as conscience allows, merging into the crowd and disappearing among them, so that they show themselves as they are, putting off all disguises with me. It is because I long to know them, so as to love them just as they are. For if I do not love them as they are, it will not be they whom I love, and my love will be unreal. . . . It is the sign of a vocation, the vocation to remain anonymous, ever ready to be mixed into the paste of common humanity.[13]

"We must share the destiny of God in the world," Rahner said.[14] "On earth, as it is in heaven" — or, in the words of Dorothy Day, "He made heaven hinge on the way we act toward him in his disguise of commonplace, frail, ordinary humanity."[15]

CALLED AGAIN

"Beyond the desert of criticism," writes Paul Ricoeur, "we wish to be called again."[16] I have long been drawn to this line from Paul Ricoeur. There is something within me that has grown tired of criticism. Maybe it's because I've lived too long in the world of academia, where so much that is undertaken is done in the name of "critique," as though everything new and creative necessarily follows a dismantling of everything old and suspect. It begins to feel like a desert after a while, or like an old house that is slowly disintegrating as everyone strips away yet another plank, which reminds me of that very haunting saying of Jesus about removing planks and neglecting splinters (Luke 6:41–42). Of course, I cannot imagine a world without critical inquiry, but I suspect that many of us — deep down — also want to feel called by a conviction that is deep and real — something that is *for us* (*pro nobis*) rather than something that is always suspiciously against. Besides, I have found that it is not *doubt* I wrestle with most of the time. Rather, it is faith that troubles me more — "I believe, help my unbelief" (Mark 9:24). I really long to live in faith — to believe — and to be called, again. Listen:

> It is not too mysterious and remote for you. It is not up in the sky, that you should say, "Who will go up in the sky to get it for us and tell us of it, that we should carry it out?" Nor is it across the sea, that you should say, "Who will cross the sea to get it for us and tell us of it, that we may carry it out?" No, it is something very near to you, already in your mouths and in your hearts; you have only to carry it out. (Deut. 30:11–14, NAB)

The poet Edmond Jabés speaks about the "roads of the book." There are paths laid out before us — in the scriptures, in our faith tradition — ways to follow, and they act like guideposts for our journey. They are like promptings — take this path, follow this way. *"The roads of the book are roads of instinct, listening, attention, reserve, and daring laid out by words and sustained by questions. Road toward the open.*"[17] The path stretches out before us, but it is sustained by questions. We follow the path by seeking, by inquiring, by attending, by instinct, by reserve, and by daring. This is what I understand by a theology that is practical — it requires a "way of life" — living it, testing it, seeking it, treasuring it, daring it.

"Strive first for the kingdom of heaven" (Matt. 6:33). Perhaps nothing sounds more impractical than these words — unless, of course, we have learned that heaven and earth are connected by a ladder that ascends and descends (Gen. 28:12). Practical theology is not simply or crudely "practical" — it knows the heights as much as it knows the descending depths. Like Jacob wrestling with the angel (Gen. 32:26–32), it knows what it means to be called "Israel" — *yisra* (to struggle with) *El* (God). As much as it strives to seek the kingdom of heaven — impassioned by the desire for God and for all that is immeasurable and *unconditional* — it knows that this striving is undertaken "on earth" — drawn by God into the depths of the human *condition.*

YOU ARE THERE

O Lord, you have searched me and known me.
You know when I sit down and when I rise up;
    you discern my thoughts from far away.
You search out my path and my lying down,
    and are acquainted with all my ways . . .

Where can I go from your spirit?
    Or where can I flee from your presence?
If I ascend to heaven, you are there;
    if I make my bed in Sheol, you are there. . . .

Search me, O God, and know my heart;
    test me and know my thoughts.
See if there is any wicked way in me,
    and lead me in the way everlasting.
                              (Ps. 139:1–3, 7–8, 23–24)

Notes

Preface

1. Ricoeur, *Critique and Conviction*, 167.
2. St. Augustine, from the Twelfth Homily of the *Homilies on the Gospel of St. John*, in *Augustine of Hippo: Selected Writings*, trans. Clark, 287. While my own preference is toward "inclusive language," throughout this work I have decided to leave citations from texts in their original form.
3. Celan, *Selected Poems and Prose of Paul Celan*, 396.
4. St. Augustine, *Sermons* 120:2; cited in Wills, *Saint Augustine*, 72.
5. See, for example, Leclercq, *The Love of Learning and the Desire for God*, 172ff.
6. See Ong's classic study, *Orality and Literacy*.
7. Leclercq, *The Love of Learning and the Desire for God*, 72ff.
8. Illich, *In the Vineyard of the Text*, 54.
9. Leclercq, *The Love of Learning and the Desire for God*, 17.
10. Ibid., 16.
11. Illich, *In the Vineyard of the Text*, 59.
12. Ibid., 57.
13. Leclercq, *The Love of Learning and the Desire for God*, 75.
14. Ricoeur, *The Symbolism of Evil*, 348.
15. Buber, *Between Man and Man*, 70.
16. Tracy, *The Analogical Imagination*, citing Eliade, 382.
17. Jabès, *The Book of Resemblances*, 1:29.

1. What Is Practical Theology?

1. See Farley, *Theologia* and *The Fragility of Knowledge*.
2. See Leclercq, *The Love of Learning and the Desire for God*.
3. Rahner, "Practical Theology within the Totality of Theological Disciplines," *Theological Investigations*, 9:104.
4. Ibid.
5. Browning, *A Fundamental Practical Theology*, 7.
6. Groome, "Theology on Our Feet: A Revisionist Pedagogy for Healing the Gap between Academia and Ecclesia," in Mudge and Poling, eds. *Formation and Reflection*, 57.

7. See Heidegger, "Being and Time: Introduction," in *Basic Writings*, 41–89.

8. See Groome's major work, *Sharing Faith: A Comprehensive Approach to Religious Education and Pastoral Ministry*.

9. Williams, *On Christian Theology*, 6–7.

10. Freire, *Pedagogy of the Oppressed*, 46.

11. *Gaudium et spes*, "Pastoral Constitution on the Church in the Modern World," no. 1.

12. For this brief biography of Gutiérrez's life and the citation from Nouwen, see Mich, *Catholic Social Teaching and Movements*, 262–63.

13. Buber, *Between Man and Man*, 12–14.

14. Ibid., 14.

15. Ibid.

16. Levinas and Kearney, "Dialogue with Emmanuel Levinas," in Cohen, ed. *Face to Face with Lévinas*, 23.

17. Levinas, *Totality and Infinity*, 78–79.

18. Weil, *Waiting on God*, 53.

19. Ibid., 60.

20. Ibid., 61.

21. Heschel, *The Prophets*, 2:268.

22. Ibid., 263–64.

23. Caputo, *Against Ethics*, 126–27.

24. Levinas, *Totality and Infinity*, 304.

25. Levinas's work will be explored further in chapter 7, "Can the Wisdom of Heaven Return to Earth?"

26. This is something I learned while studying Talmudic texts under the wise guidance of Professor Michael Rosenak at the Hebrew University of Jerusalem. Readers may like to consult his works, *Commandments and Concerns: Jewish Religious Education in Secular Society; Roads to the Palace: Jewish Texts and Teaching; Tree of Life, Tree of Knowledge: Conversations with the Torah*.

27. Augustine, *On Christian Doctrine*, bk. 1.36.41.

28. Gadamer, *Gadamer in Conversation*, 40–42.

29. Heidegger, "What Calls for Thinking?" in *Basic Writings*, 355–56.

30. *Phronesis* is a term that Gadamer borrows from Aristotle (see *Nicomachean Ethics*, Bk. 6). For Gadamer's reflections, see *Truth and Method*, 312ff. In *Theologia*, Farley focuses on theology as a *habitus*, a practical knowing having the primary character of wisdom.

31. Levinas, *Basic Philosophical Writings*, 158.

32. The participants were Evelyn and James Whitehead, Bernard Lee, Robert Schreiter, Robert Kinast, Don Browning, Sue Gallagher, Joe and Mercedes Iannone, Tom Ryan, Mary Carter Waren, Terry Veling.

33. Dykstra and Bass, "A Theological Understanding of Christian Practices," in Volf and Bass, eds., *Practicing Theology*, 18.

34. Rahner, "Practical Theology within the Totality of Theological Disciplines," *Theological Investigations*, 9:104.

35. Tracy, "Practical Theology in the Situation of Global Pluralism," in Mudge and Poling, eds., *Formation and Reflection*, 140.

36. Groome, *What Makes Us Catholic?* 2.

37. Woodward and Pattison, eds., *The Blackwell Reader in Pastoral and Practical Theology*, 7.

38. Killen and de Beer, *The Art of Theological Reflection*, 2–3.

39. Cowan and Lee, *Conversation, Risk and Conversion: The Inner and Public Life of Small Christian Communities*, 71.

40. Bevans, *Models of Contextual Theology*, 11.

41. Freire, *Pedagogy of the Oppressed*, 46.

42. Williams, *On Christian Theology*, 6–7.

43. Browning, *A Fundamental Practical Theology*, 7.

44. Williams, *On Christian Theology*, xii.

45. See chapter 8 in this work, "Go and Study—Go and Do Likewise."

46. Williams, *On Christian Theology*, 8.

47. Elizondo, "Foreword" to Casarella and Gómez, eds., *El Cuerpo de Cristo: The Hispanic Presence in the U.S. Catholic Church*, 20.

48. Levinas, *Nine Talmudic Readings*, 27.

49. Gutiérrez, "Liberation, Theology and Proclamation," in Geffré and Gutiérrez, eds., *The Mystical and Political Dimension of the Christian Faith*, 63.

50. Schreiter, *The Ministry of Reconciliation*, 20–21.

51. Burton-Christie, *The Word in the Desert*, 135.

52. Whitehead and Whitehead, *Method in Ministry*, 11.

53. Kinast, *What Are They Saying about Theological Reflection?* 61.

2. Scripture and Tradition — Heaven's Door

1. Tracy, *Plurality and Ambiguity: Hermeneutics, Religion, Hope*, 9.

2. See my own review of this literature in *Living in the Margins: Intentional Communities and the Art of Interpretation.*

3. Gadamer, *Truth and Method*, 265–379.

4. Ibid., 270–85.

5. In his book *The Dignity of Difference*, Sacks offers the following caution: "In recent years we have been reminded that religion is not what the European Enlightenment thought it would become: mute, marginal and mild. It is fire—and like fire, it warms but also burns. And we are the guardians of the flame" (11).

6. Gadamer, *Truth and Method*, 362–79.

7. Ibid., 361.

8. Ibid., 297.

9. Metz, "The Future in the Memory of Suffering," in Metz and Moltmann, *Faith and the Future*, 3–16. See also Metz, *Faith in History and Society.*

10. Ricoeur, *Hermeneutics and the Human Sciences*, 131–44.

3. On Earth — Reading the Signs of the Times

1. Jabès with Cohen, *From the Desert to the Book*, 27.
2. Ricoeur, *Hermeneutics and the Human Sciences*, 131–44.
3. Buber, *Between Man and Man*, 10.
4. Williams, *On Christian Theology*, 40.
5. Gutiérrez, *Gustavo Gutiérrez: Essential Writings*, 137.
6. Augustine, *Confessions*, Bk. VIII, Ch. 12, 177.
7. Buber, *Between Man and Man*, 9–10. The only phrase that is not Buber's in this paragraph is the phrase "ever-present-everywhere," which I borrow from a Van Morrison song titled "Warm Love."
8. See, for example, Neusner's study, *What Is Midrash?*
9. Gadamer, *Truth and Method*, 299.
10. Ibid., 297.
11. Ibid., 309.
12. Ibid., 328.
13. Ricoeur, *Hermeneutics and the Human Sciences*, 142.
14. Ibid., 143.
15. Tracy, *The Analogical Imagination*, 102.
16. Heschel, *The Prophets*, 2:264.
17. Soelle, *The Silent Cry*, 293.
18. LaCugna, *God for Us*, 6.
19. Cited in Pearl, "When Will the Messiah Come?" in *Theology in Rabbinic Stories*, 145–46.

4. Between Heaven and Earth

1. Tracy, "Part Two," in Grant and Tracy, *A Short History of the Interpretation of the Bible*, 170.
2. Browning, "Practical Theology and Religious Education," in Mudge and Poling, eds. *Formation and Reflection*, 80.
3. Edgerton, *The Passion of Interpretation*, 117.
4. Buber, *I and Thou*, 11.
5. Ibid., 39.
6. Gadamer, *Truth and Method*, 295.
7. Ibid., 367–69, 383–88.
8. Ibid., 268.
9. Ibid., 299.
10. Ibid., 356.
11. Ibid., 362.
12. Ibid., 366.
13. Ibid., 383.
14. Ibid.
15. Jabès, *The Book of Dialogue*, 21.
16. Gadamer, *Truth and Method*, 324.
17. Gadamer calls this the "fusion of horizons"; see ibid., 306–7.

18. Jabès, *The Book of Resemblances*, 1:11.

19. Jabès, *The Book of Questions*, 1:31.

20. Jabès, *The Book of Margins*, 40.

21. See my work, *Living in the Margins: Intentional Communities and the Art of Interpretation.*

22. Jabès, *The Book of Questions*, 1:291.

23. Holtz, "Introduction," in Holtz, ed., *Back to the Sources: Reading the Classic Jewish Texts*, cited on 28.

24. Barthes, *The Pleasure of the Text*, 167.

25. Ricoeur, *Hermeneutics and the Human Sciences*, 142.

26. Gadamer, *Truth and Method*, 306.

27. I explore this image of "the margins" in my work, *Living in the Margins: Intentional Communities and the Art of Interpretation.*

28. Bokser and Bokser, "Introduction: The Spirituality of the Talmud," *The Talmud: Selected Writings*, 7–14.

29. Ibid., 11.

30. Ibid., 9.

31. Heilman, *The People of the Book*, 1.

32. Ibid., 124–25.

33. Charry, *By the Renewing of Your Minds*, 185–86.

34. Tracy, "On Theological Education: A Reflection," in Petersen with Rourke, eds., *Theological Literacy for the Twenty-First Century*, 15.

35. Illich, *In the Vineyard of the Text*, 14.

36. See, for example, Charry, *By the Renewing of Your Minds.*

37. Tracy, "On Theological Education," 20.

38. Chenu, *Aquinas and His Role in Theology*, Translator's Introduction, vii.

39. Leclercq, *The Love of Learning and the Desire for God.*

40. Jabès, *The Book of Questions*, 1:16.

41. Edgerton, *The Passion of Interpretation*, 45.

42. Bernstein, *Beyond Objectivism and Relativism*, 229.

43. Jabès, *The Book of Resemblances*, 1:29.

5. *"We Will Do and We Will Hear"*

1. Cited in Levinas, *Nine Talmudic Readings*, 30.

2. Ibid., 45.

3. Ibid., 42.

4. Levinas, "Philosophy and the Idea of the Infinite," in Peperzak, *To the Other*, 88.

5. Ibid., 89.

6. Levinas, *Totality and Infinity*, 33.

7. Levinas, *Nine Talmudic Readings*, 34.

8. Ibid., 35.

9. Ibid., 36.
10. Cited in Derrida, "Force of the Law," 26. See also Caputo, *Against Ethics*, 103–6.
11. Leff, "Lech Lecha," e-mailed sermon.
12. Anselm, *Proslogion*, 115.
13. Augustine, *On the Trinity*, 15:2.2.
14. Derrida, *Memoirs of the Blind*, 129. Cited in Caputo, *The Prayers and Tears of Jacques Derrida*, 311.
15. Levinas, *Otherwise Than Being or Beyond Essence*, 146; *Outside the Subject*, 44.
16. Heschel, *God in Search of Man*, 283.
17. Ibid.
18. Ibid., 282.
19. Bakhtin, *Toward a Philosophy of the Act*, 40–42.
20. Heschel, *God in Search of Man*, 413.
21. Levinas, *Otherwise Than Being or Beyond Essence*, 114.
22. Levinas, *Outside the Subject*, 35.
23. Wojtyla, *The Acting Person*, 11.
24. Ibid.
25. Heschel, *Who Is Man?* 94.
26. Lee, "Classical and Practical Theology," unpublished paper, 3.
27. Ibid., 7.
28. Ibid., 11.
29. Heschel, *God in Search of Man*, 281.
30. Heschel, *Who Is Man?* Page references are provided in parentheses.
31. Derrida, *Deconstruction in a Nutshell*, 27.
32. Caputo, *The Prayers and Tears of Jacques Derrida*, 256.
33. Arendt, "Labor, Work, Action," in *The Portable Hannah Arendt*, 181.
34. Ibid.
35. Ibid.
36. See Caputo, *Against Ethics*, 111–12.
37. I am indebted to Robert Schreiter's insightful reading of this passage, *The Ministry of Reconciliation*, 83–96.
38. See Rosenak's works, *Commandments and Concerns: Jewish Religious Education in Secular Society; Roads to the Palace: Jewish Texts and Teaching; Tree of Life, Tree of Knowledge: Conversations with the Torah.*
39. Burton-Christie, *The Word in the Desert*. Page references are provided in parentheses.
40. Levinas, *Nine Talmudic Readings*, 42.
41. Leff, "Lech Lecha," e-mailed sermon.
42. Heschel, *God in Search of Man*, 314–19.
43. Ibid., 309.
44. Ibid.
45. Ibid., 284.
46. Merton, *The Seven Storey Mountain*, 12.

47. Levinas, "Prayer without Demand," in *The Levinas Reader*, 230.
48. Heschel, *Man Is Not Alone*, cited 243–44.

6. *"Ecce Homo"*

1. Gutiérrez, "Bartolomé de Las Casas: Defender of the Indians," *Pacifica* 5 (1992): 272.
2. Accounts and context for the controversy can be found in de Las Casas, *The Devastation of the Indies: A Brief Account* and *In Defense of the Indians*.
3. Gutiérrez, "Bartolomé de Las Casas," 272.
4. Heschel, *Who Is Man?* 119 (adapted for inclusive language).
5. Buber, *I and Thou*, 103.
6. Buber, *Between Man and Man*, 70.
7. Williams, *On Christian Theology*, 288.
8. Tracy, *The Analogical Imagination*, 435.
9. Heschel, *Between God and Man*, 112.
10. Gutiérrez, *Gustavo Gutiérrez: Essential Writings*, 131.
11. Heschel, *Between God and Man*, 105.
12. Primo Levi, "Shema," in Forché, ed., *Against Forgetting: Twentieth-Century Poetry of Witness*, 375.
13. Kohák, *The Embers and the Stars*, 125.
14. Berdyaev, *Slavery and Freedom*, 21.
15. Dussel, *Ethics and Community*, 9.
16. Gutiérrez, *Gustavo Gutiérrez: Essential Writings*, 54.
17. Berdyaev, *Slavery and Freedom*, 34.
18. Ibid., 23–24.
19. This is the title of a parable by Franz Kafka; we will explore the parable further in chapter 10, "Justice and Mercy at the Gates of the City."
20. Groody, *Border of Death, Valley of Life*, 79. The question of the immigrant and refugee will be explored further in chap. 12.
21. Berdyaev, *Slavery and Freedom*, 31.
22. For further reflections on this theme, see this volume, chap. 10.
23. Caputo, *The Prayers and Tears of Jacques Derrida*, 140.
24. Heschel, *The Prophets*, 2:266 (adapted for inclusive language).
25. Schillebeeckx, *God Is New Each Moment*, 59 (adapted for inclusive language).
26. This is also a key theme of Catholic social teaching. See *Gaudium et spes*, nos. 25–28.
27. Henriot et al., *Catholic Social Teaching*.
28. Schillebeeckx, *Church: The Human Story of God*, 4.
29. Coleman, "The Two Pedagogies: Discipleship and Citizenship," in Boys, ed., *Education for Citizenship and Discipleship*, 56. Coleman is commenting on Schille-beeckx's claim that the fundamental symbol of God is the living human being (see *The Schillebeeckx Reader*, 174).
30. Schillebeeckx, *Church: The Human Story of God*, 4.
31. Heschel, *Who Is Man?* 103.

32. Buber, *Eclipse of God*, 23.
33. James Nickoloff, "Introduction" to *Gustavo Gutiérrez: Essential Writings*, 17.

7. *"Can the Wisdom of Heaven Return to Earth?"*

1. Levinas, *Basic Philosophical Writings*, 158.
2. A biographical sketch of Levinas's life can be found in Peperzak, *To the Other*, 1–12.
3. Levinas, *Is it Righteous To Be?*, 41. See also *Difficult Freedom*, 151–53.
4. Levinas, *Existence and Existents*, 15.
5. Levinas, *The Levinas Reader*, 29–36.
6. Levinas, *In the Time of the Nations*, 163.
7. Levinas, *Difficult Freedom*, 291.
8. Levinas, *Is It Righteous to Be?*, 73–79.
9. Ricoeur, "In Memoriam Emmanuel Levinas"; Derrida, "Adieu."
10. Blanchot, *The Writing of the Disaster*, 47.
11. Levinas, *Is It Righteous to Be?*, 126; *Alterity and Transcendence*, 162.
12. Levinas, *Is It Righteous to Be?*, 97, 163.
13. Levinas, *Outside the Subject*, 48, 92.
14. Levinas, *Beyond the Verse*, 4.
15. Levinas, *Is It Righteous to Be?* 171.
16. I am drawing here upon one of my own previously published essays, "In The Name of Who? Levinas and the Other Side of Theology." The references to Levinas's major works will be abbreviated in the text as: *TI* (*Totality and Infinity*) and *OBBE* (*Otherwise Than Being or Beyond Essence*).
17. Gutiérrez, "Liberation, Theology, and Proclamation," in Geffré and Gutiérrez, eds., *The Mystical and Political Dimension of the Christian Faith*, 59.
18. Tracy, "Theology and the Many Faces of Postmodernity," 108.
19. Levinas, *Of God Who Comes to Mind*, xii.
20. Levinas, *The Levinas Reader*, 190–210.
21. Ibid., 193.
22. Levinas and Kearney, "Dialogue with Emmanuel Levinas," in Cohen, ed., *Face to Face with Lévinas*, 19.
23. Ibid., 21.
24. Ibid., 28.
25. Levinas, *The Levinas Reader*, 208. See also *Of God Who Comes to Mind*, 50.
26. Levinas, *The Levinas Reader*, 209.
27. Levinas, *Is It Righteous to Be?* 53.
28. Ibid., 58.
29. Levinas and Kearney, "Dialogue with Emmanuel Levinas," 30.
30. Ibid., 31.
31. Levinas, *Outside the Subject*.
32. Levinas, *Ethics and Infinity*, 86.
33. Levinas, *Is It Righteous to Be?* 170, 215.
34. Ibid., 55.

35. Levinas, *Ethics and Infinity*, 106.

36. Levinas, *Of God Who Comes to Mind*, 168.

37. Levinas, *The Levinas Reader*, 207.

38. Tracy, "Response to Adriaan Peperzak on Transcendence," in Peperzak, ed., *Ethics as First Philosophy*, 194.

39. Geffré and Gutiérrez, eds., *The Mystical and Political Dimension of the Christian Faith*, 11.

40. Ibid., 63.

41. Levinas, *Proper Names*, 92.

42. Levinas, *The Levinas Reader*, 247.

43. Gutiérrez, *Gustavo Gutiérrez: Essential Writings*, 105.

44. Derrida, *The Gift of Death*, 54–56.

45. Levinas, *Outside the Subject*, 92.

46. Lingis, "The Sensuality and the Sensitivity," in Cohen, ed., *Face to Face with Lévinas*, 225.

47. Derrida, *The Gift of Death*, 68.

48. Levinas, *Outside the Subject*, cited 35.

49. Derrida, *The Gift of Death*, 51.

50. Caputo, *Against Ethics*, 27.

51. Levinas, "Philosophy and the Idea of the Infinite," in Peperzak, *To the Other*, 110.

52. Levinas, *Of God Who Comes to Mind*, 165.

53. Levinas, "Philosophy and the Idea of the Infinite," in Peperzak, *To the Other*, 110.

54. Ibid., 111–12.

55. Levinas, *Outside the Subject*, 87.

56. Kafka, *Letters to Friends, Family, and Editors* 16.

57. Wyschogrod, *Saints and Postmodernism: Revisioning Moral Philosophy*, 65ff.

58. Peperzak, *Beyond: The Philosophy of Emmanuel Levinas*, 184–85.

59. Wyschogrod, *Saints and Postmodernism*, page references given in parentheses.

60. Caputo, *Against Ethics*, 126–27.

61. Levinas, "The Trace of the Other," 351, 353.

62. Levinas, *Ethics and Infinity*, 106–7.

63. Levinas, *Of God Who Comes to Mind*, 75.

64. Westphal, "Levinas's Teleological Suspension of the Religious," in Peperzak, ed. *Ethics as First Philosophy*, 152.

65. I am relying here on Nehama Leibowitz, *Studies in Bereshit (Genesis): In the Context of Ancient and Modern Jewish Bible Commentary*, 161ff.

66. Ibid., 161.

67. Levinas, *Nine Talmudic Readings*, 27.

68. Levinas, *Of God Who Comes to Mind*, 167.

69. Levinas, *Difficult Freedom*, 18, 26.

70. Levinas, *Ethics and Infinity*, 89.

8. *"Go and Study" — "Go and Do Likewise"*

1. Heidegger, *Poetry, Language, Thought*, 102–3.
2. Kundera, *The Unbearable Lightness of Being*, 5.
3. Ibid., 30, 33, 244.
4. Cupitt, "The Radical Christian Worldview," in *Cross Currents*, 57, 60, 64–65.
5. See Leo Tolstoy's classic story, *The Death of Ivan Ilych*.
6. Plato, *Phaedrus*, 67c–d.
7. Hadot, *Philosophy as a Way of Life*, 33, 93–101, 138.
8. Ibid., 20.
9. Plato, *The Republic*, 518b–d.
10. Hadot, *Philosophy as a Way of Life*, 21.
11. Ibid., 23.
12. Ibid., 20.
13. Ibid., 21.
14. Ibid., 32, 129.
15. Charry, *By the Renewing of Your Minds*, 19.
16. Ibid., 236.
17. Ricoeur, *Critique and Conviction*, 145.
18. Ibid., 169.
19. Ibid.
20. Ibid., 144.
21. Ibid., 146.
22. Ibid., 145.
23. Derrida, *Points*, 198.
24. Tracy, "On Theological Education: A Reflection," in Petersen and Rourke, eds., *Theological Literacy for the Twenty-First Century*, 15.
25. Holtz, "Introduction: On Reading Jewish Texts," in Holtz, ed., *Back to the Sources: Reading the Classic Jewish Texts*, cited 11.
26. Shanks, ed., *Christianity and Rabbinic Judaism: A Parallel History of Their Origins and Early Development*.
27. Ryan, *Thomas Aquinas as Reader of the Psalms*, 94.
28. Levinas, *Nine Talmudic Readings*, 73.
29. Ibid., 85.
30. Ibid.
31. Ibid., 86.
32. Ibid., 85.
33. Cohen, "If It Be Your Will," from the album, *Various Positions*.
34. Gandhi, *Essential Writings*, 89, 91.
35. Mandela, *Long Walk to Freedom*, 751.
36. Freire, *Pedagogy of the Oppressed*, 44.
37. Levinas, *Nine Talmudic Readings*, 114–15.
38. Kohák, *The Embers and the Stars*, 52.
39. Ricoeur, *Figuring the Sacred*, 305.

40. A Buddhist verse cited by Thich Nhat Hanh, "The Fourteen Mindfulness Trainings of the Order of Interbeing," in Gottlieb, ed. *Liberating Faith*, 453.

41. Kushner, *The Book of Words*, 51.

9. *"The Field Is the World"*

1. Pollan, *The Botany of Desire*, 10–11.
2. Sacks, *The Dignity of Difference*, 20–21.
3. Eagleton, *The Idea of Culture*, 1.
4. Ibid.
5. Gallagher, *Clashing Symbols*, 7–8.
6. See Bird, ed., *The Stolen Children*.
7. Sacks, *The Dignity of Difference*, 21.
8. Ibid., cited 1.
9. Bevans, *Models of Contextual Theology*, 10.
10. Ibid., 4.
11. Heschel, *God in Search of Man*, 5.
12. Daloz et al., *Common Fire*, 115.
13. Derrida, "Living On," in Bloom et al., *Deconstruction and Criticism*, 81. My thanks to Kevin Hart for steering me toward this reference.
14. Cited in Gallagher, *Clashing Symbols*, 48.
15. Ibid., 50.
16. *Vatican II: The Conciliar and Post Conciliar Documents*, "Decree on Missionary Activity," no. 11.
17. Tracy, *On Naming the Present*, 5.
18. Geertz, *The Interpretation of Cultures*, 89.
19. Halevi, *At the Entrance to the Garden of Eden*, 1. References to this text are provided in parentheses.
20. Benjamin, *Illuminations*, 256.
21. Gallagher, *Clashing Symbols*, 48.

10. *Justice and Mercy at the Gates of the City*

1. Cowan and Lee, *Conversation, Risk, and Conversion*, 117.
2. Ibid., 120.
3. Kafka, *The Complete Stories*, 3–4.
4. King, *A Testament of Hope*. References to this speech are provided in parentheses.
5. Gutiérrez, *Gustavo Gutiérrez: Essential Writings*, 128.
6. Ibid., 144–45.
7. A similar theme is echoed in Leonard Cohen's song/poem, "Bird on a Wire."
8. Gutiérrez, *Gustavo Gutiérrez: Essential Writings*, 323.
9. My thanks to Tom Ryan for providing this translation.
10. Schillebeeckx, *Church: The Human Story of God*, 6.
11. Schillebeeckx, *Jesus*, 177.
12. Chappell, "Conversion *By* Mercy."

13. Ibid., 6.
14. Schillebeeckx, *Jesus*, 165–66.
15. Chappell, "Conversion *By* Mercy," 6.
16. Levinas, *Totality and Infinity*, 300.
17. Levinas, *Is It Righteous to Be?* 217.
18. Levinas, "Peace and Proximity," in *Basic Philosophical Writings.*
19. Peperzak, *To the Other*, 31.
20. Levinas, *Is It Righteous to Be?* 206.
21. Ibid.
22. Levinas, *Otherwise Than Being or Beyond Essence*, 157.
23. Levinas, *Is It Righteous to Be?* 207.
24. Ibid., 146.
25. Ibid., 206–7.
26. Ibid., 168.
27. Ibid., 169.
28. Ibid.
29. Chappell, "Conversion *By* Mercy," 14.

11. To Dwell Poetically in the World

1. Kearney, *Poetics of Imagining*, 8.
2. Berger, *The Sacred Canopy*, 3–51.
3. Rich, *What Is Found There*, 28–30.
4. See Heidegger's essay "...Poetically Man Dwells..." in *Poetry, Language, Thought*, 213–29.
5. Rich, *What Is Found There*, 241.
6. Ibid., xiv.
7. Ibid., 250.
8. Jabès, *The Book of Dialogue*, 20–21.
9. Jabès, *The Book of Questions*, 1:328.
10. Rahner, "Poetry and the Christian," in *Theological Investigations*, 4:357. Subsequent references provided in parentheses.
11. Heidegger, *On the Way to Language*, 57.
12. Ibid., 63.
13. Ibid., 59.
14. Eliot, *Four Quartets*, 30–31.
15. Celan, *Selected Poems and Prose of Paul Celan*, 395–96.
16. Ibid., 187.
17. Heidegger, "Discourse on Thinking," in *Basic Writings*, 55.
18. Cixous, "Coming to Writing," 140.
19. Steiner, *Real Presences*, 176. Subsequent references provided in parentheses.
20. Meland, "The Appreciative Consciousness," 48–78.
21. Maritain, *Creative Intuition in Art and Poetry*. Subsequent references provided in parentheses.
22. Lee, *The Galilean Jewishness of Jesus*, 28.

23. Metz, *Followers of Christ*, 42.
24. Forrester, *Truthful Action*, 26–27 (citing Lobkowicz).
25. Tracy, *The Analogical Imagination*, 405–21.
26. Menocal, *The Ornament of the World*, 182.
27. Rahner, "Poetry and the Christian," 365.
28. Whitehead, *Process and Reality*, 351.
29. Kohák, *The Embers and the Stars*, 162.
30. Ibid.
31. Ibid., 102.
32. Cited in Lewis, "Translator's Introduction," in Chrétien, *Hand to Hand*, xiv.
33. Handelman, *Fragments of Redemption*, 197.
34. Soelle, *The Silent Cry: Mysticism and Resistance*, 3.
35. Maritain, *Creative Intuition in Art and Poetry*, 74.
36. Ibid., 241.
37. Rahner, "Poetry and the Christian," 365.
38. Fine, "Kabbalistic Texts," 327–29.
39. Chenu, *Aquinas and His Role in Theology*, 45.
40. Rilke, *Rilke's Book of Hours*, 141–42.
41. Brueggemann, *Hope within History*, 16–20.
42. Rich, *What Is Found There*, 241–42.
43. Ibid.
44. Matt, *The Essential Kabbalah*, 102.
45. Kushner, *The Book of Letters*, 17.
46. Matt, *The Essential Kabbalah*, 103.
47. Freire, *Pedagogy of the Oppressed*, 88.
48. Ibid., 88–90.
49. Maritain, *Creative Intuition*, 124.
50. Rilke, *Rilke's Book of Hours*, 47.
51. Tracy, *The Analogical Imagination*, 382.
52. Maritain, *Creative Intuition*, 127.
53. Rahner, "Poetry and the Christian," 362.
54. Ibid.
55. Irigaray, *Marine Lover of Friedrich Nietzsche*, 182–83.

12. Practical Theology Is *"Like a Rolling Stone"*

1. Bob Dylan, lyrics from his song/poem, "Like a Rolling Stone."
2. Lee, *The Catholic Experience of Small Christian Communities*, 15.
3. Metz, "Facing the Jews: Christian Theology after Auschwitz," in Schüssler Fiorenza and Tracy, eds., *Concilium: The Holocaust as Interruption*, 31.
4. Tracy, "Naming the Present," in *On Naming the Present* and *The Analogical Imagination*, 339.
5. Gutiérrez, *The Density of the Present*.
6. Hopkins, *Poems and Prose*, 27.
7. Frost, *Selected Poems*, 44.

8. United States Conference of Catholic Bishops and Conferencia del Episcopado Mexicano, *Strangers No Longer: Together on the Journey of Hope — A Pastoral Letter Concerning Migration from the Catholic Bishops of Mexico and the United States*.

9. *Strangers*, no. 39; *The Love of Christ*, no. 8.

10. Dummett, *On Immigration and Refugees*, 46.

11. Ibid., 32.

12. Ibid., 43.

13. Brennan, *Tampering with Asylum*.

14. Dummett, *On Immigration and Refugees*, 69.

15. Arendt, *The Portable Hannah Arendt*, 25.

16. Blume, "Migration and the Social Doctrine of the Church."

17. Dummett, *On Immigration and Refugees*, 71.

18. Ibid., 67–68.

19. Derrida, *Deconstruction in a Nutshell*, 106–7.

20. *Strangers*, no. 40.

21. Feiler, *Abraham*, 21.

22. Ibid., 25.

23. Seale, *The Desert Bible*, 121–24.

24. Levinas, *Nine Talmudic Readings*, 27.

25. Brueggemann, "Welcoming Strangers," in *Interpretation and Obedience*, 291–93.

26. Pineda, "Hospitality," in Bass, ed., *Practicing Our Faith*, 29–31.

27. Burton-Christie, *The Word in the Desert*, 266.

28. Ibid., 265.

29. Ward, *The Desert Fathers*, 134–36.

30. Pohl, *Making Room*, 105.

31. Vanier, *Community and Growth*, 199–200.

32. Derrida, "On Cosmopolitanism," in *On Cosmopolitanism and Forgiveness*, part 1.

33. Derrida, "Discussion with Richard Kearney," in Caputo and Scanlon, eds., *God, the Gift, and Postmodernism*, 133.

34. Derrida, "A Word of Welcome," in *Adieu: To Emmanuel Levinas*, 15ff.

35. Pineda, "Hospitality," in Bass, ed., *Practicing Our Faith*, 33.

36. Derrida, *Deconstruction in a Nutshell*, 108.

37. Cheah and Robbins, *Cosmopolitics*; Puri, *Encountering Nationalism*.

38. Vanier, *Becoming Human*, 48–49.

39. Derrida, "A Word of Welcome," in *Adieu*, 64.

40. Ibid., 70–71. See the 2003 Annual Report of the Jesuit Refugee Service.

41. Derrida, "A Word of Welcome," in *Adieu*, 71.

42. Ibid., 101.

43. Derrida, "The Villanova Roundtable: A Conversation with Jacques Derrida," in *Deconstruction in a Nutshell*, 12.

Epilogue

1. Hadot, *What Is Ancient Philosophy?* 176. Subsequent references are cited by page number in the text.
2. Ibid., cited, 29 (Plato, *Apology,* 366).
3. *Phaedrus,* 64.
4. Derrida, *Points,* 339ff.
5. Metz, *Faith in History and Society,* 184.
6. Elie, *The Life You Save May Be Your Own,* 434.
7. Metz, *Faith in History and Society,* 51.
8. Van Morrison, *Hard Nose the Highway,* CD title track.
9. Heschel, *God in Search of Man,* 281.
10. Rahner, *A Rahner Reader,* 211–14.
11. Milosz, *To Begin Where I Am,* 314.
12. Jabès, *The Book of Resemblances,* vol. 3: *The Ineffaceable, The Unperceived,* 31.
13. Weil, *Waiting on God,* 6–7.
14. Rahner, *Foundations of Christian Faith,* 305.
15. Elie, *The Life You Save May Be Your Own,* cited, 225.
16. Ricoeur, *The Symbolism of Evil,* 349.
17. Jabès, "There is such a thing as Jewish writing…," in Gould, ed., *The Sin of the Book,* 29.

Bibliography

Anselm. *Proslogion.* Trans. and introduced by M. J. Charlesworth. Notre Dame, Ind.: University of Notre Dame Press, 1979.

Aquinas, Thomas. *Selected Philosophical Writings.* Trans. Timothy McDermott. Oxford: Oxford University Press, 1993.

Arendt, Hannah. *The Portable Hannah Arendt.* Ed. Peter Baehr. New York: Penguin Books, 2000.

Aristotle. *Ethics: The Nicomachean Ethics.* Trans. J. A. K. Thomson. London: Penguin Books, 1953.

Augustine. *Confessions.* Trans. R. S. Pine-Coffin. London: Penguin Books, 1961.

————. *Augustine of Hippo: Selected Writings.* Trans. Mary T. Clark. New York: Paulist Press, 1984.

Bakhtin, M. M. *Toward a Philosophy of the Act.* Trans. Vadim Liapunov. Austin: University of Texas Press, 1993.

Ballard, Paul, and John Pritchard. *Practical Theology in Action.* London: SPCK, 1996.

Barth, Karl. *The Humanity of God.* Richmond, Va.: John Knox Press, 1960.

Barthes, Roland. *The Pleasure of the Text.* Trans. Richard Miller. New York: The Noonday Press, 1975.

Bass, Dorothy, ed. *Practicing Our Faith: A Way of Life for a Searching People.* San Francisco: Jossey-Bass, 1997.

Bellah, Robert, et al. *Habits of the Heart.* New York: Harper & Row, 1985.

Benedict. *The Rule of Saint Benedict.* Ed. Timothy Fry. New York: Vintage Books, 1981.

Benjamin, Walter. *Illuminations.* Ed. with an Introduction by Hannah Arendt. New York: Schocken Books, 1968.

Berdyaev, Nikolai. *Slavery and Freedom.* Trans. R. M. French. New York: Charles Scribner's Sons, 1944.

Berger, Peter. *The Sacred Canopy: Elements of a Sociological Theory of Religion.* New York: Anchor Books, 1967.

Berger, Peter, and Thomas Luckmann. *The Social Construction of Reality: A Treatise on the Sociology of Knowledge.* New York: Anchor Books, 1979.

Bergson, Henri. *The Two Sources of Morality and Religion.* New York: Doubleday & Co., 1935.

Bernstein, Richard. *Beyond Objectivism and Relativism: Science, Hermeneutics, and Praxis.* Philadelphia: University of Pennsylvania Press, 1983.

261

Bevans, Stephen. *Models of Contextual Theology*. Maryknoll, N.Y.: Orbis Books, 1992.

Bird, Carmel, ed. *The Stolen Children: Their Stories*. Sydney: Random House, 1998.

Blanchot, Maurice. *The Writing of the Disaster*. Trans. Ann Smock. Lincoln: University of Nebraska Press, 1986.

———. *The Infinite Conversation*. Trans. Susan Hanson. Minneapolis: University of Minnesota Press, 1993.

Blume, Michael. "Migration and the Social Doctrine of the Church." Paper presented at the First International Conference on Migration and Theology: "Migration and Religious Experience in the Context of Globalization." Tijuana, January 25, 2002.

Bokser, Ben Zion, and Baruch M. Bokser. "Introduction: The Spirituality of the Talmud." In *The Talmud: Selected Writings*. Trans. Ben Zion Bokser. New York: Paulist Press, 1989.

Boys, Mary, ed. *Education for Citizenship and Discipleship*. New York: Pilgrim Press, 1989.

———. *Has God Only One Blessing? Judaism as a Source of Christian Self-Understanding*. New York: Paulist Press/Stimulus Book, 2000.

Brennan, Frank. *Tampering with Asylum: A Universal Humanitarian Problem*. Brisbane: University of Queensland Press, 2004.

Breton, Stanislas. *The Word and the Cross*. Trans. Jacquelyn Porter. New York: Fordham University Press, 2002.

Browning, Don. "Practical Theology and Religious Education." In *Formation and Reflection: The Promise of Practical Theology*. Ed. Lewis Mudge and James Poling. Philadelphia: Fortress Press, 1987.

———. *A Fundamental Practical Theology: Descriptive and Strategic Proposals*. Minneapolis: Fortress Press, 1991.

Brueggemann, Walter. *Hope within History*. Atlanta: John Knox Press, 1987.

———. *Interpretation and Obedience*. Minneapolis: Fortress Press, 1991.

Buber, Martin. *Eclipse of God: Studies in the Relation between Religion and Philosophy*. Atlantic Highlands, N.J.: Humanities Press, 1952/1988.

———. *I and Thou*. Trans. Ronald Gregor Smith. New York: Scribners/Collier, 1958.

———. *Between Man and Man*. New York: Collier Books, 1965.

Burton-Christie, Douglas. *The Word in the Desert: Scripture and the Quest for Holiness in Early Christian Monasticism*. New York: Oxford University Press, 1993.

Caputo, John D. *Against Ethics: Contributions to a Poetics of Obligation with Constant Reference to Deconstruction*. Bloomington: Indiana University Press, 1993.

———. *The Prayers and Tears of Jacques Derrida: Religion without Religion*. Bloomington: Indiana University Press, 1997.

———. *On Religion*. London: Routledge, 2001.

Casarella, Peter, and Raúl Gómez, eds. *El Cuerpo de Cristo: The Hispanic Presence in the U.S. Catholic Church*. New York: Crossroad, 1988.

Celan, Paul. *Selected Poems*. Trans. Michael Hamburger. London: Penguin Books, 1995.

———. *Selected Poems and Prose of Paul Celan.* Trans. John Felstiner. New York: W. W. Norton, 2001.

Chappell, Heather. "Conversion *By* Mercy and *For* a Praxis of Mercy." Paper presented at the Catholic Theological Society of America, June 8, 2001.

Charry, Ellen. *By the Renewing of Your Minds: The Pastoral Function of Christian Doctrine.* Oxford: Oxford University Press, 1997.

Cheah, Pheng, and Bruce Robbins, eds. *Cosmopolitics: Thinking and Feeling beyond the Nation.* Minneapolis: University of Minnesota Press, 1998.

Chenu, Marie-Dominique. *Aquinas and His Role in Theology.* Collegeville, Minn.: Liturgical Press, 2002.

Chrétien, Jean-Louis. *Hand to Hand: Listening to the Work of Art.* Trans. Stephen E. Lewis. New York: Fordham University Press, 2003.

Cixous, Hélène. *"Coming to Writing" and Other Essays.* Ed. Deborah Jenson. Trans. Sarah Cornell et al. Cambridge, Mass.: Harvard University Press, 1991.

Cohen, Leonard. "If It Be Your Will." From the CD *Various Positions.* Columbia/Sony Music, 1984.

———. "Bird on a Wire." From the CD *Field Commander Cohen: Tour of 1979.* Sony Music, 2000.

Cohen, Richard A., ed. *Face to Face with Lévinas.* Albany: State University of New York Press, 1986.

Cowan, Michael A., and Bernard J. Lee. *Conversation, Risk, and Conversion: The Inner and Public Lives of Small Christian Communities.* Maryknoll, N.Y.: Orbis Books, 1997.

Crick, Bernard. *In Defense of Politics.* Chicago: University of Chicago Press, 1962.

Cupitt, Don. "The Radical Christian Worldview." *CrossCurrents* (Spring/Summer 2000).

Daloz, Laurent A. Parks, et al. *Common Fire: Leading Lives of Commitment in a Complex World.* Boston: Beacon Press, 1996.

De Certeau, Michel. *The Practice of Everyday Life.* Berkeley: University of California Press, 1984.

———. *The Devastation of the Indies: A Brief Account.* Trans. Herma Briffault. Baltimore: John Hopkins University Press, 1992.

Derrida, Jacques. "Living On." In Harold Bloom et al. *Deconstruction and Criticism.* New York: Continuum, 1986.

———. "Force of the Law: The 'Mystical' Foundation of Authority." In *Deconstruction and the Possibility of Justice.* Ed. Drucilla Cornell, Michael Rosenfeld, and David Gray Carlson. London: Routledge, 1992.

———. "Circumfession: Fifty-nine Periods and Periphrases." In Geoffrey Bennington and Jacques Derrida, *Jacques Derrida.* Chicago: University of Chicago Press, 1993.

———. *Memoirs of the Blind: The Self-Portrait and Other Ruins.* Trans. Pascale-Anne Brault and Michael Naas. Chicago: University of Chicago Press, 1993.

———. *The Gift of Death.* Trans. David Wills. Chicago: University of Chicago Press, 1995.

———. *On the Name.* Ed. Thomas Dutoit. Stanford, Calif.: Stanford University Press, 1995.

———. *Points... Interviews, 1974–94.* Ed. Elisabeth Weber. Trans. Peggy Kamuf et al. Stanford, Calif.: Stanford University Press, 1995.

———. "Adieu." *Philosophy Today* (Fall 1996): 331–40.

———. *Deconstruction in a Nutshell: A Conversation with Jacques Derrida.* Edited with a commentary by John D. Caputo. New York: Fordham University Press, 1997.

———. *Adieu: To Emmanuel Levinas.* Trans. Pascale-Anne Brault and Michael Naas. Stanford, Calif.: Stanford University Press, 1999.

———. "Discussion with Richard Kearney." In *God, The Gift, and Postmodernism.* Ed. John Caputo and Michael Scanlon. Bloomington: Indiana University Press, 1999.

———. *On Cosmopolitanism and Forgiveness.* London: Routledge, 2001.

Descartes, René. *Discourse on Method* and *Meditations on First Philosophy.* Trans. Donald A. Cress. Indianapolis/Cambridge: Hackett Publishing Company, 1993.

Dummett, Michael. *On Immigration and Refugees.* London: Routledge, 2001.

Dunne, Joseph. *Back to Rough Ground: "Phronesis" and "Techne" in Modern Philosophy and in Aristotle.* Notre Dame, Ind.: University of Notre Dame Press, 1993.

Dussel, Enrique. *Ethics and Community.* Trans. Robert R. Barr. Maryknoll, N.Y.: Orbis Books, 1988.

Dykstra, Craig, and Dorothy Bass. "A Theological Understanding of Christian Practices." In *Practicing Theology: Beliefs and Practices in Christian Life.* Ed. Miroslav Volf and Dorothy C. Bass. Grand Rapids: William B. Eerdmans, 2002.

Dylan, Bob. "Like a Rolling Stone." From the album *Highway 61 Revisited.* Columbia Records/CBS, 1965.

Eagleton, Terry. *The Idea of Culture.* Malden, Mass.: Blackwell, 2000.

Edgerton, W. Dow. *The Passion of Interpretation.* Louisville: Westminster/John Knox Press, 1992.

Elie, Paul. *The Life You Save May Be Your Own: An American Pilgrimage.* New York: Farrar, Straus and Giroux, 2003.

Eliot, T. S. *Four Quartets.* San Diego: Harvest/Harcourt, 1943/1971.

Farley, Edward. *Theologia: The Fragmentation and Unity of Theological Education.* Philadelphia: Fortress Press, 1983.

———. *The Fragility of Knowledge: Theological Education in the Church and the University.* Philadelphia: Fortress Press, 1988.

Feiler, Bruce. *Abraham: A Journey to the Heart of Three Faiths.* New York: Perennial, 2004.

Fine, Lawrence. "Kabbalistic Texts." In *Back to the Sources: Reading the Classic Jewish Texts.* Ed. Barry W. Holtz. New York: Simon and Schuster, 1984.

Forché, Carolyn, ed. *Against Forgetting: Twentieth-Century Poetry of Witness.* New York: W. W. Norton, 1993.

Forrester, Duncan. *Truthful Action: Explorations in Practical Theology.* Edinburgh: T. & T. Clark, 2000.

Freire, Paulo. *Pedagogy of the Oppressed.* Ringwood, Victoria: Penguin Books, 1972.

Frost, Robert. *Selected Poems.* Ed. Ian Hamilton. New York: Penguin Books, 1973.

Gadamer, Hans-Georg. *Truth and Method.* Trans. Joel Weinsheimer and Donald Marshall. 2nd rev. ed. New York: Crossroad, 1989.

———. *Gadamer on Celan: "Who Am I and Who Are You?" and Other Essays.* Trans. and ed. Richard Heinemann and Bruce Krajewski. Albany: State University of New York Press, 1997.

———. *Gadamer in Conversation: Reflections and Commentary.* Trans. and ed. Richard E. Palmer. New Haven: Yale University Press, 2001.

Gallagher, Michael Paul. *Clashing Symbols: An Introduction to Faith and Culture.* New York: Paulist Press, 1998.

Gandhi, Mohandas. *Essential Writings.* Selected with an Introduction by John Dear. Maryknoll, N.Y.: Orbis Books, 2002.

Geertz, Clifford. *The Interpretation of Cultures.* New York: Basic Books, 1973.

Geffré, Claude, and Gustavo Gutiérrez, eds. *The Mystical and Political Dimension of the Christian Faith* (*Concilium* 6/10). New York: Herder and Herder, 1974.

Górecki, Henryk Mikolaj. *Miserere.* New York: Elektra Entertainment, 1994. Jacket notes by Adrian Thomas.

Gottlieb, Roger, ed. *Liberating Faith: Religious Voices for Justice, Peace, and Ecological Wisdom.* Lanham, Md.: Rowman & Littlefield Publishers, 2003.

Gould, Eric, ed. *The Sin of the Book: Edmond Jabès.* Lincoln: University of Nebraska Press, 1985.

Grant, Robert, and David Tracy. *A Short History of the Interpretation of the Bible.* Philadelphia: Fortress Press, 1984.

Groody, Daniel. *Border of Death, Valley of Life: An Immigrant Journey of Heart and Spirit.* Lanham, Md.: Rowman & Littlefield Publishers, 2002.

Groome, Thomas. "Theology on Our Feet: A Revisionist Pedagogy for Healing the Gap between Academia and Ecclesia." In *Formation and Reflection: The Promise of Practical Theology.* Ed. Lewis S. Mudge and James N. Poling. Philadelphia: Fortress Press, 1987.

———. *Sharing Faith: A Comprehensive Approach to Religious Education and Pastoral Ministry.* San Francisco: Harper, 1991.

———. *What Makes Us Catholic?* New York: HarperSanFrancisco, 2002.

Gutiérrez, Gustavo. "Liberation, Theology, and Proclamation." In *The Mystical and Political Dimension of the Christian Faith.* Ed. Claude Geffré and Gustavo Gutiérrez. *Concilium* 6, no. 10 (June 1974).

———. *A Theology of Liberation.* 15th anniversary ed. Maryknoll, N.Y.: Orbis Books, 1988.

———. "Bartolomé de Las Casas: Defender of the Indians." *Pacifica* 5 (1992).

———. *Gustavo Gutiérrez: Essential Writings.* Ed. James B. Nickoloff. Minneapolis: Fortress Press, 1996.

———. *The Density of the Present: Selected Writings.* Maryknoll, N.Y.: Orbis Books, 1999.

Hadot, Pierre. *Philosophy as a Way of Life: Spiritual Exercises from Socrates to Foucault.* Oxford: Blackwell, 1995.

————. *What Is Ancient Philosophy?* Trans. Michael Chase. Cambridge, Mass.: Belknap Press of Harvard University, 2002.

Halevi, Yossi Klein. *At the Entrance to the Garden of Eden: A Jew's Search for Hope with Christians and Muslims in the Holy Land.* New York: Perennial, 2002.

Handelman, Susan A. *Fragments of Redemption: Jewish Thought and Literary Theory in Benjamin, Scholem, and Levinas.* Bloomington: Indiana University Press, 1991.

Hanson, Paul. *The People Called: The Growth of Community in the Bible.* San Francisco: Harper & Row, 1986.

Heidegger, Martin. *Discourse on Thinking.* Trans. John M. Anderson and E. Hans Freund. New York: Harper and Row, 1966.

————. *On the Way to Language.* Trans. Peter D. Hertz. San Francisco: Harper, 1971.

————. *Poetry, Language, Thought.* Trans. Albert Hofstadter. New York: Harper & Row/Perennial, 1971.

————. *Basic Writings.* Ed. David Farrell Krell. New York: HarperCollins, 1977.

Heilman, Samuel. *The People of the Book.* Chicago: University of Chicago Press, 1983.

Henriot, Peter J., et al. *Catholic Social Teaching: Our Best Kept Secret.* Maryknoll, N.Y.: Orbis Books, 1988.

Heschel, Abraham. *Man Is Not Alone: A Philosophy of Religion.* New York: Farrar, Straus and Giroux, 1951.

————. *God in Search of Man: A Philosophy of Judaism.* New York: Farrar, Straus and Giroux, 1955.

————. *Between God and Man: An Interpretation of Judaism from the Writings of Abraham J. Heschel.* Selected and ed. Fritz A. Rothschild. New York: Free Press, 1959.

————. *The Prophets.* Vol. 1. New York: Harper Torchbooks, 1962.

————. *The Prophets.* Vol. 2. New York: Harper Torchbooks, 1962.

————. *Who Is Man?* Stanford, Calif.: Stanford University Press, 1965.

Holtz, Barry W., ed. *Back to the Sources: Reading the Classic Jewish Texts.* New York: Simon and Schuster, 1984.

Hopkins, Gerard Manley. *Poems and Prose.* Selected and ed. W. H. Gardner. New York: Penguin Books, 1953.

Illich, Ivan. *In the Vineyard of the Text: A Commentary on Hugh's Didascalicon.* Chicago: University of Chicago Press, 1993.

Irigaray, Luce. *Marine Lover of Friedrich Nietzsche.* Trans. Gillian C. Gill. New York: Columbia University Press, 1991.

Jabès, Edmond. *The Book of Questions.* I, II, III. *The Book of Questions: The Book of Questions, The Book of Yukel, Return to the Book.* Published as vol. 1. Trans. Rosmarie Waldrop. Hanover, N.H.: University Press of New England/Wesleyan University Press, 1972.

————. *The Book of Questions.* IV, V, VI. *Yaël, Elya, Aely.* Published as vol. 2. Trans. Rosmarie Waldrop. Middletown, Conn.: Wesleyan University Press, 1983.

————. *The Book of Questions.* VII. *El (or the last book).* Trans. Rosmarie Waldrop. Middletown, Conn.: Wesleyan University Press, 1984.

―――. *The Book of Dialogue.* Trans. Rosmarie Waldrop. Middletown, Conn.: Wesleyan University Press, 1987.

―――. *The Book of Resemblances.* I. *The Book of Resemblances.* Trans. Rosmarie Waldrop. Hanover, N.H.: University Press of New England/Wesleyan University Press, 1990.

―――. *The Book of Resemblances.* II. *Intimations, The Desert.* Trans. Rosmarie Waldrop. Hanover, N.H.: University Press of New England/Wesleyan University Press, 1991.

―――. *The Book of Resemblances.* III. *The Ineffaceable, The Unperceived.* Trans. Rosmarie Waldrop. Hanover, N.H.: University Press of New England/Wesleyan University Press, 1991.

―――. *The Book of Margins.* Trans. Rosmarie Waldrop. Chicago: University of Chicago Press, 1993.

Jabès, Edmond, with Marcel Cohen. *From the Desert to the Book.* Trans. Pierre Joris. Barrytown, N.Y.: Barrytown/Station Hill Press, 1990.

Jesuit Refugee Service. *2003 Annual Report.* Ed. Hugh Delaney and James Stapleton. Jesuit Refugee Service.

Kafka, Franz. *Franz Kafka: The Complete Short Stories.* Ed. Nahum N. Glatzer. New York: Schocken Books, 1971.

―――. *Letters to Friends, Family, and Editors.* New York: Schocken Books, 1978.

Kearney, Richard. *Poetics of Imagining: Modern to Postmodern.* New York: Fordham University Press, 1998.

Kierkegaard, Søren. *Works of Love.* Trans. Howard and Edna Hong. New York: Harper Torchbooks, 1962.

―――. *Fear and Trembling* and *The Sickness unto Death.* Trans. Walter Lowrie. Princeton, N.J.: Princeton University Press, 1968.

―――. *Provocations: Spiritual Writings of Kierkegaard.* Ed. Charles Moore. Farmington, Pa.: Plough, 1999.

Killen, Patricia O'Connell, and John de Beer. *The Art of Theological Reflection.* New York: Crossroad, 1994.

Kinast, Robert. *What Are They Saying about Theological Reflection?* New York: Paulist Press, 2000.

King, Martin Luther. *A Testament of Hope: The Essential Writings and Speeches of Martin Luther King Jr.* Ed. James M. Washington. New York: HarperSanFrancisco, 1986.

Kohák, Erazim. *The Embers and the Stars: A Philosophical Inquiry into the Moral Sense of Nature.* Chicago: University of Chicago Press, 1984.

Kundera, Milan. *The Unbearable Lightness of Being.* Trans. Michael Henry Heim. New York: Harper Perennial, 1984.

Kushner, Lawrence. *The Book of Letters: A Mystical Alef-bait.* 2nd ed. Woodstock, Vt.: Jewish Lights Publishing, 1990.

―――. *The Book of Words: Talking Spiritual Life, Living Spiritual Talk.* Woodstock, Vt.: Jewish Lights Publishing, 1993.

LaCugna, Catherine Mowry. *God for Us: The Trinity and Christian Life*. San Francisco: HarperSanFrancisco, 1991.

Las Casas, Bartolomé de. *In Defense of the Indians*. Trans. Stafford Poole. DeKalb: Northern Illinois University Press, 1992.

Leclercq, Jean. *The Love of Learning and the Desire for God*. New York: Fordham University Press, 1961.

Lee, Bernard. *The Galilean Jewishness of Jesus: Retrieving the Jewish Origins of Christianity*. New York: Paulist Press/Stimulus Books, 1988.

————. "Practical Theology: Its Character and Possible Implications for Higher Education." *Current Issues in Catholic Higher Education* 14, no. 2 (Winter 1994).

————. *The Future Church of 140 BCE: A Hidden Revolution*. New York: Crossroad, 1995.

————. *The Catholic Experience of Small Christian Communities*. New York: Paulist Press, 2000.

————. "Classical and Practical Theology," unpublished paper.

Leff, Barry. "Lech Lecha." E-mailed sermon.

Leibowitz, Nehama. *Studies in Bereshit (Genesis): In the Context of Ancient and Modern Jewish Bible Commentary*. Jerusalem: Eliner Library, no date.

Levinas, Emmanuel. *Totality and Infinity: An Essay on Exteriority*. Trans. Alphonso Lingis. Pittsburgh: Duquesne University Press, 1969.

————. *Existence and Existents*. Trans. Alphonso Lingis. The Hague: Martinus Nijhoff, 1978.

————. *Ethics and Infinity: Conversations with Philippe Nemo*. Pittsburgh: Duquesne University Press, 1985.

————. "The Trace of the Other." In *Deconstruction in Context*. Ed. Mark C. Taylor. Chicago: University of Chicago Press, 1986.

————. *The Levinas Reader*. Ed. Sean Hand. Oxford: Blackwell, 1989.

————. *Difficult Freedom: Essays on Judaism*. Trans. Sean Hand. Baltimore: The John Hopkins University Press, 1990.

————. *Nine Talmudic Readings*. Trans. Annette Aronowicz. Bloomington: Indiana University Press, 1990.

————. *Otherwise Than Being or Beyond Essence*. Trans. Alphonso Lingis. Dordrecht: Kluwer Academic Publishers, 1991.

————. *Outside the Subject*. Trans. Michael B. Smith. Stanford, Calif.: Stanford University Press, 1993.

————. "Philosophy and the Idea of the Infinite." In *To the Other: An Introduction to the Philosophy of Emmanuel Levinas*. Adriaan Peperzak. West Lafayette, Ind.: Purdue University Press, 1993.

————. *Beyond the Verse: Talmudic Readings and Lectures*. Trans. Gary D. Mole. Bloomington: Indiana University Press, 1994.

————. *In the Time of the Nations*. Trans. Michael B. Smith. Bloomington: Indiana University Press, 1994.

————. *Basic Philosophical Writings*. Ed. Adriaan T. Peperzak, Simon Critchley, and Robert Bernasconi. Bloomington: Indiana University Press, 1996.

————. *Proper Names.* Trans. Michael B. Smith. Stanford, Calif.: Stanford University Press, 1996.

————. *Of God Who Comes to Mind.* Trans. Bettina Bergo. Stanford, Calif.: Stanford University Press, 1998.

————. *Alterity and Transcendence.* Trans. Michael B. Smith. New York: Columbia University Press, 1999.

————. *Is It Righteous To Be? Interviews with Emmanuel Levinas.* Ed. Jill Robbins. Stanford, Calif.: Stanford University Press, 2001.

Levinas, Emmanuel, and Richard Kearney. "Dialogue with Emmanuel Levinas." In *Face to Face with Lévinas.* Ed. Richard A. Cohen. Albany: State University of New York Press, 1986.

Levinas, Emmanuel, and Edith Wyschogrod. "Interview with Emmanuel Levinas." *Philosophy and Theology* 4, no. 2 (Winter 1989).

Lingis, Alphonso. "The Sensuality and the Sensitivity." In *Face to Face with Lévinas.* Ed. Richard A. Cohen. Albany: State University of New York Press, 1986.

Mandela, Nelson. *Long Walk to Freedom.* London: Abacus, 1994.

Mannheim, Karl. *Ideology and Utopia: An Introduction to the Sociology of Knowledge.* San Diego: Harcourt Brace Jovanovich Publishers, 1936.

Marcel, Gabriel. *Homo Viator: Introduction to a Metaphysics of Hope.* New York: Harper Torchbooks, 1962.

————. *Being and Having: An Existentialist Diary.* New York: Harper Torchbooks, 1965.

————. *Creative Fidelity.* New York: Fordham University Press, 2002.

Maritain, Jacques. *Creative Intuition in Art and Poetry.* New York: Pantheon Books, 1953.

Matt, Daniel. *The Essential Kabbalah.* San Francisco: HarperSanFrancisco, 1996.

Meland, Bernard. "The Appreciative Consciousness." In *Higher Education and the Human Spirit.* Chicago: Chicago University Press, 1953.

Menocal, María Rosa. *The Ornament of the World: How Muslims, Jews, and Christians Created a Culture of Tolerance in Medieval Spain.* Boston: Back Bay Books/Little, Brown and Company, 2002.

Merton, Thomas. *Silence in Heaven.* New York: The Studio Publications in association with Thomas Y. Crowell Company, 1956.

————. . *Conjectures of a Guilty Bystander.* New York: Image Books/Doubleday, 1965.

————. *The Seven Storey Mountain.* New York: Harvest/HBJ, 1976.

Metz, Johannes-Baptist. *Followers of Christ: Perspectives on Religious Life.* New York: Paulist Press, 1978.

————. *Faith in History and Society: Toward a Fundamental Practical Theology.* Trans. David Smith. New York: Seabury Press, 1980.

————. "Facing the Jews: Christian Theology after Auschwitz." In *Concilium: The Holocaust as Interruption.* Ed. Elisabeth Schüssler Fiorenza and David Tracy. Edinburgh: T. & T. Clark, 1984.

Metz, Johannes-Baptist, and Jürgen Moltmann. *Faith and the Future: Essays on Theology, Solidarity, and Modernity.* Maryknoll, N.Y.: Orbis Books, 1995.

Mich, Marvin L. Krier. *Catholic Social Teachings and Movements*. Mystic, Conn.: Twenty-Third Publications, 1998.

Milosz, Czeslaw. *To Begin Where I Am — Selected Essays*. New York: Farrar, Straus and Giroux, 2001.

Morrison, Van. "Warm Love" and "Hard Nose the Highway." From the album *Hard Nose the Highway*. Exile Productions, 1973.

Mudge, Lewis S., and James N. Poling, eds. *Formation and Reflection: The Promise of Practical Theology*. Philadelphia: Fortress, 1987.

Neusner, Jacob. *What Is Midrash?* Philadelphia: Fortress Press, 1987.

O'Brien, Davis, and Thomas Shannon, eds. *Catholic Social Thought: The Documentary Heritage*. Maryknoll, N.Y.: Orbis Books, 1999.

Ong, Walter. *Orality and Literacy: The Technologizing of the Word*. London: Routledge, 1982.

Pearl, Chaim. *Theology in Rabbinic Stories*. Peabody, Mass.: Hendrickson Publishers, 1977.

Peperzak, Adriaan. *To the Other: An Introduction to the Philosophy of Emmanuel Levinas*. West Lafayette, Ind.: Purdue University Press, 1993.

————, ed. *Ethics as First Philosophy: The Significance of Emmanuel Levinas for Philosophy, Literature, and Religion*. New York: Routledge, 1995.

————. *Beyond: The Philosophy of Emmanuel Levinas*. Evanston, Ill.: Northwestern University Press, 1997.

Petersen, Rodney L., with Nancy M. Rourke, eds. *Theological Literacy for the Twenty-First Century*. Grand Rapids: William B. Eerdmans, 2002.

Pineda, Ana María. "Hospitality." In *Practicing Our Faith*. Ed. Dorothy Bass. San Francisco: Jossey-Bass Publishers, 1997.

Pinkerton, James. "Deadly Journey to the North." *The Houston Chronicle*, June 13, 2000.

Pirkei Avos, Ethics of the Fathers. Commentary by Rabbi Meir Zlotowitz. New York: Mesorah Publications, 1989.

Plato. *Symposium* and *Phaedrus*. Trans. B. Jowett. New York: Dover Publications, 1933.

————. *The Republic of Plato*. Trans. Francis MacDonald Cornford. London: Oxford University Press, 1945.

————. *The Great Dialogues of Plato*. Trans. W. H. D. Rouse. Ed. Eric H. Warmington and Philip G. Rouse. New York: Mentor Books, 1956.

Pohl, Christine. *Making Room: Recovering Hospitality as a Christian Tradition*. Grand Rapids: William B. Eerdmans, 1999.

————. "A Community's Practice of Hospitality: The Interdependence of Practices and of Communities." In *Practicing Theology: Beliefs and Practices in Christian Life*. Ed. Miroslav Volf and Dorothy Bass. Grand Rapids: William B. Eerdmans, 2002.

Pollan, Michael. *The Botany of Desire: A Plant's-Eye View of the World*. New York: Random House, 2001.

Pontifical Council for the Pastoral Care of Migrants and Itinerant People. *Refugees: A Challenge to Solidarity.* Vatican City, 1992. Retrieved from Vatican Web site: www.vatican.va.

Pontifical Council for the Pastoral Care of Migrants and Itinerant People. *Erga migrantes caritas Christi — The Love of Christ towards Migrants.* Vatican City, 2004. Retrieved from Vatican Web site: www.vatican.va.

Pope John Paul II. *Dives in misericordia — Rich in Mercy.* Vatican City, 1980. Retrieved from Vatican Web site: www.vatican.va.

———. "Message of the Holy Father for the World Migration Day 2000." Retrieved from the Vatican Web site: www.vatican.va.

Puri, Jyoti. *Encountering Nationalism.* Malden, Mass.: Blackwell, 2004.

Purves, Andrew. *Pastoral Theology in the Classical Tradition.* Louisville: Westminster John Knox Press, 2001.

Rahner, Karl. "Practical Theology within the Totality of Theological Disciplines." In *Theological Investigations* 9. New York: Herder and Herder, 1972.

———. *A Rahner Reader.* Ed. Gerald A. McCool. London: Darton, Longman & Todd, 1975.

———. *Foundations of Christian Faith.* London: Darton, Longman & Todd, 1978.

———. "Poetry and the Christian." In *Theological Investigations* 4. New York: Crossroad, 1982.

Rich, Adrienne. *What Is Found There: Notebooks on Poetry and Politics.* London: Virago, 1993.

Ricoeur, Paul. *The Symbolism of Evil.* Trans. Emerson Buchanan. Boston: Beacon Press, 1967.

———. *Essays on Biblical Interpretation.* Ed. Lewis Mudge. Philadelphia: Fortress Press, 1980.

———. *Hermeneutics and the Human Sciences: Essays on Language, Action, and Interpretation.* Trans. and ed. John B. Thompson. Cambridge: Cambridge University Press, 1981.

———. *Figuring the Sacred: Religion, Narrative, and Imagination.* Minneapolis: Fortress Press, 1995.

———. "In Memoriam Emmanuel Levinas." *Philosophy Today* (Fall 1996).

———. *Critique and Conviction: Conversations with François Azouvi and Marc de Launay.* Cambridge, Mass.: Polity Press, 1998.

Rilke, Rainer Maria. *Rilke's Book of Hours: Love Poems to God.* Trans. Anita Barrows and Joanna Macy. New York: Riverhead Books, 1996.

Rosenak, Michael. *Commandments and Concerns: Jewish Religious Education in Secular Society.* Philadelphia: Jewish Publication Society, 1987.

———. *Roads to the Palace: Jewish Texts and Teaching.* Providence, R.I.: Berghahn Books, 1995.

———. *Tree of Life, Tree of Knowledge: Conversations with the Torah.* Boulder, Colo.: Westview Press, 2001.

Ryan, Thomas. *Thomas Aquinas as Reader of the Psalms.* Notre Dame, Ind.: University of Notre Dame Press, 2000.

Sacks, Jonathan. *The Dignity of Difference: How to Avoid the Clash of Civilizations.* London: Continuum, 2002.

Schillebeeckx, Edward. *Jesus: An Experiment in Christology.* Trans. Hubert Hoskins. New York: Crossroad, 1979.

———. *God Is New Each Moment.* In conversation with Huub Oosterhuis and Piet Hoogeveen. Trans. David Smith. New York: Seabury Press, 1983.

———. *The Church with a Human Face.* Trans. John Bowden. London: SCM Press, 1985.

———. *The Schillebeeckx Reader.* Ed. Robert Schreiter. New York: Crossroad, 1987.

———. *Church: The Human Story of God.* Trans. John Bowden. New York: Crossroad, 1990.

Scholem, Gershom. "Tradition and Commentary as Religious Categories in Judaism." *Judaism* 15 (Winter 1966).

———. *Kabbalah.* New York: Dorset Press, 1974.

Schreiter, Robert. *Constructing Local Theologies.* Maryknoll, N.Y.: Orbis Books, 1985.

———. *The Ministry of Reconciliation: Spirituality and Strategies.* Maryknoll, N.Y.: Orbis Books, 1998.

Seale, Morris. *The Desert Bible: Nomadic Tribal Culture and Old Testament Interpretation.* London: Weidenfeld and Nicolson, 1974.

Sells, Michael. *Mystical Languages of Unsaying.* Chicago: University of Chicago Press, 1994.

Shanks, Hershel, ed. *Christianity and Rabbinic Judaism: A Parallel History of Their Origins and Early Development.* Washington, D.C.: Biblical Archaeology Society, 1992.

Soelle, Dorothee. *The Silent Cry: Mysticism and Resistance.* Trans. Barbara and Martin Rumscheidt. Minneapolis: Fortress Press, 2001.

Steiner, George. *Real Presences.* Chicago: University of Chicago Press, 1989.

Stern, David. *Parables in Midrash: Narrative and Exegesis in Rabbinic Literature.* Cambridge, Mass.: Harvard University Press, 1991.

The Talmud: The Steinsaltz Edition. Vols. 2 and 3. *Tractate Bava Metzia Part II and Part III.* New York: Random House, 1990.

Taylor, Charles. *Multiculturalism.* Princeton, N.J.: Princeton University Press, 1994.

Tolstoy, Leo. *The Death of Ivan Ilych and Other Stories.* New York: Signet Classics, 1960.

———. *Walk in the Light and Twenty-Three Tales.* Farmington, Pa.: Plough, 1998.

Tracy, David. *The Analogical Imagination: Christian Theology and the Plurality of Cultures.* New York: Crossroad, 1981.

———. "Theological Method." In *Christian Theology: An Introduction to its Traditions and Tasks.* Ed. Peter Hodgson and Robert King. Philadelphia: Fortress Press, 1985.

———. *Plurality and Ambiguity: Hermeneutics, Religion, Hope.* San Francisco: Harper & Row, 1987.

————. "Practical Theology in the Situation of Global Pluralism." In *Formation and Reflection: The Promise of Practical Theology.* Ed. Lewis S. Mudge and James N. Poling. Philadelphia: Fortress Press, 1987.

————. *On Naming the Present: God, Hermeneutics, and Church.* Maryknoll, N.Y.: Orbis Books, 1994.

————. "Theology and the Many Faces of Postmodernity." *Theology Today* 51, no. 1 (1994).

————. "Response to Adriaan Peperzak on Transcendence." In *Ethics as First Philosophy: The Significance of Emmanuel Levinas for Philosophy, Literature, and Religion.* Ed. Adriaan Peperzak. New York: Routledge, 1995.

————. "On Theological Education: A Reflection." In *Theological Literacy for the Twenty-First Century.* Ed. Rodney L. Petersen with Nancy M. Rourke. Grand Rapids: William B. Eerdmans, 2002.

United States Conference of Catholic Bishops. *People on the Move: A Compendium of Church Documents on the Pastoral Concern for Migrants and Refugees.* United States Catholic Conference, 1988. Retrieved from the United States Conference of Catholic Bishops Web site: www.usccb.org.

————. "Welcoming the Stranger among Us." United States Catholic Conference, 2000. Retrieved from the United States Conference of Catholic Bishops Web site: www.usccb.org.

United States Conference of Catholic Bishops and Conferencia del Episcopado Mexicano. "Strangers No Longer: Together on the Journey of Hope — A Pastoral Letter Concerning Migration from the Catholic Bishops of Mexico and the United States." Issued by USCCB, January 22, 2003. Retrieved from the United States Conference of Catholic Bishops Web site: www.usccb.org.

Vanier, Jean. *Community and Growth.* Sydney: St. Paul Publications, 1979.

————. *Becoming Human.* New York: Paulist Press, 1998.

Vatican Council II: The Conciliar and Post Conciliar Documents. Ed. Austin Flannery. Collegeville, Minn.: Liturgical Press, 1975.

Veling, Terry. "Theological Hermeneutics in the Works of David Tracy." *Compass Theology Review* (Summer 1993).

————. "Practical Theology: A New Sensibility for Theological Education." *Pacifica* 11, no. 2 (June 1998).

————. "In The Name of Who? Levinas and the Other Side of Theology." *Pacifica* 12, no. 3 (October 1999).

————. "Questions of Religious Identity: Who Are You Facing Me? Who Am I Facing You?" *New Theology Review* 14, no. 3 (August 2001).

————. *Living in the Margins: Intentional Communities and the Art of Interpretation.* Eugene, Ore.: Wipf and Stock Publishers, 2002. (Originally published by Crossroad, 1996.)

————. "Theology after Disaster." *The Living Light* 38, no. 4 (Summer 2002).

Visotzky, Burton. *Reading the Book.* New York: Anchor/Doubleday, 1991.

Volf, Miroslav, and Dorothy Bass, eds. *Practicing Theology: Beliefs and Practices in Christian Life.* Grand Rapids: Eerdmans, 2002.

Ward, Benedicta, trans. *The Sayings of the Desert Fathers: The Alphabetical Collection.* London: Mowbrays, 1975.

————, trans. *The Desert Fathers: Sayings of the Early Christian Monks.* London: Penguin Classics, 2003.

Weil, Simone. *Waiting on God: Letters and Essays.* London: Fount/HarperCollins, 1950/1977.

Weiman, Henry Nelson. "Creative Good." In *The Source of Human Good.* Cardondale, Ill.: Southern Illinois University Press, 1946.

Westphal, Merold. "Levinas's Teleological Suspension of the Religious." In *Ethics as First Philosophy: The Significance of Emmanuel Levinas for Philosophy, Literature, and Religion.* Ed. Adriaan Peperzak. New York: Routledge, 1995.

Whitehead, Alfred North. *Adventures of Ideas.* New York: Free Press, 1933.

————. *Process and Reality.* Corrected ed. by David Ray Griffin and Donald W. Sherburne. New York: Free Press, 1978.

Whitehead, Evelyn and James. *Method in Ministry: Theological Reflection and Christian Ministry.* New York: Seabury Press, 1983.

————. *Community of Faith: Crafting Christian Communities Today.* Mystic, Conn.: Twenty-Third Publications, 1992.

Williams, Rowan. *On Christian Theology.* Oxford: Blackwell, 2000.

Wills, Garry. *Saint Augustine.* New York: Viking/Penguin, 1999.

Wojtyla, Karol. *The Acting Person.* Trans. Andrzej Potocki. Dordrecht, Holland: D. Reidel, 1979.

Woodward, James, and Stephen Pattison, eds. *The Blackwell Reader in Pastoral and Practical Theology.* Malden, Mass: Blackwell, 2000.

Wyschogrod, Edith. *Saints and Postmodernism: Revisioning Moral Philosophy.* Chicago: University of Chicago Press, 1990.

Young, Brad. *Jesus the Jewish Theologian.* Peabody, Mass.: Hendrickson Publishers, 1995.

Zohar: The Book of Enlightenment. Trans. and introduced by Daniel C. Matt. Mahwah, N.J.: Paulist Press, 1983.

Index

Also of interest

Doing Local Theology
A Guide for Artisans of a New Humanity
Clemens Sedmak
FOREWORD BY Robert J. Schreiter

ISBN 1-57075-452-7

"Approaches theology not as a content to be mastered or produced but as a process."

—*Stephen B. Evans*

Models of Contextual Theology
REVISED AND EXPANDED EDITION
Stephen B. Bevans

ISBN 1-57075-438-1

"Stephen Bevans has done us a great service in proposing a way to think more clearly about the interaction of the Gospel message and culture, and about honoring tradition while responding to social change."

—*Robert J. Schreiter, C.PP.S.*

History, Theology & Faith
Dissolving the Modern Problematic
Terrence W. Tilley

ISBN 1-57075-568-X

"Another stone in the edifice Tilley is building that showcases 'practice' as a key to doing theology."

—*Elizabeth A. Johnson*

Please support your local bookstore or call 1-800-258-5838
For a free catalog, please write us at
Orbis Books, Box 308
Maryknoll, NY 10545-0308
or visit our website at www.orbisbooks.com